A STONE OF
HOPE

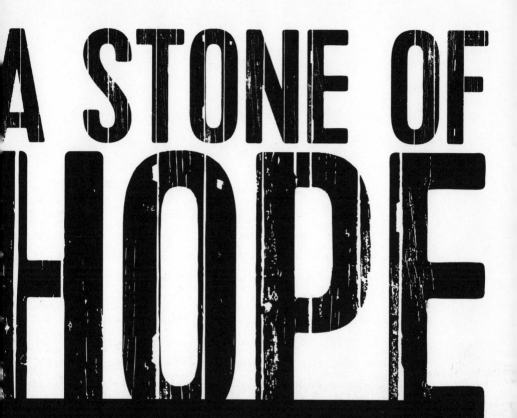

A STONE OF HOPE

A MEMOIR

JIM ST. GERMAIN

WITH JON STERNFELD

HARPER

An Imprint of HarperCollins*Publishers*

This is a work of nonfiction. The events and experiences detailed herein are all true and have been faithfully rendered as I have remembered them, to the best of my ability. Some names, identities, and circumstances have been changed in order to protect the anonymity of individuals involved. Though conversations come from my keen recollection of them, they are not written to represent word-for-word documentation; rather, I've retold them in a way that evokes the real feeling and meaning of what was said, in keeping with the true essence of the mood and spirit of the event.

HarperCollins books may be purchased for educational, business, or sales promotional use. For information, please email the Special Markets Department at SPsales@harpercollins.com.

FIRST EDITION

Designed by William Ruoto

Library of Congress Cataloging-in-Publication Data has been applied for.

ISBN 978-0-06-245879-7

17 18 19 20 21   LSC   10 9 8 7 6 5 4 3 2 1

THIS BOOK IS DEDICATED TO MY SON, CALEB JIM ST. GERMAIN.
YOU'RE MY SANCTUARY; YOUR LOVE STRENGTHENS ME AND
ENCOURAGES ME TO KEEP FIGHTING.

Any society, any family, which cannot share or take seriously the pain of its children, and views that pain as something normal or to be expected, is a society condemned to remain a hostage to itself.[1]

—POPE FRANCIS, CURRAN-FROMHOLD
CORRECTIONAL FACILITY, PHILADELPHIA

CONTENTS

CONTENTS

PART I
BROOKLYN, USA

We teach what we know, but we reproduce what we are.
-John C. Maxwell

1

Front-Row Seat

As the aircraft descended, I pushed my ten-year-old face up against the tiny window, in thrall to the light: flickering orange, yellow, and red. A planetary system down there. Bright and beautiful jewels sprinkled in the dark sky, millions of candles stretching out past the horizon. It was such a stark contrast from where I'd come, a town called Bon-Repos in La Plaine, Haiti, where most of the population lives in darkness.

As kids, our world was small. We didn't even know about other places. Being dirt poor, we had to create fun and distraction out of what was lying around—mostly discarded wood and metal. We'd make our own toys, stacking rubber tires, aluminum, wood, and a milk can to make cars. We'd make our own kites using loose plastic and string. We'd put blades at the ends of the kites to cut the other kids' kite wires so they couldn't fly anymore. That's how you'd win.

When the wheels touched down and we felt that thump and then the loud whirring, I exhaled. It was like I had been holding my breath for ten years and the relief made me light-headed. We had made it—no more hunger, no more beatings, no more of the uncertainty that had become a fact of my life. Landing on a tarmac at LaGuardia Airport made me feel free. America, New York City, was where dreams were made and I would make mine here. I'd heard that from everyone, so it must be true.

A friend of my grandfather picked us up at the airport in his black Lincoln Town Car and we packed tight in the leather seats and carpeted floor. I piled with my siblings in the back and watched the flashing reds and blues streak across the windshield, mesmerized by the speed and electricity of the highway, the buildings stretching up into the darkness, the skyline in the distance as large as any mountain. We crossed a bridge that stretched for what felt like miles and I thought we were going over the ocean.

My mother wasn't with us—and she hadn't been for a long time. Soon after my younger brother Roothchild was born, my father beat her pretty badly. He was in a rage, suspecting her of being with another man, even though he had lots of his own women on the side. While my mother was lying on the floor, he picked up a piece of metal and held it over her like he was going to hit her. Luckily he hesitated long enough for his friend Kesner to hear the commotion and run into the house; he grabbed my father's arm and wrested the metal from his hand. My mother told me later she was afraid he was going to kill her.

A few days later, she woke early, packed what she could, and left for provinces in the rural north. She had family with some means up there in a town called Lascahobas—her dad was mayor and chief judge—and she started up again. Over the years, she'd send things back to us: a bag of rice, maybe some beans, a gift or two. Occasionally we'd go up and visit though she often sent me back to my father for causing too much trouble. When my siblings and I finally got visas to come to America, we sent word to her and she came down to say good-bye to all of us.

I was too overwhelmed to think of her, though, as we pulled off the highway and plunged down into local streets, slower and packed with parked cars in every conceivable spot. We pulled up to a traffic light, dangling red in the quiet.

"Why we stopping?" I asked in Creole, looking around. "No one's coming."

The driver, a slim older gentleman with gray hair, looked back and smiled at me. "Well, it's the law," he said. His voice was calm, matter-of-fact.

I was not sure what that meant.

"I have to pay money if they catch me," he explained, eyes latched on me in his rearview. "It's like a hundred dollars."

"Oh," I said, turning around to look through the rear windshield. "But how would they know?"

"They're always watching, Jim," he said, eyes ahead. "Even if you can't see them." I understood who they were, but I couldn't figure out where they were hiding.

I turned and pressed my forehead against the window, which was cool and wet. On the glass I blew my breath and streaked out a circle in the fog, a head with eyes and a smiling mouth. Then I wrote my name: "JIM."

Even off the highway there was still so much light. Bright whites under awnings and in the windows, yellows and reds coming off the street. It would take weeks for me to adjust to the unnatural night-time light, fluorescent and buzzing and constant.

"What's this?" I said, jumping forward again. "Where are we now?"

"Home," my grandfather said.

"Here?" I didn't hide my disappointment. I'd imagined it would look like the street in *Home Alone*, which I had watched obsessively on a staticky videotape in Haiti, dreaming of the big house, the nice neighborhood, the Christmas season. It all spelled America.

"Almost," he said.

"What's it called?"

"Crown Heights," he said.

Older kids, electric with energy and confidence, ran the sidewalks. They were pushing one another and laughing, blasting music and yelling at people passing by. They sat on the hoods of parked cars, thick brown cigarettes dangling from their lips engulfing them in smoke. Under the streetlights I spotted dark hoodie sweatshirts and Timberland boots, red do-rags, pristine NBA caps, and fitted skullies, clothes I'd only seen before when my cousin Rodlin had visited us from the States.

The car came to a stop and we poured out onto Crown Street. I eyed a perimeter of jagged fencing above a large stone wall, block and bright graffiti blanketing every inch—names and signs I couldn't decipher. I spotted my grandma coming outside, tall and healthy, big for a woman. My father, who'd moved up here the year before, followed behind her. Teenagers and older guys were everywhere: on the corner, in front of the park, outside the building, sitting on the stoop. Just about everyone threw us a look as we passed; some stared us down—earrings reflecting and gold teeth sparking. A few yelled things I didn't understand. I couldn't tell if they were welcoming us, making jokes at our expense, or just greeting my grandmother, whom they all seemed to know.

One kid sitting on the stoop, hair braided tight against his head, said hello to my grandmother in Creole. This was Serge—Jigga—who would become one of my best friends. Sitting next to him was a kid named Kino. Short and fiery, he grilled us pretty hard. I tried not to break eye contact with him. Though I was a "just come" in America, I knew fear was a universal language and instinctively understood that I couldn't break first. He spit out a laugh and looked away.

My eyes widened as I looked up at the mass of faded red brick, almost half a block wide. It was bigger than any building I'd ever seen and I thought my grandparents owned the whole thing. Bright red metal bars zigzagged from the top and made their way down across the windows. Single trees popped up like soldiers on square dirt patches. It was jarring because I couldn't shake the image of the kid's block from *Home Alone*. I had expected grass and trees, a white wood fence, hello-neighbor types watering their lawns, garbage pails stacked at the ends of long black driveways.

As we entered the building the thick smell of marijuana wafted toward us. A group of teenagers were in the lobby puffing and rolling dice. I slowed down to get a closer look at the game. Five guys were circled up and bent down, some on their knees, spread around dirty green cash on the floor. Dice skittered across the linoleum, yells ricocheted off the cinder block. My grandma yanked my arm. *"An nale,"* she whispered. "Let's go."

"Just ignore them, Jim," she said as we passed. That first interaction—me straining to look, Grandma protesting—was a preview of things to come.

My father smacked me lightly on the back of the head.

"Look at you here five minutes and already looking for trouble," he said, half-joking. My brothers laughed. *"Sou moun,"* my dad said. *Always in someone else's business.* The rest of my family seemed fearful, but I was curious. Something was going on there and I wanted in.

My father's sister Michelle, who had lived with us in Haiti and helped us out a great deal, also moved into that apartment with her two children a year earlier. Aunt Michelle's son Wikley met us in the lobby and grabbed some of our bags. They had been here for two years already; he'd gone through puberty since I last saw him so he looked filled out and seemed to move different, more New York. Light-skinned with permed coolie hair, Wikley no longer looked like he belonged in the family. He swaggered like he thought he was a stud as he led us into the elevator. The ride was jittery, and the elevator smelled like stale urine, but I thought it was cool: this small metal box that took us to our floor at the push of a button. It was the most American thing I'd seen.

We walked off the elevator into the dim lights of the hallway. I ran my finger along the thick cinder blocks, faded white with carved symbols, gang signs I didn't yet recognize. We entered through the door of my grandmother's apartment: a narrow hall leading out into a cramped space. My family was about to increase the population of that apartment exponentially and the moment we walked in, it felt like it.

There were unpainted wood doors off a tight hallway and the thick smell of artificial Haitian cuisine: canned meat and garlic powder. Grandma was preparing a dinner for our arrival but I went straight for the kitchen; I'd been dreaming about the clean white light of that refrigerator. The reality was a smack in the face. It was near empty: an opened bag of hot dogs, a giant bottle of dark soda, and some wrapped meat up in the freezer. I snatched one of the hot dogs and devoured it cold.

An hour later an older gentleman with a mustache came out of a door off the kitchen. Wilfred was one of the renters who lived in my grandmother's place and stayed in that side room with his wife. He opened the fridge and started ranting that someone ate one of his hot dogs, how hard he worked to be able to buy food. Every eye automatically lit toward me; they knew I was the only one bold and careless enough to touch things without asking, within minutes of entering my new home.

At the time, the master bedroom housed another two renters, who had their own bathroom. My sister, Geraldine, would sleep in my grandmother's bedroom off the kitchen. The other large room was split into two by a giant curtain. My aunt; her boyfriend; and Wikley's little sister, Jenny, slept in a bed there on one side. The other half had a bunk bed for Wikley, with my dad on the bottom bunk. My brothers Colin and Roothchild and I would share space with some comforters on the floor, lined up like mummies.

The life my grandparents had in Haiti in the 1970s was almost middle-class. But, like most immigrants, when they migrated to America it was downgraded. The apartment was rugged, old paint peeling off thin walls, holed-out furniture ratty from use. When we opened the kitchen cabinets roaches would fall out with the dishes. At night when I flicked the lights on in the kitchen, I'd hear *chhhh*, *chhhh*, *chhhh* as they scattered under the oven. I'd have to chase them around with a slipper on my hand. Sometimes we'd have to take a metal dustpan to the rats, turtle-size things with spiky hair and dead eyes.

I was grateful to have a home, but over time, I resented my grandmother's apartment. It was a stinging reminder of the gap between what I thought America was and the reality I had stepped into. Our ceiling was always leaking, and water would seep into the kitchen, the bathrooms, sometimes the bedrooms. The problems piled up and took months to fix, if ever. The doorbell never worked and that filthy elevator was a death trap. It would get stuck every other week, forcing someone to call the fire department to get them out. People would get jumped in there too. One time I got in the elevator and a guy waiting there put a .45 Glock to my forehead and took the little bit of money I had. After that, I started to take the stairs.

Still, we were used to worse. In Haiti, during the rainy season, flooding is the norm. And not water-filling-a-basement-type flood. It is like a Katrina every year. Houses, animals, whole families are swept away. What was a national tragedy in the United States is just a season of the year there.

Our house there was a small rickety nothing, scrap aluminum roof over wooden beams, two overcrowded and dusty rooms with no plumbing and sporadic electricity. We had a narrow bed made for one person, which we stretched to the limit. I'd pile on there with Colin and Roothchild, or Geraldine, or sleep alone with just a sheet on the dirt floor. It was so dry and dusty we'd pour water on it to keep it moist. As I got older I would sleep out when I could, on other people's beds and floors, sometimes in abandoned cars, sometimes just outside.

But there is another smaller Haiti along the coastline with exquisite beaches and expensive resorts, where elite Haitians and rich foreigners don't even have to know what's going on in the rest of the country. I didn't even know about this Haiti until I was six and went to a resort in Wahoo Bay with my uncle Reynold's family, who were visiting from America. The resort itself was immaculate, not a spot of anything anywhere. Even the garbage cans and ashtrays were clean. Sky blue and yellow pastel hotels, private beach bungalows, waiters carrying colored cocktails by an enormous pool, waterfalls cascading around bright wooden bars. And underneath the push-up umbrellas, shading themselves from the sun, white tourists. White tourists were everywhere. Of course, *I* felt like the tourist, there in my own country. It seemed everything rich and powerful was associated with white skin.

Now, I quickly learned there were two Americas too. And in New York they're side by side, virtually on top of each other. I could see both out of my grandmother's second-story window: Nostrand Avenue cut right through my neighborhood, a clear dividing line. On one side were gangs, poverty, violence, crowded apartments, drugs, broken families, and incarcerated fathers. But on the other side—

approximately fifty feet away—lived Brooklyn's middle class, the Hasidic Jews. They owned brownstones or had nice little lawns; their children went to private schools, had tutors, and lived in a stable environment. I had come to the land of opportunity and *bam*, I had a front-row seat to the America that wasn't mine.

My exposure to white people had been so limited that the sight of Orthodox Jews was a shock. When I first heard that Jews owned all of the buildings in Crown Heights I asked, "What the hell is a Jew?" I'd soon meet a kid in school whose father was a black Orthodox Jew, which blew my mind. Around the neighborhood I'd see the Orthodox traveling around in thick groups in their wide-brim black hats, curly sideburns, and long beards. They wore thick black wool suits throughout the year, insulated from the weather and everything else. They lived in their own world within our world.

In the months after we arrived, my grandmother ferried me around to doctors for blood work and health checkups and to government offices: social security, identification, forms and more forms. All the loops immigrants go through. The way they welcome the huddled masses in the modern age. The language barrier was thick, the processes were repetitive, and my grandmother was in uncharted territory. My grandfather traveled back and forth to Haiti a lot and just wasn't around enough to be in charge. It was half the year before I could even start school, putting me even further behind than I already was.

Even so, our lives in New York were an improvement. In Haiti, we'd almost always wake up in the morning without food. Late spring and summer is mango season and they just about grow everywhere, full green-and-orange bunches. During those months I could climb those big blooming trees or throw rocks to knock them down—often getting chased by whoever owned that tree. The rest of the time I'd forage around and look for things to eat. Forage describes animal behavior, I know, but that's what I did. I'd go around the neighborhood and scout things out, searching for anything on the ground or in the ravines that I could wipe off and eat. I'd hang out in different homes to see who would have something to give me. Or I'd figure out a way to hustle myself a meal. Once I took the food from a voodoo ceremony, the gift to the spirits, which was just not done. Another time I passed a chicken as it was laying eggs—I scooped up the eggs in my shirt and ran, boiling them over a fire in the dirt. Somebody must've told my father because he whipped me with a belt when I got home.

I quickly fell in love with the urban landscape of New York: Stepping over the underground trains rumbling up through the vents, dodging the cars like an athlete, making sense of the tangled colored lines on the subway map. On a typical block in Brooklyn, there's an entire economy: restaurants, barbers and beauty salons, Laundromats and grocery stores, check cashing next to the liquor stores, electronics alongside two-for-one suits. Chinese restaurants, fried chicken establishments, and a few Caribbean takeout spots. The corner store would make any sandwich you wanted behind a wall of chips and candy, things I'd only seen smuggled in diaspora suitcases. And I caught a glimpse at the hidden illegal world unfolding in the backs of stores owned by Arabs and Hispanics.

I had an optimistic, even naive sense that with school, things were going to improve. I didn't realize that moving away from Haiti wasn't going to solve all my problems. So many issues that I thought I left behind in La Plaine weren't geographical; they traveled with me.

Back in Haiti, I was known as a vagabond, a reckless kid wary of authority, forever wandering, always pushing boundaries and limits. I had a reputation for being aggressive and angry—a constant fighter; if there was a fight in the neighborhood, I was usually involved.

People in the neighborhood would say, *"Jim gen gwo san,"* which literally translates to "Jim has 'big blood'" but means I had anger issues, a bad temper. I'd be playing with someone and just like that, we'd be fighting. Parents would tell their kids not to play with me; even my dad would warn kids not to play with me.

By the time I was nine years old I was fighting teenagers. It was the only way I knew how to communicate. But I never thought myself the instigator—I was protecting someone, retaliating for something unfair, or trying to prevent or right a wrong. I was meting out what I saw as justice, defending my family members or other kids who wouldn't fight back.

If there was a fight with ten kids, and one of the kids wouldn't fight, I would go back into the scuffle and fight for that person. I defended my older brother Colin all the time; if he got hit, I'd ask him to point out who did it and no matter that kid's size, I'd go at him—with rocks, a bottle, or just my fists. I absolutely refused to back down, which is a whole lot more important than any fighting skills.

Considering the tightness of our living quarters in La Plaine, I was fighting my own brothers as well. When I was about eight, I grabbed a jagged rock from the ground and smashed it into Colin's head. It busted open and left a hole there that was gushing with blood. I had to go on the run for days because my father was looking for me. When I returned he made Colin whack at me with a tree branch. My dad was all about evening things out like that. I almost felt bad for Colin, though. He couldn't defy my father but he knew that once my father was out of sight I would beat the hell out of him.

In Brooklyn, even among the black and Latino immigrants, Haitians were singled out. We were picked on, called things like "Haitian booty scratcher," laughed at for being too foreign. I didn't know back then about my country's proud history, that it was home to the most successful slave rebellion in history. I just reacted.

The barriers were thick. Adolescence is challenging anyway, but not being able to communicate, not knowing how to interact with other kids, is isolating. The world became a threat, and the most common and effective interaction was through my fists, the most effective voice I had.

The first real schooling I ever got was in an American sixth grade classroom. Lefferts Junior High School was an enormous, industrial-looking building with endless white tiles, caged-in windows, and humming fluorescent lights. And it was chaotic: squeaking sneakers, metal slamming, guys wrestling, bells ringing, kids scattering. I was on high alert at all times and everything mystified me: the classroom setup, the winding hallways, the vending machines, things like fire drills and assemblies.

And I was totally lost in the classroom. In my eleven years in Haiti, I attended maybe two years of formal school total. If my grandparents in America sent money we could go to school for a couple of months. But it would always run out or have to be used for something else—usually food or medicine—and then we'd miss the rest of the year. Then maybe my father would hit the lottery numbers or win a cock-fight, and we'd go back for a few months. At one point my father's friend, Mr. Eddy, started a free school with homemade wood benches outside, a blackboard hung from the back of a brick wall, a few out-of-date books, but the pay schools found a way to shut him down.

Brevity and instability were the only constants throughout my education. School was too inconsistent to ever hold my interest or teach me anything. Since my mind had nothing to attach to, no concepts that the information could build on, my mind would wander.

In Brooklyn, not asking for help—not wanting anyone to know I needed any—set me back even further. I was trying to process this new world and answer my own questions, all the while wearing a tight mask that showed none of this. Adolescence is one big blending game. No one could know this was the biggest school I'd ever seen, that I barely understood what anyone was saying, that even the food and the clothes were totally alien to me. But no matter what, my face stayed stone.

I recently found my passport picture, a faded black-and-white image of a little boy, locked in time. I'm wearing my father's dark suit from when he was a kid, slightly baggy, his old shirt and tie, crookedly knotted. I recognize that expression I wear, remember it from the inside. It's a fierce look, like someone was trying to take my soul from me with that picture. But I can tell it's a front, what I put out to the world to make sure everyone knew I was serious. At school my face was always like that passport photo—I wouldn't let anyone know what was going on inside. I wouldn't let them use that knowledge to take from me.

Recess was held after lunch in an enclosed cement space surrounded by trash and metal. Kids flooded into the playground that spilled out and rubbed up against the city sidewalks. The boundary was fluid and the street element leaked in: older brothers, unemployed fathers, hustlers, and junkies. Some boys snuck off to the apartment buildings next door with their girlfriends or to get high.

On my very first day I was playing football outside and keeping an eye on Colin, watching him on the basketball court through the holes of the metal fence. I might've been the younger brother but since I could stand I'd been Colin's protector. He was just too soft to take care of himself in that environment; we used to call him Butter. At some point that day I lost track of him and scanned the schoolyard. When I spotted him again he was walking back to the entrance, head down. I tossed the football back and stormed across the asphalt. I could tell from his body that he was crying.

"Butter!" I yelled. "Wait. Slow up, man. What happened?" I caught up to him and grabbed his shirt. He looked away, his sleeve covering half his face.

"What's going on?" I said. I reached for his arm and he yanked it away. A big mark hugged the outside of his eye and a small cut was trickling blood.

"What the fuck, man?"

"Got punched in the face," he said.

"Wait, what?!" My blood simmered. When I was upset, things got biological. My body changed: my face tensed and I was incapable of hiding anything. "Hold the fuck up. Who?"

"Some kid—"

"Show me." I dragged him by the shirt back to the basketball court. He dragged his feet at first, but that was just pride. He wouldn't have told me unless he wanted me to take care of it. Colin pointed to a quick kid with braids who was dribbling the ball.

I stormed right out onto the court and shoved him in the chest. The ball rolled off and the kid stumbled back.

"What's good, man?" I said. "Why you hitting my brother?"

Adrenaline focused me. After a morning of being totally lost, I was back in my element. Fighting is what they call a transferable skill, able to travel across all boundaries.

The kid whipped his jacket off and came back at me with a cocked half smile.

"You touch my brother, I fucking kill you," I said, my English still sharply accented.

The rest of the kids circled around us, shouting, egging him on:

"Shut him up, Devon."

"He trying to play you, D!"

"Fuck him up!"

Devon spread his legs apart, bent slightly at the knees, and put his hands up in a boxer's stance, rolling his fists in a little circle.

I froze.

Back in Haiti, we'd kick, bite, wrestle, put someone in a headlock, throw him to the ground, go Van Damme on each other. I never saw anyone put his hands up like that—except maybe in a Muhammad Ali poster.

"C'mon, man," he said, spitting on the ground. "Let's get it crackin'."

I had to look like I knew what I was doing, so I mirrored him, fists up and out. We traded punches back and forth but it felt like I was holding back. I was used to ambushing people, going all out, dirty as hell, clawing and tossing in the dirt. This was like fighting in a straitjacket.

After a couple of minutes of trading punches, the dean of the school, Mr. Walton, came running out of the lunchroom door.

"Yo! Stop it now! What you all doing?!" he yelled.

He jumped in between us and stuck his muscled arms into each of our chests. A big guy with thick dreads like tight ropes, he cut an imposing figure in his fresh dark suit.

"Hey, hey!" he bellowed in his deep voice. Mr. Walton could silence a crowd with a word.

He dragged us both by the back of our jackets and led us upstairs to his office. We sat down across from his desk and he turned to Devon first.

"Devon, we've been here too many times, man," Mr. Walton said, hands folded, exasperated but calm. Devon didn't even make eye contact. He stared at the windows, playing with the shoelaces on his new Jordans. Those jumped out at me. I wondered where he got them, where the money came from, how I could get them.

"If this pattern doesn't stop," Mr. Walton was saying, "I have no choice but to expel you. Is that what you want?" Devon behaved like he had already checked out. "You hear me?"

Stone silence.

"Devon?" His head swiveled to Mr. Walton, as if noticing him for the first time. "We good?"

"Yep," Devon said, already pulling himself up.

I was polite when the dean turned to me. I tried to show him that I was willing to try, lots of "No, sir" and "Yes, sir," and a "thank you." But Devon had already graduated beyond adolescent mischief. He was embedded in the gang life, drinking, smoking, and hustling with guys twice his age. He was a known quantity, willing to break jaws at the slightest provocation. Kids I didn't know came up to me in the hall after that fight. "Aw man," they said, "I can't believe you trying to fight Devon."

The first thing they tell you in the streets is to hit the biggest guy to send a message to everyone else. Respect was crucial. If I hadn't retaliated, I would have given everyone a free pass on my brothers and me. But it was a lose-lose: once I went at him, everyone came after me.

In public school conflicts spill out of those halls and follow you home: to the playground, the sidewalks, the walk home, the parks near your house, off your stoop and outside your window. Devon lived on my block. That first day was a domino: more fights with him, his brothers, then his friends, then kids who wanted Devon to have their back.

Devon was aligned with the Crips, a gang that ran much of my neighborhood, and things escalated quickly. I had to worry about much bigger dudes who carried knives, guys who could go to their OGs and borrow a gun; street-hardened guys with chains, hammers, and brass knuckles, who had to prove themselves to one another. I was already a tough kid but those months hardened me into something solid. It was impossible to focus on schoolwork while I was consumed with getting home in one piece.

Growing up in Haiti, the fights were one-on-one, a winner and a loser, a closed loop. In a tight-knit community like that things get solved. But Crown Heights didn't care about fair fights. Everyone's clique got involved once you fought any one of them. Going anywhere alone became dangerous—it's why gangs evolved in the first place. It was like I had declared war on a bunch of people I didn't even know—but who all knew me.

The school lunchroom was an unruly arena, at a constant roar. A woman named Miss Bess would patrol, yelling "Sit down!" and "Stop it!" in a piercing wail. I learned about free lunch, and was even more baffled when I saw how it was treated. Kids would take those hamburgers and pizzas and toss most of them in the garbage. As shocking as it first was—I had just left a place where food was a luxury—I soon had the same reaction to the free food. There were rules about how to behave and blend in, and lunch was a prime example of how powerful those forces were. Most kids brought lunch, or money for the vending machines, and the last thing they wanted to do was take the free lunch. It was the stamp on the forehead, which is the kiss of death at that age.

"Line up!" Miss Bess would yell. The kids who got on the free lunch line were usually from other countries and wore hand-me-downs and no name brands. The girls didn't talk to them and they got picked on in the halls and punched in the schoolyard. They were on display in that cafeteria, and mocked ruthlessly for it, carrying their stigma like heavy chains. The cool cliques would knock the trays out of their hands, throw plastic utensils and ketchup packets at them, and mock them across the lunchroom. That harassment was brutal; society makes kids pay twice for being poor.

Adolescents work against their own self-interest all the time and I was no exception. Already stigmatized for being new and in the bilingual classes, I wouldn't eat. I was starving, and I'd come from a place with barely any food at all, but America can do that to people, make them question their worth or measure it in strange ways. It's why you'll see Mercedes in a public housing lot, or kids, like me, starving but thinking about brand-name sneakers.

My saving grace was that I was a born adapter, trained in the dirt roads and shanty houses of one of the poorest places in the Western Hemisphere. I'd grown up where adapting was a matter of life and death. So at school I caught on quickly and mirrored all of it: the glide through the packed hallway, the tone that skirted trouble but didn't make you a punk, the casual flirtation with the girls. I learned enough English slang to get by, though I'm sure the teachers thought I understood more than I did.

That first fight with Devon helped develop my reputation as a fighter, and gained me some respect. Other guys would step in and bargain for me. "Nah, man, chill out," they'd say. "Leave him alone. He just got here." Or, "Shoot him a fair one"—meaning let me fight one-on-one, give me a chance at least. In the schoolyard I quickly absorbed football, a more physical version of soccer. I was always pounding kids on the soccer field anyway so it was a natural fit. Like water taking the shape of its container, I formed into my world.

2

Five Square Blocks

It is easier for a lot of young people in this city and in some of your communities to buy a gun than buy a book. It is easier in some communities to find a gun than it is to find some fresh vegetables. . . . That's just a fact.

—PRESIDENT BARACK OBAMA

Bless her soul, my grandmother did the best she could. But she couldn't teach a boy about becoming a man. That was a hectic apartment: constant and escalating arguments over space, clothes, and food; fights that quickly got physical and ugly. If someone came in late at night, they'd get dead-bolted out and have to bang on the door, screaming for someone to open up. No one would answer, mostly out of spite. There was a lot of that in that house: *You did this to yourself.* Many times I slept in that cold hallway under the window, waiting for the morning.

My grandmother had enough to worry about—my grandfather left the day to day of that house to her—and I was a willful kid. She told me to stay off the streets, avoid the circles that drew the wrong kind of attention. But my adolescent mind couldn't comprehend that there was more available to me beyond the five square blocks of my world.

From a young age I'd been a social chameleon with a survival mentality. Dropped into this world, I made the choice to assimilate, to absorb the surrounding culture and habits, and to wear it like a shield. I had to make a name for myself or people would do it for me at my expense.

There is luck, there are exceptions, and there is the reality of your four walls, and your five square blocks. The boundaries of your world. Your "no" has no power and no reach; your only agency comes from your "yes." You said yes the day you moved in. For many, it was the day they were born. The residue of generations piling thick and heavy around us. Those who grow up in the right household, with the right role models, find access to resources and beat the odds. They develop the engine to get out and find the tracks to lead the way. That just didn't happen for me. At least, not then.

I was not even thirteen years old and every day was some kind of initiation. The combination of my inexperience, the street environment, and my frenzied home life pushed me with overwhelming force in one direction. I was just swimming with the current, trying not to drown. I had to defend myself when threatened, ally myself with those who took charge. Kids do what they know; they navigate based on what they have available to them. The adolescent mind isn't capable of seeing the end result, especially when their world is a concentrated threat.

That summer I was fighting Devon again, this time scuffling on the sidewalk in front of my building. My brother Colin and Devon's friend Pana were there too. Pana was a Latin King, not a Crip, but he and Devon were close. When Pana tried to jump in, my brother stuck his arm out to grab him.

"Yo, what you doing?" Colin said.

Boom! Pana turned and hit my brother quick and hard on the side of the head. Colin dropped the issue so quick it was almost comical. He was called Butter for a reason. He held the side of his head and walked off to watch with the rest of the small crowd.

I had started carrying a work knife in my pocket for protection, a box cutter with an orange handle and a sliding button. I was tired of looking over my shoulder on every sidewalk and the knife showed I meant business. Once Pana jumped in, I pulled the knife out and held it tight in my left hand, close to my body. In the ensuing scramble I got the knife up near Devon's throat. Pana was trying to pull me off from the side as Devon pushed my hand back, and we struggled like that, locked tight.

Devon and I were frozen, tussling. He was holding; I was cornered against the spiked railing, pushing the knife toward his neck, him holding my arm back. At some point the knife dropped out of my hand and someone in the crowd yelled, "The boys coming!"

Then the siren, one quick and jarring whoop. With that chirp, the spectators scattered.

A police car pulled up and two cops rushed at us. It was my first run-in with cops, so the uniforms and swirling lights still had the power to scare me. My eyes darted around looking for the knife; I spotted it five feet away, on the other side of a low railing, its shiny tip in a grass patch below a window. I looked for Colin, hoping he might read my mind and grab it. A weapon was a guaranteed ride to the precinct and a booking.

A barrel-chested white cop grabbed me and forced me to sit down on the sidewalk. "What's the story here, guys?" he said.

Devon immediately mentioned the knife and I tried to talk over him to distract them. "Officer, they were jumping me," I said, sticking with a polite and scared pose. As I rose the cop pushed me back down. "Both of them. I was protecting myself. I—"

"Okay, just calm down," the officer said.

"But I didn't do anything wrong."

The other cop, a stocky Latino, took Devon aside. Then my cop yelled over, "What's going on, Devon?" The fact that they knew him relaxed me.

"He pulled a knife on me, man," Devon said. "Trying to stab me."

The cop escorted Devon over to the police car and propped him up against it, his hand pinned to Devon's chest.

"Yeah?" his cop said.

"Oh yeah?" my cop said. "This one?" He pointed at me sitting on the ground, not yet thirteen. I guess I didn't look like much. "What knife? Where's this knife?" he said.

"Right there," Devon said, pointing to the grass strip. "He just dropped it." Devon started to walk toward it, but the cop fixed him back to the car.

"Hold it, hold it, Devon," he said. "Stay right there."

"He had it at my neck, man," Devon said, imitating the motion.

His cop went over by the bushes to look for it, kicking his feet around in the grass. My heart pounded fast, and then rose up into my throat. The moment my grandmother had repeatedly warned me about was inevitable and I couldn't stop it.

But the knife was gone.

The cops' radio rumbled alive, a staticky voice calling out numbers, and they let us go. I walked inside, trying to get my heart to slow. The culture hits snitches pretty hard, marks them forever. I didn't want to get arrested, but I didn't want Devon locked up either. Devon's arrest would've rippled and made me even more of a target. Things could've been fatal—for either of us—if he hadn't held me off.

A few nights later I was in my lobby about to walk up the stairs. A Puerto Rican woman named Maria who lived on the first floor called me over. She knew me from around the building; I used to throw the football in the hallway with one of her sons. Standing at her door in a nightgown, she motioned with her finger to come close. I anticipated her giving me a hard time for making too much noise.

From her open door I could see through her apartment. Her window looked right out onto the sidewalk, a straight shot to where Devon and I had been fighting a few days before.

"You live upstairs?" she said.

I nodded.

"What's your name?"

"Jim," I said, my voice cracking a bit. Female authority figures had the strange effect of pinning me down more than any male could.

"You're the one with the knife. I took it away. Did you know that?" she said.

"What knife?"

She gave me a *save your shit* look. "The other day," she said, "when the police came up."

"Oh yeah." I looked up at her. "You took it?"

She nodded.

"Why?" I asked.

She waved her hand like that didn't matter. "Just be smart," she said.

"Yes, ma'am."

"You're young. Be careful. That boy—" She pointed as if Devon were still outside. "That boy is bad news."

"Yes, ma'am."

She eyed me tight. "I know your grandmother. You seem like a decent kid," she said. "Don't become bad news."

I nodded and ran up the stairs.

That was the first time I felt like my building was its own community, a compacted version of what I had had in La Plaine. Haitians embrace the idea of shared responsibility and selflessness. The people reject the idea that in order for me to have more, you need to have less; it's more like if you don't have enough then *no one does*. People in Haiti don't just mind their own. Anyone could discipline you, look after you, feed you. We were all family to a certain degree—the terms "aunt," "uncle," and "cousin" all hung loosely around anyone you knew well. That moment with Maria was like a bridge back to that world. She didn't want any of us arrested because an us-versus-them mentality pervaded. People would rather protect a guilty neighbor than help the police.

There was a vampire-like element to what was happening to me, like I'd been bitten. I was getting into scuffles with Crips and Bloods, or allies of someone I fought in school, or enemies of someone I was seen with. A network of gangs and cliques was orbiting around me. Exposure leads to curiosity.

I wanted to know about these gangs, their prevalence and necessity. About their red and blue bandannas, their tags that blanketed concrete walls and electrical boxes. About their hierarchies of workers and bosses. About the music that blasted and thumped out of their parked cars. I tried to absorb the whole culture, learn the differences between a Crip and a Blood and a Latin King, understand what triggered certain beefs and who was involved. From my window, I'd watch the rise of their smoke, the rattling energy of their dice games, their intricate greetings. I could see the entire front and side of my block, with a view of the whole neighborhood. That window exposed an entire world to me and gave me an itch that kept me awake at night.

I hitched myself to the right people, those experienced enough to know the map and generous enough to look out for me. Pierre was about eighteen at the time, with light caramel skin and swollen cheeks. Everyone called him Big Head. He lived with his uncle in my building and they welcomed me into their home, sharing their food even when they didn't have extra and their clothing that had gotten too small. Pierre had also moved from Haiti to Brooklyn as a young kid, so there was comfort in talking to him, like I could retread tracks he had already made. Watching him was like looking ahead to a future I wanted to mold for myself.

Pierre and his friend Mackenzie taught me the lingo of the street, how to mimic the swag and decode the gang language kids spoke on sidewalks. I picked up which blocks were fighting, who were the robbers versus who were the shooters, what certain girls would let you do and what others wouldn't. I had no swagger and couldn't afford the kinds of things that signaled to girls that I was somebody. Listening to their stories about women's bodies—what they were going to do to them, what they had done—was like a peek to the other side of the mountain.

"Mack thinks he's got her, but I got the jump. Trust me." Pierre was talking about a girl on our street he was eyeing. We were sitting outside the stoop of my building in the hazy evening, the sun drifting down and the block coming to life.

"Why? What she say?" I asked.

"She didn't have to. Shorty was *having* it. I could tell." He touched his temple. "Sixth sense, cuz."

"You called her?" I asked.

"Nah man, you can't just do that." Pierre was scanning the block with slight moves of his eyes. "You just get her digits and then say 'I'll see you around' or something. Or else you look like you're interested."

"Yeah, but aren't you?"

"Shit, yeah. You see that onion butt?"

I'd heard this before. Makes a grown man cry.

"But you just say 'what's up' when she passes," he said, "and then go back to what you're doing. Even if I'm doing nothing. Make it like I got business to take care of."

Success on the street was linked to never being tied down. Mobility, deniability, ghosting. I would pick this up quickly.

Mackenzie came out of the bodega drinking a Mountain Dew, which he would down all day long. "What happened with Shorty up the block?" he asked.

"The one with the—" Mackenzie put his hands out in front of his chest. They both laughed. I laughed a half a beat behind.

"You saw that?" Pierre threw his hand out and gave him a dap. "I was trying to get her to come over to my crib."

"And?"

"She was frontin', said she had to work."

"I hate that *bullshit*," Mackenzie said, spiking both syllables. "That's some bullshit right there."

My experience with girls was limited, but the desire was there. It was a hard, biological fact, just sloppy and unformed. My arrival in New York coincided with the arrival of my hormones and it was like an overload. In Haiti, most of the girls were ones I had grown up with and they fell into two categories: family and practically family. In Brooklyn, the number of available girls and opportunities exploded. Every one was a question, a possibility, a door.

"Shorty, you got a fat ass!" Pierre yelled out to a girl passing by— tight jeans, large hoop earrings. He meant it as a compliment. Usually they ignored him, but this one turned around, flirting it up, moving her ass around. Then she kept walking.

"Damn, bro, you see that ass?" Pierre asked me. "Shorty got a fat ass, bro."

It was rare that a girl walked by and we didn't say something to her. I learned the language from these guys, who were persistent until one left earshot and a new one passed.

Yo Shorty what's good?

Can I walk with you?

Shorty, can I talk to you for a second?

Let me holla at you. Shorty, can I get your number?

You looking fine, Shorty. Where you going?

You look sexy, girl. Let me get your math.

Pierre was relentless.

When we got bored or restless, we'd drive around the block blasting Nas or Jay-Z, our heroes who grew up poor and troubled a couple of miles away. They didn't just rap about the street and violence but about police, racism, and oppression. Jay-Z wrote about being raised by a single mother, about his missing father and the hole left there. DMX rhymed about being lonely, growing up homeless and hungry. I lived vicariously through him, his voice and stories mirroring my own. *To live is to suffer,* he said, *but to survive is to find meaning in the suffering.* Nas was gritty, gutter-angry, and resilient. He mixed street gospel with honest pain. His lyrics became my mantras, his voice my guide, his world my ghetto sanctuary.

An older group of guys on the block also took me under their wings. Jay was in his midtwenties and had lived on Crown Street his whole life. Solidly built with a goatee, Jay had real style: smooth tailored suits for the workweek and North Face bubble jackets or Polo hoodies on the weekend. He was educated and street-smart, Haitian roots with American swag. As a young child I attached myself to older figures to get fed; now in Brooklyn, I shadowed mentors to learn the street. I was forming an American identity, looking to these guys to decipher this world to me. They didn't try to be my father or give me lectures, and because of that, I took heed of the lines they drew. The respect, the lack of condescension in that crowd, made me all the more willing to listen. I was drawn magnetically to Jay, his calm intelligence, his hawklike awareness of his world.

Jay's crowd hung out on the Orthodox side of Nostrand at a spot in front of a Hebrew school we called the Jewish Steps. On summer nights, twenty or so of us would pile around those steps, smoking blunts and drinking malt liquor, rolling dice on the sidewalk, blasting music from parked cars. I was the youngest but being around the older crowd conferred some maturity on me.

As long as we respected the Orthodox who lived nearby, they left us alone. They owned the few buildings on that side that still had black residents but they never gave any of us a hard time about the noise, smoke, or late hours. If we were sitting in front of the school's doors they'd say, "Excuse us, please," and we'd move out of the way.

On Saturdays, the Sabbath, they couldn't use any electricity, so they would ask us to come inside their homes and press the elevator button or turn on their lights. I was intrigued to see the inside of those houses and always jumped at the opportunity while the older guys sat back. They were more spacious than our small apartments and the only other kind of living space I had ever seen in America. I was half curious and half frightened, but I was always willing to help and learn, and figured this was my opportunity. I didn't know a thing about Jewish people except that they lived in their own isolated world, dressed the same, prayed a lot, and owned the buildings we lived in. For various reasons they were able to build a level of self-reliance and economic independence that I admired.

We coexisted peacefully with the Jewish population, both sides letting the other be. We were both a forgotten class, both with histories of oppression from not being wanted anywhere, and that shared experience created some kind of unity. We were both pushed into a specific corner and, in Brooklyn, our corners were side by side.

Jay and his friends would tell stories—the ongoing saga of the hood—and I soaked it all up. It was history absent from the school textbooks but the kind that shaped my world: it was embedded into the sidewalk and built into the asphalt. Most of those guys also accumulated the kind of conspicuous wealth that I found seductive: Gucci clothes, Rolex watches, Benzes and Lexuses and Range Rovers. I'd sit in their parked cars with one leg dangling out, and change the music on their sound systems. I'd press into that smooth interior, check myself in the rearview. As I switched out CDs and messed with the bass and treble, spaceship lights beaming, a sensation would shoot into my fingers. *I wanted this.*

Jay stood out by being low-key, with a steady job and little interest in the illegal side of that world. He could tell I was getting captivated by the extravagant and tried to bring me balance. When he noticed I was getting into too much trouble, he told me about a football program run by the city. It was designed to both get at-risk kids off the street and to prepare them for high-school football, which could bring structure and discipline, and perhaps counteract the street temptations. In that world, any activity that keeps a child off the streets is lifesaving. Sometimes the activity is called warehousing—literally putting them somewhere else, eating up their hours that could be spent in danger or hustling. Other times, the activity is more root-based, establishing new expectations and new assumptions. Football was both and it also gave impressionable kids the mentorship of a coach, the type of male role model they may not encounter anywhere else.

There's an identity element at work too—we can only conceive of available options. When we watch television the only successful people that look like us are professional athletes and entertainers. Television's largest role in a lot of our homes is not as distraction or escape. It is as a mirror.

So for over a year I traveled on a bus on Rockaway Parkway out to Canarsie High School, a well-known football powerhouse in Brooklyn. We played a few games—it was mostly practice—but I took to it. At first I thought organized football was nuts: Why were they running into one another? Why not run through the open spaces? But I caught on easily, becoming a disciplined defender, and the coaches encouraged me. I turned into an imposing strong safety and felt like I had a shot to turn it into something. Some players from the New York Giants came out to talk to us and run some drills, and the effect on me was palpable. It broke through the wall that I had put up regarding my future.

Sports, especially at the youth level, are the great equalizer, a true democratic activity. Everyone knows who can play and neither your family nor your money impress on the field. It's played in the poorest slums in the world because it costs nothing—all you need is a ball and another person. You create everything else yourself. On the weekends and after school on Crown Street, we played behind the school on my block. It was touch football on gravel but everyone would always trip and get cut up. You had to learn how to plant yourself, how to roll when you fell. There'd be crowds along the sidelines, sitting on the metal benches, burger wrappers and beer cans strewn everywhere. It was a raucous scene down there and fights would break out from time to time.

I was younger than just about everyone, with a big chip on my shoulder. One cold Sunday morning, I was on the sidelines, trying to get in on the next game. A wiry teenager named Laurence started to yell back at me when I was calling next. He was eighteen and always talking shit on and off that field.

"He thinks he getting in," Laurence said in his squeaky voice, which sounded like Eazy-E. He turned to me, smoking his cigarette like he had never held one before. "You can't play, little man. What about kickball? They got kickball at the nursery school."

"Fuck out of here," I said. "I can play. I can fuck you up, too."

"Shit, you don't even know what you doing." He was peacocking at my expense, talking for other people's benefit. "You're into that Haitian soccer shit."

"Fuck out of here. What you got?" I said, walking toward him. "You ain't got shit, you pussy."

"Pussy?" He flicked his cigarette and started toward me, chest out. "You're the pussy. Fuckin' booty scratcher. Let's get it."

As he ran forward I caught him in a headlock and started to swing his body from the neck. We both fell to the ground and rolled, tussling over by the wooden picnic benches. When we got up I swung at him. As he blocked my punch with his forearm something popped in my right wrist, like I had punched concrete. The nerve pain shot up my arm like fire flowing through my body. I had never felt such pain. I walked off shouting backward at him, all adrenaline and agony, holding my arm like a dead kitten.

I knew no one at home would take me to the doctor, and I was so accustomed to getting hurt that I assumed it would heal the next day. But every day that week I woke up with a howling, throbbing pain inside my hand. Six days later it hurt even worse. I was hanging out at the Jewish Steps when Jay noticed me trying to zipper my jacket with one hand. He asked me what was wrong and I told him about the fight behind the school, the blocked punch.

He took my arm and extended it out, slowly. "Close your hand," he said.

I started to but couldn't, like a clamp was tightened on my wrist. I winced even trying to move it.

"Shit." He shook his head and pulled at my coat. "Let's go," he said, exasperated.

"Where?" I asked, but he just kept walking. "Where we going!" I followed him over to his car.

We got in and the car started up smooth and syrupy, lights aglow.

A sudden thump and then the raw spurt of Nas's voice, rhyming *tactics*, *defects*, and *hyperactive*.

"Don't you know to go to the doctor when you're hurt?" he said.

I was embarrassed. It was just one of the thousands of little things that a normal home life would have provided. "Yeah, but I—"

"It's fine," he said, the car pulling like water onto Crown Street. "Somebody's got to take you."

Kings County Hospital is a beast of a building, and as chaotic a place as you'll find in New York. People whirling through on gurneys, doctors running and calling out codes, everything just a hair away from going off the rails. It's one of the US hospitals where army medics are trained before being sent off to places like Iraq and Afghanistan. At Kings County doctors get experience with the speed, volume, and wounds of battle. This says more about my community than just about anything else.

My wrist barely merited a look there so we had to wait a long time. Jay and I flipped through magazines and watched TV for hours. We sat in the waiting room crunched among the walking wounded—a guy holding a thick bandage to his bleeding ear, a gunshot victim with his leg wrapped, a jittery guy limping around and yelling at the air, sleeping bodies pushing out a rancid smell, and countless of Brooklyn's sick and maimed. Cops scattered in and out, some trying to catch parole violators, which is common.

As Jay and I watched *Judge Judy* with the sound too low to hear, Jay turned to me. "That's some dumb shit, man," he said. "You got size, you're quick. You could make varsity if you could just get your shit together. That's the path, right there."

Unnecessary risk bothered Jay. He'd seen people lose so much over little things; he knew how easily the fight with Laurence could've snowballed into bloodshed or prison. Most of our conversations consisted of him trying to talk sense to me.

I was worried about my hand, but I tried to play it off. "It's fine."

"Oh, you a doctor now? You diagnose yourself?" he asked. "Walking around with a broken hand isn't too smart. Shit, I thought you were smart."

"I am smart," I said defensively. I hated when people even implied this.

"Yeah? I think the jury's still out," he said, picking up a magazine. A woman came running into the ER, yelling about her mother on the sidewalk. EMTs rushed the electric doors whirling a wheelchair. The rest of the waiting-room eyes didn't stray from the TV. That ER was a show they'd seen before, a channel they were tired of.

"What's that mean?" I asked, but Jay ignored me, flipping through pages. "J—what's that mean?"

"Look," he said, turning to face me. "I live where you live and I been there a lot longer. I'm not your fucking dad. I'm not your guidance counselor. I understand if someone approaches you, you gotta do what you gotta do—"

"Damn right—"

"—I'm not saying be a punk. But don't seek it out. You're like a heat-seeking missile. Always seeking it out. You feed off it—that part's gonna get you killed."

I had no argument. But there's a giant difference between understanding something and willing yourself to change because of it.

"Looking out for yourself doesn't always mean warring." He rolled the magazine and pointed it above my eyes. "Use your head."

It was dark outside by the time we saw a doctor. A hand threw open the green curtain with a snap and an older white guy, trimmed beard and glasses, stepped in. He asked me to stretch out my arm, turned it slightly, and saw the expression on my face. He watched my eyes more than my arm. "We can X-ray, but I can tell it's broken."

"What is?" Jay asked.

"The ligament here." He pointed and started to write on his chart. "The wrist."

"Shit," Jay said, more upset than I was.

"How long ago did this happen?" the doctor asked.

I started to answer, but Jay cut me off. "But can't you cast it?"

"It's too late to really do anything," the doctor said.

The doctor started turning my hand over, slowly. I winced. "Well, we can. So it won't break again. But it's not likely to matter. It's already settled into place."

"But you can cast it?" Jay said again.

"Sure, we can fit him for a cast." He swiped the curtain open and called for a nurse. Then he turned to me. "What's your name, son?"

"Jim," Jay said.

The doctor eyed Jay, then looked back at me. "What's your name?" he said again.

"Jim," I said, my voice hoarse.

They put me in a cast but, ignorantly, I took it off less than a week later. With that, my football career ended before it began. To this day I have to do push-ups on my fingers because my palm won't go down. Once that single path was closed off—even the hope of it snuffed out—the trap of my circumstances got that much tighter.

I rarely went to school and when I did, I was a terror. The bilingual classes were taught mostly by Haitian women, trying their best with few resources in overcrowded rooms. I was like my own weather system in there, a magnetic field pulling things toward me. Strolling in late and arrogant, swinging on kids at the slightest provocation, yelling and tossing things across the room. Friends would pop in from the hallway and interrupt class to give me a dap, let me know the latest news. Just like when I was younger, teachers hung that vagabond label on me. This time I embraced it.

There was a stigma to being in those bilingual classes and once my English was good enough, I wanted out and the teachers were more than willing to help. Early on in eighth grade, Dean Walton switched me to the regular-track classes, hoping the change would work to everyone's benefit. The fact that Mr. Walton had faith I could succeed was something of a motivator. I didn't want to let him down and I put together a well-behaved streak, even tried to do some homework. I sat at the kitchen table with my books trying to make sense of Ancient Egypt while Colin threw food at Roothchild and Roothchild screamed back and my grandmother screamed at everyone as she tried to pay bills. I tried to decipher algebra textbooks while my cousins and aunt argued over the television. My dad complained that he couldn't sleep, the street noise high and tight like it was there in the room with us. You couldn't even hear your own thoughts in that place.

But I didn't last long as an eager student. The gravity was just too powerful. In fact, moving me into the main-track classes actually made things worse: it extended my circle, so now I was mixing it up with kids in the regular classes and still the protector of those left behind. If anyone took the bilingual kids' money or threatened them, they would come to me and I would sort it out. It was a feedback loop: as my stature grew, people came to me for help and I got into more trouble because I would get involved. Now I was the center of another orbit and I liked it.

3

Hustle

The United States is really terrible at turning boys into men.

—DAVID BORKOWSKI

I gazed out that window of my grandmother's apartment and things started to crystallize. The quick exchanges tucked-inside handshakes, the tight-jeaned girls catching hollers, the corner dudes who reeked of grit and hustle, the diamond shine of the cars, the solid force of those who ran the street. There were those who "held things down," were respected and feared in equal measure, and there were chumps. I didn't even consider it a choice.

The more time I spent time with Jay and his crew, and with Pierre, Mackenzie, and their clique, the more my burgeoning mind understood things for what they were: I needed money. To get what I wanted, even to be *who* I wanted. It was a fact as solid as the bricks stacked high and the concrete spread wide.

But I didn't even have money for the vending machine or a subway ride. I began taking on odd jobs or, as we called them, hustles. A hustle is about putting yourself where the money is, squeezing something hard enough or from the right angle to find the money inside of it.

In Haiti, panhandlers are a rarity, despite the poverty blanketing the country. There's a work ethic in our blood and in our history— the same ethic that galvanized an island of slaves over two hundred years ago to do the unprecedented: take down their colonial masters and reinstate their freedom. It coursed through my veins too.

Even as a young kid with nothing, I didn't expect anything for free: I wanted to work. By the time I was six, I was already working for the local taxi service in Haiti, called a tap tap. It was a used converted pickup truck with a Technicolor top, people scrunching in that tight space, passengers up on the windowsills, bodies spilling out. I'd sit above the tailgate and collect the fares, scoring free lunch and maybe ten dollars. In Brooklyn, I kept my eyes open, my ears pushed tight to the ground, studied the way money exchanged hands, and put myself in between those transactions. I became a student, keeping a watch over what went on, what was paid for, and where I might fit into the mix. And in that, I found the value in myself.

I washed the exteriors of cars and vacuumed the interiors, carried boxes down stairwells, and loaded furniture onto trucks. In the summer I ran water bottles to sweating drivers at stoplights. In the winter I high-stepped through packed snow with a shovel, knocking on doors behind driveways buried in white. I'd get eighty dollars for twelve hours demolishing an entire brownstone with a sledgehammer, exhausting and unhealthy work. Pierre was plugged in to the odd-job economy around the neighborhood. He brought me along when he needed a second pair of hands, and vouched for me on those early jobs.

"Just don't talk. Don't say nothing," Pierre said, as we ventured one Saturday deep into the Hasidic side of Crown Street. It was late summer. On compact lawns, other lives reared their heads: teenage boys spraying one another with a hose, a family blowing up a kiddie pool, a girl pulling a red wagon with pristine white dolls lined up straight, a Hasidic man unloading straw and plywood from a truck. Not a thousand feet away were the faded bricks of my apartment building; I could turn around and still just about see my window. That's how New York unfolds—you look up and you're in another country, with its own rules and population. You're a local on one block and a tourist on the next.

An Orthodox family had offered Pierre four hundred dollars to paint their small one-story house. "Let me do the talking," he said. "I know these white folks."

"What if they ask my name?" I said. I was always polite to adults, of all stripes.

"They won't," he said. "Don't say nothing unless they ask you a direct question. They ask if you want water, something to drink. You say 'No, sir.'"

"What if it's a woman?"

Pierre quick-punched my arm. "Then it's 'ma'am,' dog. But it won't be. The Jews don't let their women talk to anyone. You can't shake their hands or even look at them. Strange shit."

I had noticed how shy and covered-up the Orthodox wives were. Pierre was right: we always dealt with the men. The women usually had multiple babies in various stages of need, dangling on them like they were the tree of life. I felt for those women. There was something meek about them and we might as well have been the wallpaper for all they talked to us.

These early hustles were all legal, but that didn't mean they were always safe. There are trip wires in that environment that can turn things quickly.

My friend Lorenzo got me a job at a supermarket out in East Flatbush where I bagged groceries at the end of the register counter; if there was an open spot, I'd go on walkabouts with him to hand out the weekly circulars. Given the choice, I'd take the fresh air every time. One time Lorenzo and I were handing out circulars a few blocks from the store, putting the pamphlets under doors and on windshields. Some of those apartment complexes were dangerous—deep out of our neighborhood and run by the Bloods. We were young and black with no work uniform, so every pair of eyes—homeowners, street gangs, law enforcement—stared us down. It was enemy territory from all angles.

We were folding and shoving coupons into mailboxes off an empty lobby, our voices traveling down cold hallways.

"I'm gonna hit Clarkson," Lorenzo said. "Make sure you do the mailboxes on the other side."

"Yup," I said.

I heard him go through a fire door off the lobby to cross between the buildings. Far from our home base, I was more alert than usual. When I heard muffled conversation from outside, I stepped back to get a look. There was no way Lorenzo ran into someone he knew.

I could see through the door into the alley: wires dangling out of back windows; broken A/C units and busted TVs. I could see Lorenzo's back and a huddle of five or six guys waiting outside the door on the railing. There was nothing loud—that's never how it goes down. It's like a shift in the air and some voices you can't place. It's a change in temperature and airflow. That's what it's like to get robbed; quiet and creeping, then smack in your face.

"Yo, hold up. Hold up," said a squirrely voice, heavy New York vowels. The words were distorted by the walls and the wind so I couldn't make out anything he said. And then I heard, "Nice kicks, man. What size you wear?"

Now, a stranger approaches you asking that, it's not a question. It's a straight-up threat. In terms of saving face, the currency of the street, there's only one way to respond. Lorenzo was no punk, so that's how he answered. "Your size," he said.

"Word?" the guy said, laughing. He flipped open a folding knife and took a step in, pointing with it. I weighed my options. Do I approach six guys with weapons in their own backyard or do I find a way to get Lorenzo out, and round up my own to come back at them? It's not as intuitive an answer as it sounds. Where I'm from the hard and fast rule is to fight—even if you're outnumbered. I started to creep their way when the guy took a swing at Lorenzo with the knife hand. Lorenzo jumped back in the air and the knife caught his North Face jacket, cut a big slash in it. The goose down flowed out, floating in the wind. Lorenzo took off and ran into me a few feet from the door's entrance, feathers trailing.

"Knife, go! Go!" he yelled, turning me around and pushing me forward. The guy took off after us, so we cut through the lobby and sprinted across the street. I could feel my heart beating into my throat, but once I looked back he was gone.

"What the fuck, man?" Lorenzo said.

"I know, shit." I turned around to check but no one was coming. I leaned against a mailbox, catching my breath. But Lorenzo kept walking, talking almost to himself.

"No way. Naw. We coming back at him," Lorenzo said. He had the devil eyes.

If Lorenzo was gangster enough to say "your size"—by himself—he certainly wasn't going to let it drop. And just by virtue of being there, I was in it too. I told him I'd grab anyone from my block and we'd have his back.

"Pussies," he said, looking back toward the building. Lorenzo stuck his finger in the big hole of his North Face. The fabric was just flapping around, the insides already blown out. "Fucking pussies. I just got this. And trying to snatch my Jordans."

The rest of the walk back to the supermarket, Lorenzo kept talking about whom he was going to round up, how quickly, and what they were going to do. It was like I wasn't even there. Back home I got sidetracked. I never did ask him if he went back there.

Most of my jobs were dull, exhausting, and dangerous, and three or four dollars an hour, less than minimum wage. But I was thirteen; I had few options and if I complained, there were literally hundreds of kids on my block who could step into my place. For a while I hung out at a barbershop down Nostrand Avenue sweeping up the hair on the floor with one of those big push brooms. I'd make piles that looked like dead animals and dustpan them up for a few bucks. The barbers were older dudes, mostly immigrants, who would give me a free fade or some of their takeout Chinese food.

A lot of buildings in my neighborhood had layers of businesses, operations hidden inside of operations. There was what the sign out front said was going on in there and then there was the rest of the onion. Often what was tucked inside was illegal, but not always. Behind the counter of the barbershop was a narrow stairwell that led to a dank basement where a husband and wife ran a cleaning business. They had seen me around the barbershop and hired me to wash and press shirts down there in a tight, hot room. I'd do six-, seven-hour shifts in that cramped basement and leave with twenty dollars. Whole weekends would roll by while I was down in that cave, buried from the world. Hours of standing up and ironing, my feet aching, my breath short, the heat from the lights inches from my head. I'd wipe the back of my neck and my hand would be painted in soot. There was no window or ventilation, so I'd step outside just to breathe and they'd give me a hard time for slacking. I just wanted oxygen. So many of my friends were making a lot more money by doing a lot less, handing out bags and vials on the street. When you're poor, young, and colored, your options don't extend much further than these.

"Keep moving, Jim. Not today."

"C'mon, just let us shoot a fair one." I was pleading to Dean Walton in the second-floor hallway of Lefferts Junior High. He'd heard I had come to school to get revenge on a crew that had jumped me at Field Day a few days prior.

Mr. Walton was right—that's why I was there. I was often at school specifically for that reason. It was the one place where I knew exactly where someone was going to be and at what time, down to the room and to the minute.

"You know I can't do that," Mr. Walton said. He was trying to catch my eyes, but I wouldn't let him. I refused to get locked in. Mr. Walton had me pinned up near the lockers, but I was somewhere else.

"Let it go, son."

As we were talking, the crew's leader, Gregory, tall and athletic, came up the stairs. Mr. Walton called him over.

"Gregory! C'mere."

"Yes, sir." Gregory looked confused.

"How about an apology?" Mr. Walton said.

"Sir?"

"I hear you and Mr. St. Germain had an altercation at Field Day. Something you were responsible for escalating?"

Gregory looked at me like he thought it was a setup. I just looked right through him, burning a hole. Mr. Walton's body blurry, his voice muffled and distant. Gregory's face just wide and open and asking for it. Mr. Walton's thick arms were between us and I was counting the seconds, waiting for him to move.

Gregory snapped to, like it all flooded back to him. He knew my crew was three times the size of his; he respected me now and Mr. Walton had nothing to do with it. He wanted my approval a whole lot more than the dean's. That disconnect—between whose approval we were seeking and whose approval we *should* have been seeking—was massive.

"Yo, it's all good. My bad," Gregory said. "Sorry." He stuck his hand out but I didn't take it. I just kept my eyes locked on him.

"All right, let's squash this gentlemen." Mr. Walton grabbed my hand and pushed us together, forcing us to shake.

As we came in, Mr. Walton relaxed his body backward. It was almost slow motion. I could see Mr. Walton's eyes pop, like his brain was telling his body to step back in. I pulled quickly out of the handshake and threw a right haymaker across Gregory's face, landed it square and clean. That satisfying contact where it's all give.

Mr. Walton's two hundred pounds were around me fast, and he grabbed me by the shirt and walked me down to his office, angrier than I'd ever seen him. If I'd been reckless enough to knock a kid out in front of the dean, right after he told me specifically *not* to, then I couldn't be talked sense to. And Mr. Walton knew it.

I was transferred—sentenced, really—for a few weeks to Pegasus, a suspension school for kids with extreme behavior problems. It was basically a small, disorganized prison for teenagers where we went home at the end of the day. Teachers had zero control over a student body that boasted rap sheets, records, and a bevy of shooting and stabbing stories. Pegasus was a way station, a warehouse to store troubled kids while the system figured out what to do with them.

Pegasus was also right across the street from the Albany projects—

Bloods territory—so I got it on both fronts: fending off classmates inside and rival gang members outside. Pegasus was like the minor leagues, a feeding pipeline for the criminal justice system eating away at black America. That place did nothing but build me a harder shell. When you're dropped in among other wolves, the choice is simple: become the alpha or get eaten. The hordes of angry and futureless young men roaming the streets and prison grounds are not inherently this way. You get through places like Pegasus by adapting. Instead of stemming any kind of bleeding, it speeds up the process of criminalization. There's no incentive to behave, to do well, to be a good person. Your reward—your survival—is based on your ability to impose your will on others.

After two months at Pegasus I got dropped back at Lefferts, but something had shifted in me. My time there drew me into a rougher crowd, a no-conscience crowd. As happens at that age, Devon and I stopped fighting and became close friends. The anger and animosity gets pulled inside out and that person becomes a brother for life, someone you can go to war with.

It's part of the process: Guys from one block sort it out and then join up to take on other blocks. It's like practice scrimmages prepping for game day. The trust creates a thick and tested bond. Those battles filter out who's going to not be there when it matters. It was cleansing: we'd get all of our shit out of the way first. We would often seek out who was closest to us, who perceived the world as we did, and Devon and I had been cut from the same mold, even down to the fact that he spoke Creole.

One Halloween night Devon and I were walking down Empire Boulevard on the way to the park next to Lefferts Junior High. It was a regular hangout where cliques got high on the swings and playground slides. The scene there was that mix of innocence and rebellion that you see in a lot of New York City parks. It was cold, and a harsh rain whipped sideways at us, flicking our cheeks. We got to the park and shielded ourselves underneath a playground bridge from the wind.

I pulled a thick blunt out of my coat pocket and was about to light it when we heard a squelching sound, gushing boots stepping on rubber. Eight to ten guys appeared in the dark. They surrounded us until Devon and I were back-to-back inside their circle.

Off the streetlights, I saw nothing but masks: Jason from *Friday the 13th*, Freddy from *Nightmare on Elm Street*, a skeleton face, a devil face, some others. The all-star team of horror movies.

Their words punched through the mouth holes in the plastic, their breath drifting out white in the cold air. Little puffs of smoke in the dark.

"What's good now, pussy?"

"What the fuck you gonna do?"

"What's up, pussy?"

Even against those numbers, we couldn't back down. And we certainly couldn't run because we lived in a cage. Being a punk knocks down your self-worth, removes the value that others give you. Getting out of one fight creates a hundred more as a consequence. It's the reason I went after Devon that first day on the basketball court. It's the reason neither of us moved from that circle.

"We're right here," Devon said. "Whatever you want. Let's get it in. Let's go."

We weren't going to start anything, but we had to stay, see if they would make the first move. It was tense, Devon's words holding in the cold air like that.

I started planning in my head: whom I was going to hit first, and how; who was going to come at me from behind, how to get out of that. I played it in my mind like in those Bruce Lee movies, though the reality was always scrambled and messy.

It was eerie being face-to-face with those masks, even though I sensed who they were. Darrell, a broad-shouldered kid we used to play football with, had one of those frozen sneers that he thought made him tough. I had recently gotten into a few fights with him in the schoolyard, then a few fights with his cousin J.J. Then his whole block was hunting me.

The masks had given them false confidence, and once they saw we weren't scared, they seemed less eager to fight. They played it like they were messing around and then just wandered off. The second they were gone Devon and I took off back up Nostrand to round up our crew. That kind of thing couldn't stand. An open case makes you look weak. People start talking about you and word leaks out. *We circled them up and they didn't do shit.* It would be open season on us.

When we got back no one was around except for an older dude named Malone, one of the sages on the block. Before we even finished telling him what happened he grabbed a gun from under his mattress, and I grabbed two meat cleavers from his kitchen.

"Aw shit," Devon said.

"All right, we're out," I said, handing one of the knives to Devon.

A few blocks down, we spotted Darrell and some of his clique on the corner. Their masks were all gone, but the jackets and hats were the same.

"Hey!" I yelled out, crossing the street toward their corner. "Hey!" They all looked up.

We all crossed against the traffic, not showing any of our weapons. If you showed them, you had to use them. And you didn't want to cut or shoot someone you knew unless there was a solid reason. They hadn't harmed us; they *violated* us. In my mind, it had to be addressed, but in proportion.

Devon and I were both talking at the same time, edgy and hyped. We were hungry and ready to go.

"What the fuck was that?"

"What's good?

"Ya'll trying to play us?"

"Let's get it crackin'. Let's go."

"Who wants?" I whipped off my jacket, trying to build momentum. Malone stood off to the side keeping watch, his chin low and his gun tucked in the back of his jeans.

There was a process to getting a gun in my neighborhood, a built-in checks-and-balances system that filtered out a lot of hotheaded nonsense. It started at the top of the tree: The older dudes, the OGs, had the gun. If you wanted to use it you had to give a reason and get permission. Then maybe as you learned your business, your clique would all share one. Later that year we all chipped in and bought an old rifle, which we hid on the roof of my building in a black plastic garbage bag. We also bought a .22 that we stashed behind the heater in the lobby of Devon's building.

With Malone and Devon standing back, Darrell and I fought it out there on the field, punching and wrestling and kicking by the metal backstop. We scrambled on the ground, rolling into the jagged fences. Just as we were getting winded, a cop car pulled up in the darkness, sneaky and soundless in the rain.

Everyone took off. I ran through the supermarket parking lot into an alley, ditching the meat cleaver. My whole arm and hand were bruised and cut—skin scraped away from the cement and sliced from the fence. It was late when I got home and I didn't know if I was being followed. I tapped on the door with my fingers, loud enough for someone to hear, not loud enough to wake someone's wrath. Roothchild opened it just a peek, looking groggy and annoyed. "What the fuck, man?"

"Just let me in, Patou. Now."

"What the fuck happened?" He saw my arm cut up, my clothes drenched.

I pushed the door open and walked past him. No way was I getting stuck sleeping in that cold hallway. I went straight to the kitchen and shook out some salt into a giant plastic bowl. For about an hour I sat in front of the TV and pushed my fist down in there, let it eat away at the cuts. I remembered when I was a kid my dad used to make me kneel on a metal grater and then kneel in salt. I had assumed it was a cruel punishment but maybe it was supposed to be a healing thing after all. Maybe it has to hurt first for it to heal. I thought about how the two things could be so close to each other, maybe even two sides of the same coin.

I fell asleep like that, with my hand in the bowl.

Devon and his friend Fernando provided a blanket of protection. Fernando was more filled out than me, with the early scribbles of a mustache. He was flashy, rocking fresh skullies, new fitteds, diamond earrings, and gold teeth. I was not immune from the peer pressure they brought—not just in taking on our enemies, but even targeting the innocent.

One night the three of us were walking through the lobby of my building when the elevator rattled open. We stopped just to see who was coming out. A quiet kid our age, who lived in the building, was standing there. He was about to walk past, but we were in his way. I saw a flicker of panic and I pounced. For no reason, I clocked him, straight and square in the face, knocking him back into the metal frame. A loud rumbling boom as he fell into it. Devon and Fernando both busted out laughing. "Oh shit!" Fernando said, as we took off up the stairs to my apartment.

I never saw that kid again, but I still remember his shocked face, his falling body, the reverberating boom, and then silence. It felt like nothing at the time but now I can't shake it from my memory.

* * *

There were no backyards in our world, so we were out in the open a lot—drinking and getting high in front of buildings, stairwells; in lobbies, playgrounds, and public parks. Neighbors would call the cops if we got too rowdy so we had escape routes and lookouts. We'd hear "Boys!" and take off, split up, cut through back alleys and parks. Cops would chase us in an endless game of cat and mouse. We'd vanish behind buildings, knowing which alleys led to which cut fences, to which backyards, to which back doors. We had those things mapped in our heads.

Of course we'd be right back an hour later. All we could see was about six inches in front of us, five minutes into the future. It was a by-product of our impulsivity, which justified our unnecessary risks. It gave us a hunger to push the limits of our newfound power.

Devon's parents drove a Camry and we discovered those keys could start other Camrys. One afternoon we stole one parked on the Jewish side. I had no idea how to drive but I faked my way slowly around the block, knowing I just had to keep the steering wheel straight. As I came back around the loop on Rogers Avenue cop cars were sitting there waiting. I blew through the stoplight, drove to the fire hydrant in front of my building, jumped out of the car while it was running, and ran inside. The older guys would nab cars and then sell them for parts, which made a lot more sense. Devon and I lacked that forward thinking.

One time there was a commotion on my block after a fight had broken out next to Medgar Evers College, which was across the street from my building. A whole squad of cops rolled up and inflamed the already chaotic scene: they pulled their guns and clubs out, were screaming and chasing people, cuffing bystanders. I was off on the corner on my bike and rolled up onto it. From my view, there was something almost comic about it all. "Yo, when the captain leaves," I yelled out, "we gonna fuck up the rookies." One of the cops heard me, holstered his radio, and gave chase. He was on me before I even had the thought to speed off.

"What the fuck did you say?" He grabbed me by my collar, spittle flying.

"What?" I said. "What'd I say?"

"You little fuck," he said. He banged me against the trunk of the car, turned me over, handcuffed me, put me in the car, and took me to the 71st Precinct down the street.

I sat in a cell for a few hours, but they couldn't really keep me—I was thirteen, ignorant of consequences, and had said something stupid. Arresting us for frivolous things like that, things that would never stick in court, was common. Because of the quota system, officers often get judged by their arrest numbers, even for minor offenses—which is what I was picked up for a lot of the time.

That was the MO: Rough us up, give us the hassle of fingerprinting and processing, the supposed scare of the cell, the nuisance of the time wasted, the call to the irritated parents, the reprimand or beating you'd get at home. I went through this a bunch of times: my father, grandmother, or Jay, posing as a family member, would come get me. It was just routine.

Over time, I drifted away from Pierre and his clique and started spending more time with Devon and Fernando, who both already had both feet planted in the street. My hustles began shifting from legal to illegal. The equation shook out simply to me underneath those hot basement lights and on those cold mornings: Why not stay on my block where everyone knows me? Why kill myself in eight hours of work for twenty bucks when up the block I can sell a package and make two hundred dollars? Devon made much more than me and he worked not even half as much. Passing out bags that got people high, gave them a good time? If I didn't do it, someone else would, so why not? I rationalized it all back then.

Julio was a Hispanic guy in his thirties who lived in a ground-floor apartment of my building. He had been selling drugs there since the day we arrived, for years before then. The neighborhood users and dealers would line up outside his apartment where his mom, younger brother, girlfriend, newborn son, and big-ass pit bull all lived. Coming into the building I'd spot a line at his door spilling into the tight hall. Julio had a market in there: drugs, guns, counterfeit clothes, boosted electronics. He would sit home, and people would come to his door and hand him money. The guy didn't have to move; he didn't even have to get up. Every six months or so the narcotics squad would smash his door down and lock him up. But he'd be back, every time, like the sun.

I'd been purchasing weed for myself from him for some time. One day, sometime in eighth grade, I stopped by to buy a quarter ounce. With his door cracked open, chain across, he handed me a bag and I handed him the money.

"Later," he said. For some reason, I hovered there for a moment. Our eyes met and he could tell what I was thinking. Word had gotten around that I'd been hustling every free minute I had.

"Yo," he said, "you looking to make some money?"

"Always," I said.

"I got some work you can flip. Bring me back half. No pressure but let me know when you're ready."

I barely let him finish. "Ready now," I said.

None of this was truly new to me. My father had connections to a lot of the drugs that flowed through Haiti. He even grew marijuana himself for some time, and all over the house I used to see these white squares, which looked like baking powder or sugar cubes. My dad and his friends would sprinkle some of the white powder into their marijuana blunts.

As a boy in Haiti, I was always doing errands for my father and plenty of times was his delivery boy for drugs. He'd hand me a package of thin brown paper, called sugar paper, and tell me where to deliver it and what to come back with and how much. I'd show up at a neighbor's house, turn over whatever was in that sugar paper, and they'd give me money or food to bring back home. I never questioned it and nothing seemed strange about it.

Julio gave me my first pack—a hundred nickel bags of marijuana. As long as I brought him back his share, he didn't care what I did with the product. I could be disciplined and sell it or smoke it with my friends, which was usually what I did. Like it does for a lot of young men in my position, the game sucked me in like a vacuum.

4

Buffett

Teenagers will disregard everything—their own fears, their parents' warnings, physical pain, the possibility of going to jail or dying—because they're convinced that social acceptance requires them not only to take risks but to do so in a cool, seemingly unconcerned manner. They exert self-control to overcome their inhibitions and more self-control to hide their negative feelings.

—ROY F. BAUMEISTER AND JOHN TIERNEY, *WILLPOWER: REDISCOVERING THE GREATEST HUMAN STRENGTH*[2]

When a kid is cutting school, hanging out on corners, dealing drugs, and getting high, society says he is *in* the streets. *On* the streets means you live there, you're homeless—it's geographical. *In* the streets means you're inside of it, surrounded on all sides. It's the identity that you wear, speak, and walk. And then you become part of it.

In New York, to be in the streets is to be engulfed. Consumed by the lifestyle, the threats, and the incentives that trap you. By thirteen I was stealing bikes and breaking into cars, getting high on marijuana and drunk on cheap liquor. Jay used to call me "street gum"—everywhere all of the time, sticking to the hard concrete.

Frank was part of Jay's crowd, in his late twenties and a little more street than Jay. He was a slick talker, spouting this rapid-fire rhythm, a musical *bitta bap* that shot out of him. The brim of his fitted cap was always pulled low, hiding his weathered face. At first I was his one-man audience, nodding and trying to follow. As my confidence grew, I'd speak up more and we'd hash things out together: trading off ideas on street philosophy, police behavior, business ventures, hip-hop lyrics. I loved that those older guys gave my ideas some weight. They gave me a sense of worth that was hard to come by at home or in school.

One Saturday afternoon after football on my block, Frank, Andre, and some others were hanging out on the Jewish Steps. The neighborhood was coming alive after a long winter. Hip-hop blasted from passing cars, reggae from open windows, and howls from dice games carried and bounced. Short girls caught hollers from platoons of men, as police worked their loop—all eyes and sneer. The thick smell of marijuana carried on the wind, while young kids chased one another in circles around elders playing dominoes on a rickety table.

Frank had just purchased a silver S500 Benz and had it parked in front to show everyone. That car just oozed. It looked to me like a sparkling toy, the sun beating and bouncing off it. I couldn't stop asking about it, but he wouldn't let me inside.

"Hell no, man," he said. "Out of work, out of school, what you want with my car?"

"But I got a job now," I protested.

"Oh yeah?"

"I'm a pharmacist."

Frank looked at me quizzically.

"Street pharmacist," I said, laughing.

"Fuck that. I don't need the cops taking my car because you got some shit on you."

The cops had trumped up some reason to impound Frank's last car and he'd been paranoid ever since.

"All right, let me see the Breitling?" I asked.

Frank held his arm out. The watch was chunky but it hung on his wrist all natural. I was always asking to look at it.

"Can I put it on?"

"Fuck outta here," he said. "It'd break your arm, cuz."

I lost myself in the whirled gold and pebbled diamonds. The face like an old train station, all Roman numerals and foreign words. I was still in my white T-shirt, secondhand jeans, thin-soled sneaks—what Jay called my uniform. My gear was so weak, off-brand and no-brand, that I was embarrassed to show up at school.

Frank saw me zoning out and put his arm around me. "You know what? I'm a call you Buffett from now on," he said.

"What?"

"Like Warren Buffett."

"Who's that?" I asked, defensive.

Frank grabbed Andre by the shoulder. "We have to educate this young one, Dre!" Frank said. Andre didn't look up from his pager, flicking Frank away like a fly.

"What's he do?" I asked.

"Stop texting that girl," Frank said, tight against Andre's ear. Frank got like that when he was revving up, all into your space. "Shorty don't like you. She trashed her phone when you got her number."

"Shut the fuck up," Andre said.

"What's he do?" I asked again, trying to knock his attention back.

"Who?" Frank asked.

"The guy. Muppet . . . Buffett, whatever his name is."

"Buffett. Warren Buffett." He broke down the sounds. "He's a value investor."

"Like oil and shit?"

"Nah, the market, man. Wall Street. A value investor is like the lone wolf. He puts money on the numbers no one else is betting on."

"You talking shit," Andre said, eyes still glued to his phone.

"Fuck you, cuz, I *read*," Frank said. "I read more than my fucking pager! You know what—fuck out of here, that's the problem! That's what I'm talking about!"

"What?" I asked.

"You ever read the tax code?" he asked me. I was thirteen and I had just learned English. So, no, I hadn't read the tax code.

"Nah, course not," Frank said. "It's written in fucking Greek—but *they* understand it." He pointed west toward Manhattan. "They wrote it! It's written for them to understand. We sitting here like suckers while they duck all of it! You think that's a coincidence?"

"No?" Andre said, half-mocking.

"Hell no!" Frank said, stomping on the Jewish Steps.

"Frank," I said, "how'd Warren Buffett get his money?"

He swung back to me and sat down. "Look, everyone goes one way: this company's the shit, that company is a piece of shit. Ninety-nine percent of those guys are sheep. Look how they dress. Look at their fucking *haircuts*! But Warren Buffett does things his own way. True gangster."

"I don't want to be named after some old white dude," I said.

"From Nebraska," he said.

"You're naming me after an old white dude who lives in *Nebraska*." I could not have told you at the time where Nebraska was.

"Cuz, Warren Buffett is *gangsta*," Frank said. "He's worth like fifty billion. That's with a *b*. You," he rubbed my head, "you gonna be filthy rich one day."

With that, I was Buffett. It was street code not to have people know "your government," and fights would break out if a real name spilled in public. You never knew who was listening or when something could lure the cops. Your name was like a paper trail leading right back to your front door. To this day, everyone I grew up with in my neighborhood still calls me Buffett.

Buffett was my street badge, my tag name, a freshly wrapped new self. The strict use of nicknames on the street is practical, but there's something bigger and psychological at work. It's a suit of armor. A gangster identity. It's someone who's you but not you. An alter ego that you put out there so no one can get in *here*. I tucked myself in tight and wrapped Buffett around me. I made sure it would be all that anyone ever saw.

I never entirely stopped going to school and I was never old enough to drop out. I'd stay home, or pretend I was going and just roam the streets. I was too independent to join a gang but a lot of my friends were Crip. Taking orders never made any sense to me and felt unjust. I didn't listen to my father, my grandmother, my dean, or my teachers: why would I take orders from some guy a few years older than me? That stubbornness served me well, might've saved my life.

We were all drawn to the luxury, but reality put it out of reach. There was a giant gap between whom we saw ourselves as and whom the world saw us as, what we had and what our heroes had. I was still early in the drug game, still dealing dime and nickel bags of mari-juana to friends, still smoking most of my supply. For me, that gap was a canyon.

Just like back in Haiti, poverty fostered creativity in the street economy—often the illegal type. One of the older hustlers on my block was a counterfeit supplier. He had a machine that churned out fake hundreds, fifties, and twenties, which he would sell to people so they could flip them for real cash. It was a ten-to-one purchase, so a hundred dollars would buy you a thousand counterfeit. He would even give the fake bills out on consignment. We'd take to the streets, exchanging the fake twenties for as much real money as possible—by buying cheap and getting change, over and over again, in as many locations as possible.

Taxi rides were ideal. Drivers didn't check the money closely, never got a look at your face, and would have trouble finding you since they didn't live in the neighborhood. I'd ride five blocks, get change, and pocket the money. Then do it again. Clubs were even better because almost everyone in there is drunk, it's dark and loud, and a bartender doesn't have the time or focus to check your money. The trick was folding the bills, scuffing them, playing with them a bit. Shuffle them between our fingers to give them that real texture. Periodically we mixed it in with real money and tried to slip it through.

Andre, Frank's friend, made out like a bandit hustling fake money, enough to buy rundown houses and flip them. He became something of an entrepreneurial hero in the hood, showing us that what it takes to be successful in the streets isn't that much different than it is in corporate America. Though there's a big discrepancy in who goes to jail when caught breaking the law.

I also joined up with a crew in their late teens and early twenties who had a hustle they called going "on the meet"—boosting. We would steal from stores and sell back the merchandise to smaller stores for half-price or whatever we could get for it. Those guys were masters, slick and ghost about it. In and out before anyone knew what happened. I boosted rarely, and usually just big chain stores. I convinced myself that stealing from billion-dollar companies wouldn't hurt anyone, and avoided local joints, mom-and-pop stores, places run by locals trying to feed their kids. I had to feel good about the decision, even if it was a bad one.

I'd grab items from supermarkets—dog food, baby formula, laundry detergent—and sell them back at the corner store. There was always a market for our stolen goods. We had a loyal customer base, mostly immigrants who ran bodegas up around Rogers Avenue. They didn't care that the products were stolen—we were extending their margins. They were making 50 percent on the markup instead of the regular five or ten. Sometimes I'd keep a sweater or jacket I swiped from a department store, but usually I just resold things for quick cash.

There was a particular hustle where we'd join up with ten or twelve guys from nearby blocks like Montgomery and Union. Beforehand we'd circle up and smoke a few blunts to get our courage up. Then we'd all take off in a pack: head down the whooshing subway entrance, like a wave into the station. We'd jump the turnstile or get a swipe from someone. My cousin Breeze taught me this trick where if I bent the MetroCard at a particular angle and swiped it about ten times it would eventually let me through. Sometimes when I needed money I'd hang out by the turnstile and do this for other people for a dollar.

Middle Easterners and Africans ran a whole counterfeit economy in Manhattan on Broadway around Thirty-Fourth Street, a commercial stretch of Midtown. We would mob the pop-up shops and grab counterfeit Nikes, Iceberg shirts, and Louis Vuitton purses and watches, and take off into the busy foot traffic, holding as much as we could carry. It was dicey because shop owners weren't afraid to chase us down with weapons. Sometimes the store would be twenty floors up a high-rise so if you got nabbed, you had nowhere to run.

We'd break off into smaller groups. One group would pretend they were interested in buying—asking questions, trying things on, keeping the employees engaged while another group would stuff items down their pants, or in their jackets or bags. At the next place we'd switch and the other group would play distracter. Success was based on speed and fearlessness, but I felt bad taking people's property in front of them.

One crowded Saturday we'd been having no luck so we met up at McDonald's and agreed on a Hail Mary plan: bum-rush a store all at once, take as much as we could hold, and run out. We picked a sports clothing store on the corner, near enough foot traffic that we'd be able to vanish into the crowds. There were football and basketball jerseys by the door and so many of us that it seemed like an easy smash and grab situation. We flew in like a bank robbery, yanked and tossed and ran.

"Hey! Hey, what the fuck!"

The burly store owner chased us down Broadway with a long knife that looked like a sword. I was holding a bunch of jerseys, some still attached to hangers, just kicking as fast as I could, dodging through tourists like a running back. He probably came as close as five feet to sticking his knife in my back. When I got to the subway station, I hopped three at a time down the stone steps and jumped over the turnstile. Just as those doors closed, I squeezed into the train, heart pounding and breath wheezing the whole ride back to Brooklyn.

Sitting there with those jerseys in my lap, some people side-eying me with their dead-right assumptions, I took some stock. My life wasn't really worth these jerseys. I wasn't even good enough at it, or motivated enough, to buffer the risk of getting a knife in my back.

When things went bad like that we'd rather the police show up because the alternative was much scarier. I'd rather a petty larceny wrap than a trip to the ICU. This was true for other encounters too: if you came up alone and unarmed on a group of gangbangers you'd be grateful if the police pulled up. You're not supposed to appreciate police presence and you would rather die than show it. But inside of your thumping heart you've never been so happy to hear those sirens and see those starchy blues.

Chuck D of Public Enemy called hip-hop "the black CNN." And that's what it began as, a satellite beaming from the ghettos of black life to the rest of the world. Hip-hop culture reflected my America to me and I reflected it back: 50 Cent and G-Unit, Jadakiss and the LOX—they took the right angles, the tight walls, and the black holes of my world and turned them into poetry, into road maps, into an anthem and a purpose. Styles P's album *A Gangster and a Gentleman* was my favorite, striking that perfect balance between reckless and thoughtful, which is how I thought of myself. We fell for the illusory too: Al Pacino in *Scarface*, Wesley Snipes in *New Jack City*, cold-blooded heroes who were self-made and entirely fictional. Fantasy heroes disguised as street reality. It's a persuasive charade and, like most, I bought it all.

The music opened up a hidden part of me. I'd curl inside head-phones and carry my portable CD player everywhere, like a pass-port. When things got too overwhelming for my young mind to cut through, I'd put on DMX and break down crying. He was open about the pain, pushing through it and thriving on it. He was a true survivor, honest about the hole carved out inside of him. I carried pain within me and disguised it with a swag and brashness that did nothing but cover the wound.

Morning to night, my friends and I were high. We would hold ci-phers, stand in a circle and pass four or five thick blunts around until everyone was way past good. If I couldn't smoke I'd get annoyed and antsy, willing to do just about anything to get high. In the evening we'd pour down cheap liquor and spend the rest of the evening inside a haze.

It was all done under the guise of having a good time; we were letting loose, partying, not giving a fuck. But we were all self-medicating. It seemed the only answer for our plight: hopelessness braided with loss, poverty, and the constant threat of violence. I was lonely, no matter how many people were around. Our clique was a loyal group but there was a thin thread keeping things together. Underneath it all, we were in a rat hole, everybody out for himself.

Handling one's liquor was about being a man—spitting testosterone and draping yourself in a machismo cape. I didn't really have the constitution for it or the internal gauge to keep things steady. I tended to heave myself over the line headfirst. My favorite drink was the Incredible Hulk, which was Hpnotiq, baby-blue liqueur that would turn green when mixed with Hennessy cognac. Straight up, the Hennessy would burn my little bird chest, but when mixed with the sugary liquor, I would pound my weight.

One night during the summer before ninth grade Devon and I threw down three or four Hulks and met up with some other guys at a party out at Kingsborough Houses. It was an off-the-rails situation, spilling into multiple apartments, the hallway, the roof, the lobby, the park out front. I mixed everything I could find in the cabinets and by the sink, anything that looked or smelled like alcohol. Around 2:00 a.m.—well past my limit—I took off, somehow making it the seven blocks to the 3 train. In the empty station I lay down on the wooden bench, waiting for the train, the ground picking up and dropping. No sound but the hollow whoosh from the tunnel and the buzz in my ears.

A train finally came and I willed myself on it, floating in and out of consciousness the whole ride. Somehow I got out at the right stop and then—nothing. I collapsed on the platform, blacked out for a minute or two. My body went limp and lifeless, nearly falling onto the tracks.

When I came to I saw a heavyset woman carrying a broom, her feet shuffling over.

"Call an ambulance! This boy just dropped! Hey!" She was yelling maybe to the guy in the booth. She dragged me by my foot away from the track and sat with me until paramedics showed up. The EMT workers loaded me onto a stretcher and carried me up the stairs. I can only remember intense dreams—water rising, my mouth swallowing and spitting—and waking up in the hospital, an IV in my arm and a beeping machine at my ear. A beautiful black woman in an all-white jacket before me, fuzzy and angelic.

"What's your name?" She had a syrup voice and bright teeth. I smiled, but I didn't really hear her. She was like a TV with the sound off.

"Can you hear me? What's your name?"

"Jim?" My voice sounded like someone else's, far away and behind glass.

"You sure?" She smiled. "Do you know where you are?"

My throat was sore, like I'd been screaming. I had dreamed that I was yelling and getting pulled underwater, pissed that I never learned how to swim. "Hospital."

"Can someone come and get you? An adult?"

The place seemed unfamiliar. "This Kings County?"

She shook her head. "Brookdale," she said. Brookdale was in Brownsville, the roughest section of Brooklyn, the reigning murder capital of New York. She checked all my vitals.

"Are you religious?" she asked.

"No," I said, "but I believe in God."

"Well, you should be thanking him. Profusely," she said. "What are you, thirteen? Ten more minutes and the coroner would've been there to pick up your body." Her eyes peered into me, tired and haunting. "You're lucky to be alive."

Looking back, that summer was like a solid gate closing behind me. Nothing felt like a crisis; I had become so inured to it that it all just rolled off. Jay had been my tether to an actual future but as I got into more dealing and boosting, I pushed him away. I couldn't wrap my head around his life, which seemed distant to me. Kids' brains are wired toward instant gratification. Jay's talk about the future clashed with everything my friends were doing—squeezing every last drop out of the day. And with that attitude came arrogance and greed and fearlessness.

We put value in everyone knowing who we were. Punks and sissies weren't worth knowing because they didn't "put in work" selling drugs, toting weapons, getting girls you didn't care about, taking from those who had what you didn't, punishing those who posed a threat, standing your ground when things got ugly, and holding your own when consequences arrived.

One way we got our names out there was literally—by tagging. Putting our names on the surfaces of the neighborhood in spray paint or big fat permanent markers. Graffiti is about rebellion and adolescent mischief, but it's also about staking claim. My clique would travel all over Brooklyn, writing our street names over everything. I tagged "Buffet"—misspelling it—on stop signs, gates, alleyways, cars, storefronts, benches, public restrooms, subways, elevators. Part of the rush was the chase—that's where the danger was. My friend T, a prolific tagger, was shot at multiple times for tagging on someone's van. Another time my cousin Breeze was chased by a guy with a knife after he got caught tagging around his front gate. Few of us had any artistic talent. It was solely about name recognition. No one gave us a voice so we had to declare ourselves. *I was here. I'm here now. I may come back.*

Across the street at Medgar Evers College, we used to hang among the stone buildings and open spaces after hours. One night some of us were out tagging and on our way back we hopped the locked fence and snuck back to get high by the trailers that were used as classrooms during the day. For whatever reason, we got revved up and started kicking in doors and smashing locks. We ransacked those trailers—

tossing drawers and papers, kicking everything over, tagging the walls and blackboards in the classroom in black spray paint, "Buffet" and "Fuck You" on just about every surface. My friend P smashed the glass for the fire extinguisher and started spraying the windows and doors in thick white foam. Outside we heard radio chatter and then saw a shadow creeping toward us, so we lit off through the courtyard. I was too dumb to realize I'd written my name just about everywhere.

A couple of days later cops approached my landlord, a short and heavyset Puerto Rican. Once he heard the name Buffett he described me, said I lived on the second floor with my grandmother. He told the cops he had just kicked me and my friends out that morning for smoking in the hallway. The cops went to talk to my grandmother and my sister, Geraldine, who was about eighteen at the time. She told them my real name and gave them a photo.

A few hours later, while I was cutting school on my block with Fernando, two officers approached me and told me to come with them to the 71st Precinct. Once there, they sat me at a table while they called my dad and found a cop who spoke Creole to translate for him. Hours later, when my dad finally arrived, the officer laid out what they found: broken doors, graffiti, "Buffet" everywhere. At the sound of that name, my dad's eyes popped.

"Eh, Buffett! Buffett Buffett! He writes Buffett all over! Everywhere!"

"Calm down, sir—" the officer said, trying to ease him.

"I knew you were a lost case! I am tired of this!" my dad said, hitting the table. "Maybe you *should* be in jail! Vagabond hanging out with other vagabonds."

"Sir—"

"Embarrassing me, your grandmother, everyone."

My father kept at it, the cops nodding patiently, the way other parents would. He talked about sending me back to Haiti, how he should've done it already, how Colin should go with me. All the anger poured out of him like from a burst valve. Once they got my dad's permission to speak to me, one of the cops read me my rights. The kindness extended to my dad faded, and the cop lit into me.

"You use the name Buffett?" he asked me.

"Yes, sir," I said. "People call me that." My dad's eyes were inflamed. I was more concerned about him hitting me than anything else.

The cop showed me a photo of the blackboard with "BUFFET" in black spray paint.

"Did you write this?"

I looked at my dad.

"Don't look at me!" my dad said in Creole. "I didn't do it! Answer their questions."

"Yes, sir."

"You wrote it?" the cop asked.

"I think so?"

"You think so?"

"Yes."

"Anyone with you?"

Silence. I looked again at my dad, but this time, the cop snapped, "*Don't* look at him. Look at me."

I stared into his eyes, beady and tight.

"Jim," the cop said, "was anyone with you?"

"I don't know."

"How can you not know?"

"I don't know."

"Did you break into the school?"

"What? No!"

"Then how—"

"I didn't! I wasn't even—"

"How'd you get in?"

"It was open," I said.

"We have a security guard," he said, "and a witness saying the gates were all locked. And we found six locks broken by the trailers."

"I told you I don't know nothing," I said, not convincingly. They arrested me for trespassing and burglary, even though nothing was missing. I told them just enough to incriminate myself but not enough to be helpful or cooperative.

I ended up missing a court date, and then another, until cops came one morning to take me down to Brooklyn Family Court. When I arrived, a petite white woman with black hair and brown glasses on a pointy nose introduced herself. "Hi," she said, smiling, "I'm Christine," and she stuck out her hand.

"Jim," I said, taking it.

"Let's talk in here. Get some privacy," she said. She brought me into a side room and we sat at a small table. In her clipped New York accent she asked me how I was, if I needed anything, and then tried to walk me through the particulars of my case. I nodded, though I didn't understand much of what she was saying.

"I mean nothing was stolen so the prosecutor will drop the burglary," Christine said. "And the trespassing charge is just ridiculous."

"It is?"

"Well, you were across the street from your house, right?"

I was hesitant. She saw it in my eyes.

"It's okay. I'm your lawyer. You can tell me anything."

"Okay."

"Plus, it's right here," she pointed to her papers.

"Yeah," I said, "it's across from my building."

"See, that's ridiculous. In the suburbs that would never have gotten you all the way to court. It's the problem with city policing. Ticks me off."

It wasn't just what Christine said to me—my understanding of the law was close to nothing. It was how she said it: the eye contact, asking questions about my life, listening to my answers, the tone of her voice, the language of her body. She treated me like an individual, not as a case or a problem to be solved. I assumed professional white people were all one thing and she shattered that.

I didn't know it but I was sitting across from a guardian angel, sent to me by the randomness of the juvenile court system. But at the time her generosity was confusing, even a bit suspicious. I had little inter-action with the white world and was led to believe there was a wall meant to keep people like me out. But here was this woman, whom I had nothing in common with, who acted almost like a mother to me. Or how I imagined a mother would act.

"Okay, this is a misdemeanor," she said. "So it's going to be fine. Now, what I care about is how do we make sure you walk out the door and go home.

"So," she said, shuffling through her bag for a pen. "When we see the judge, we need to tell him we'll put you in the care of a responsi-ble adult who can take you home. Who can make sure you make the next court date. You live with your dad? Your grandmother? Can they come get you?"

"I doubt it." I gave her my home number. "You can try."

It rang and rang until someone picked up, probably my grand-mother. For whatever reason, she couldn't come.

"Is there any adult we can call?"

She tried Jay, Pierre's uncle, and a few others. Then I thought of my neighbor, whom we called Black, who worked downtown. Chris-tine tracked him down and convinced him to show up at my hearing. I didn't tell Christine that Black was a regular customer of mine. We'd smoke together in his apartment, and I'd sit there rapt as he told me stories about his well-connected days up in Harlem.

Black came down to the courthouse and talked to Christine, tell-ing her what he knew about my home situation, how I'd come knock on his door sometimes for food. Christine later told me that was the first red flag that things were tough at home: I was reaching out to other adults for basic needs like being fed.

After a few more court dates that fall Christine got the judge to drop the case. After one of our court sessions, I was on my way down the steps of the courthouse and she yelled after me. "Jim!" She came closer. "How are you getting home?"

"The 3," I said, pointing to the station. "Taking the 3 train."

A slight smirk because she knew I'd be jumping the turnstile. She reached into her purse and put five dollars in my hand. "Look at me," she said. "Use this to pay your ride."

"Okay, thanks."

That was the pattern with her for all the court dates. If she could tell I hadn't eaten, and it was going to be a long wait to see the judge, she'd give me money for breakfast or lunch, sometimes money to get home. Before court or during breaks she'd ask about my home life— not really prying, but poking around. I remember once she mentioned something about a group home, which I'd heard of. Andre and Frank had both been in group homes, as had some of Devon's friends. I said it sounded like a good idea and asked how to get into one. She looked surprised. She hadn't been recommending it, she said, she was just talking about various services provided by the city. I was the first kid she met who actually requested to be remanded; it raised even more flags for her. She talked me out of going into the juvenile system that time, saying that it wasn't always the best idea. So once the case was dismissed, we hugged good-bye, and that was it. I was released back to the street.

But I'd see Christine again soon enough.

5

Survival Mode

It's not the load that breaks you down, it's the way you carry it.

—LENA HORNE

Once the court proceedings ended, my dad made good on his threat, buying plane tickets to send Colin and me back to Haiti. He knew a family friend—Jacqueline or Louloun—would take us in. It was a strategy to keep me from getting killed or going to prison, though I couldn't see his reasoning. And I couldn't even conceive of returning to La Plaine. I was a New Yorker now. There was no way I was going back. I'd rather take my chances here, even with nothing, than climb mango trees for food and work the back of the tap tap again.

The night before our flight, my brother and I were packing our bags, Colin seesawing between yelling and crying, cursing out my dad, throwing a tantrum. My grandmother and sister were crying too, but still acknowledging this was just better for everyone. My father would peek into the room once in a while, flash us a look like he was about to say something, and then walk off. That apartment was overflowing with bad feelings, grudges, and no room to breathe.

I was calm, while formulating an escape plan in my head. When no one was looking, I dropped my bag in the hallway, then approached my dad, who was heating something up in the kitchen.

"I got to pick up some shirts," I said.

"Where?"

"The dry cleaner. I got my jerseys there. Can I get ten dollars?"

Dad hesitated, looking suspicious, but pulled out his wallet and gave me a twenty.

"Be right back," I said.

When I got into the hallway, I grabbed my bag and took off for the stairs. My building had a lot of abandoned apartments; my friends and I would often hang in them, drinking and smoking, trying to bring girls by. On the other side of our building there was an abandoned apartment on the fourth floor where I'd been getting high with Devon and Fernando. The lock was busted and no one had lived there for a while. That night I emptied out some clothes on the floor for a pillow, plugged in my portable radio, and claimed my new home.

Winter was creeping in and that place was hollow, empty walls staring back at me, hardwood echoing in the night like the sound of death. At night I welcomed the sirens piercing the air; they pointed to a life outside, even a treacherous one. I holed up in that apartment, in a strange no-man's-land. My friends came by with food, liquor, and weed and kept me occupied. All I had to do was wait it out until the plane ticket was no longer good and then deal with the fallout.

When I strolled back into my grandmother's apartment a week later, everyone was furious: my grandmother for giving her more heartache than she could hold, my father for wasting his money, my cousins and aunt for making their household so combative.

My grandmother sat me down on the side of her bed. "You can't live here anymore," she said, apologetic but firm. "It's too hard. Your grandfather's not around and I can't do this. You don't care and you don't listen. You're on your own." Looking into her eyes, weary and aged, I felt bad. She had given me a life in America and I had spit it back at her.

So I took all my stuff into that abandoned apartment and just continued my day-to-day. I still popped in on school once in a while. My friends were there; there was drama and girls and dice games. Soon enough, word about my home life leaked out. One morning Mr. Walton found me during first period and brought me to his office.

"Have a seat, big son. Where you living now?"

"What do you mean?"

"Well, I know you're not with your grandmother. I hear things. You on your own?"

"I'm fine. It's good," I said. I was embarrassed that things had deteriorated so badly at home. School was a respite, a place where I didn't have to deal with that world.

"I'm not asking how you are, son. I'm asking where you're living. Where are you staying?"

"Here and there. I got a place."

"Wait, which is it?"

"What do you mean?" I asked.

"'Here and there' or your own place?"

Mr. Walton was good at catching people in contradictions. He had the confidence of a lawyer mixed with the experience of the street. It's what made him so effective as a dean.

"I'm good," I insisted.

"Yeah? Where do you sleep?"

"I got a place." I wasn't sure what he was getting at. "Am I in trouble, sir?"

"What place?"

"An apartment in my building." Mr. Walton's face dropped. "No, it's like no one's apartment but it like belongs to everyone."

"An abandoned apartment?"

"Kind of. It's—"

He shook his head. "I can't have one of my students homeless." At first, I thought he was going to kick me out of school for having no home. But it was the opposite. "You're coming home with me today," he said.

"What?"

"Meet me here after school."

At the end of the day, Mr. Walton drove me to his one-bedroom house in Rosedale, Queens. He let me sleep on an air mattress in his front room for a couple of weeks. It was unspoken that I shouldn't tell anyone.

This was a huge risk, endangering his career, and I was too walled off to even appreciate it. While living with him I made it to school every day so in that sense, it was good for me. But eventually I couldn't stay there anymore; people at school were talking and he just couldn't risk it.

Even my brief stint of being homeless didn't turn me around. I crashed with Pierre, with Jay, a night here and there with others, until my grandmother eventually let me back in. But it was different. I was different. I was my own broken limb now, hardening and settling into place. And I was throwing off helpful people and second chances like they were chains slowing me down.

* * *

The decision to push me along to high school the next year was baffling. Though I'd always had a share of natural intelligence, I was practically illiterate when I started at Lafayette High School. But like thousands of unprepared kids, I got promoted to high school because of the system's momentum. For kids of color in poor neighborhoods, it's like signing their death warrant at fourteen. The factory mentality pushes kids along, the clock ticking down on their adolescence, the chances for a meaningful intervention narrowing to nothing. The solution was to pass us on to another failed institution, become someone else's headache.

Lafayette High School was in the Bensonhurst section of Brooklyn, and it was a ninety-minute trek to get out there. I'd take the 2 train to Atlantic Avenue, hop on the Brooklyn-bound D-train express, and get off at Ninety-Fifth Street.

Bensonhurst was a dramatic shift in environment. A quiet, well-kept neighborhood consisting mostly of family homes filled with elderly residents and immigrants who'd been there for generations. Asian and Russian women watering gardens, sweeping porches, lining trash cans on the sidewalk. It looked closer to the streets of *Home Alone* than anything I'd seen yet in New York.

The sense of safety in the air was palpable, the same way that the threats were back on Crown Street. The only visible problems in the neighborhood were from us, a fraction of the commuting student body. We brought the unrest with us in our backpacks and inside our jackets, five days a week, from Crown Heights, Bed Stuy, and Brownsville. With the commute, my troubles in the classroom, and my broken wrist that prevented me from even trying out for football, I had little reason to show up at all.

When I did go, I got caught in the chaotic stream: cliques clashing over gang activities; fights over which colors someone was wearing and who said what to whom; conflicts with Lincoln and John Dewey High Schools, which were minutes away and formed a sort of triangle.

The street had taught me that the only way to keep others from imposing their will on me was to impose it on them first, so I became reckless. I would attend school extremely high, tipsy, and carrying my knife inside my North Face jacket. I discovered that being under the influence emboldened me. Often I'd pick a fight with another student, go to the locker room to take someone's money in a dice game, then maybe smoke a joint in the stairwell. School safety officers would give chase and I would exit the school building through a side door and vanish for a few weeks.

Once I returned to school, suspension would await. The principal, wise to the fact that I wanted out of school, began to give me in-school suspensions. They'd hand me a packet to complete and lock me up in a small room with three or four other students whom I ended up fighting with. I dug myself in such a hole that there was no way out and I'm sure that knowledge was simmering underneath. Little things would gnaw and gnaw at me until the anger would fill my body—run up my legs, my arms, heavy in my chest. Electric and thick and coursing through my veins.

One afternoon I was cutting class and playing dice—cee lo—in a small hallway behind the gym with this kid from Bed Stuy we called Rummy. He was quiet and kept to himself, but he'd bet wild and heavy at dice. In cee lo you hold the money you're betting in your left hand and roll the dice with the right. Rummy would lie all the time about what he was holding—ass betting.

When the bell rang I picked up the dice to leave before the halls flooded. "That's one-twenty you owe," I said. "Is that all of it?" I reached for the stack in his hand but he pulled it back, stuffing it in his jeans pocket.

Rummy threw his backpack over his shoulder. "Nah, it was twenty."

"The bank was at one-twenty. I'm the bank. You pay me."

"Nah, I never said one-twenty. I said *twenty*. You heard wrong, man."

I hadn't heard wrong and he knew it. Like "What size you wear?" this was a dare. He was saying *come and get it.*

I was like a Bugatti, zero to sixty in a blink. His mouth didn't move, but it was as if I heard him say, *What you gonna do about it, pussy?*

A teacher popped in. "Boys, where are you supposed to be?"

We didn't respond, keeping our stares locked.

"Boys!"

Silence.

"Should I bring you to the principal?"

But I could barely hear him. This was the line for me: under no circumstances could you allow someone to get over on you, or it opens the floodgates. *You don't need to pay Buffett, he's not going to do shit about it.* I was. I had to.

"You gonna pay me," I mouthed. "You gonna pay me."

"Fuck. Outta. Here," he mouthed back.

I charged him, linebacker style, right into the wall, and started whaling on him. The teacher got in between us and before I knew it, two school safety officers and the principal, Mr. Siegel, were pulling me off.

"You spit on me, man," Rummy said. "Fucking pussy."

I pushed through and swung at him again. The principal grabbed me and pinned my arms back. He was stronger than he looked.

"Stop. Stop! What's going on?" Mr. Siegel said.

"He owes me money," I said, trying to shake off his hold.

"Look at me. Calm down. Jim, calm down."

"He owes me—"

"First off," Mr. Siegel said, "you shouldn't be playing dice in school."

That just made me angrier. It was beside the point. I kept swinging my arms to free myself and both officers ran up to grab me again. During the struggle my gold chain popped off and fell on the floor. It was less than a hundred bucks and probably fake, but it was mine. The officer went over to pick it up as I was being taken away.

"My chain, man. That's mine!" I said.

"I'll put it in the office safe," Mr. Siegel said. "Someone from home can come and get it."

When I got that angry, all the emotions opened up so I started crying too. My face locked and my breath got tight, like I was hyperventilating. Their reactions went from puzzled to alarmed to terrified. Everyone's faces told me that I looked like a demon.

"We gotta get this kid to a hospital," Mr. Siegel said.

A nurse called the ambulance and the school safety officer put me in handcuffs just to keep me contained.

Coney Island Hospital was a faded place with walls like dirty water and bright lights that buzzed my brain. It was creepy in there, as if poor souls were passing their lives away. I didn't want to touch anything or look at anyone, least of all doctors.

Everyone spoke to me cautiously. Mr. Siegel reported that I had exhibited abnormal and dangerous behavior. The young doctor went through a checklist, trying to get me to talk. I zoned out during the questions, thinking about getting my money, smashing Rummy's teeth out on the curb, figuring out who could pick up my chain from school. My dad wasn't even at home anymore; he was living with a girlfriend in Queens. We had been fighting constantly and one night he smacked me in the mouth, striking blood. Someone called the police, children's services showed up, and he was removed from the house.

And no way my grandmother was going to travel over an hour to pick up my chain.

"Why are you so angry?" the doctor asked.

I peered out the windows, or what the bars let me see through. "What?"

"You seem angry. Why are you so angry?"

"I don't know."

I offered them little, but the psychiatric evaluation determined I was depressed much of the time, irritable and angry most of the time, and had trouble concentrating all of the time. I was low energy and worn out, though I never had thoughts of self-harm or suicide. I did wonder *Why me?* a lot. Why are we drenched in poverty while others have so much? Why are violence and hopelessness so prevalent in my world? What's the purpose of living if this is all there is?

They kept me overnight to be safe. I slept in a rickety metal bed, so narrow I couldn't move without falling. I woke to some kid yelling in his sleep and rain pelting the long barred windows.

My grandmother picked me up the next morning. On the drive home, staring out the window, I was quiet. A threshold had been crossed. There was no going back for me, both literally—I was done with school—and mentally. I wouldn't listen to anyone. I understood that I couldn't have one foot in the street and one foot out—you lose a foot that way. There was no more halfway for me. There couldn't be.

The less time I spent in school, the more I was attracted to the older crowds that seemed to be doing fine without it. They took me to some clubs. Around midnight, there'd be two lines in front, one for men and the other for women. Sleek cars would pull up, women dressed in just about nothing but high heels, rancorous dudes smoking and shouting obscenities at the ladies. A heavy police presence right around the perimeter. We would get searched and one of the older guys would slip the bouncer a twenty to let me in, though I soon got a fake ID.

Inside you couldn't see much in front of you. The club would be filled with smoke and dancing bodies. The DJ would swivel between reggae and hip-hop: Sean Paul, Vybz Kartel, Mavado, Sizzla, 50 Cent, Jay-Z, and others were on heavy rotation. On the dance floor the guys would go from woman to woman and compete to see who could grind against the most and get as many numbers as possible. If you left with someone, you were crowned the champ.

Like clockwork, once everyone's buzz topped out, there'd be a huge fight in the club. Cliques fighting over old beefs or someone's girl or ice grilling in the club. Broken bottles would fly and someone might get stabbed or shot out on the sidewalk. Most of the time it would spill into the street where the police would get involved. After too many of these fights, the older guys began to frequent more upscale clubs in Manhattan, which I couldn't sneak into. I would stay on the block and hustle all night until the sun came up. I'd see them driving through the neighborhood after a night out, looking for a parking spot, bleary-eyed and hundreds of dollars lighter.

Friday nights I joined the younger clique at the roller rink on Empire Boulevard, the prime spot in Brooklyn for teenagers. The skating rink was our stage, the hub to display what we pretended to have. We'd hustle all week just to have enough for the rink. A New York City landmark, the Empire roller rink had been there since the 1940s. It was the "Birthplace of Roller Disco," as a neon sign bragged. Friday nights were teen nights so we'd put on our best outfits, smoke some blunts, and pound Hennessy and Hpnotiq.

The place drew all types, not just low-level peddlers like me. Among typical schoolyard fighters and weekend hustlers were hardened young men whose lifestyle demanded constant armed protection. Late night, out front, things usually turned fierce—too many different cliques thrown together in one spot—so we'd come prepared. Beforehand we'd grab knives, brass knuckles, hammers, and then roll thick over to Empire Boulevard. We were emboldened by the rink's proximity to our neighborhood. Somewhere by the gas station on the corner we'd stash our weapons in trash cans, bushes, and Dumpsters.

Outside the rink, we'd get on the long line, the Ebbets Field public housing rising tall and industrial in the distance, the funeral home and liquor store across the street. We'd be searched and pay our fifteen dollars, security guards eyeing us tight as we passed. The place had a frozen-in-time look: slippery wood floor, cheesy neon palm trees, walls lit in bright fluorescents. The DJ would play hip-hop at a deafening volume so everyone had to shout. The tables and hangout area was a small square inside the rink and we'd be in there watching the skaters circle around us. After 11:30 they would end the skating and the entire rink would become a dance floor. When it closed, and we emptied out, the fights would start like they were part of the schedule. Too many young cliques thrown into one spot full of raging testosterone mixed with alcohol and marijuana. It was the perfect recipe for disaster.

One night on my way out there was a big brawl between gang members from my neighborhood and one from Bedford Stuyvesant. After I passed through and started walking home, empty-handed and alone, I got jumped by a group. They knocked me onto the sidewalk, and one of them repeatedly stomped on my face with his Timberland boots until I was out cold. I was laid up for a few days. It could have been a wake-up call; a turning point, even; but it was those five blocks of my world again. I couldn't see past them so I just thought about revenge.

6

T and T's

I think about this show I saw on the Nature channel the other day about elephants. About how despite weighing up to twenty-five thousand pounds and standing thirteen feet tall, they can still be chained . . . It starts when they're babies. Some asshole puts a metal chain attached to a wooden peg nailed into the ground around the baby elephant's foot. The baby elephant struggles but fails to break free and learns at that very moment not to struggle, that struggle is useless. Later on, even when the elephant can easily break free, it doesn't.

—MK ASANTE, *BUCK*

By fourteen I was stuck inside a trap that I mistook for freedom, driven by a sense of power that was likely to bury me. As a young riser in the drug trade, I was driven to plant my feet in all of it: the money, the fashion, the respect, the girls. It didn't even occur to me that there was anything else out there.

The lobby of Devon's building was our sanctuary. We would spend hours there, slinging drugs from broken mailboxes and selling off boosted clothes and electronics hidden in his family's first-floor apartment. In the winter we'd lose whole days on the thick steps and metal railing, smoking weed and passing a bottle of E&J cognac.

The streets strip away much of who you are, but it does give you a sharpness and an intuition about people. I can still look at someone, chat with them for a minute, and unwrap them, read something significant about them: desires, fears, and motivators. It was a skill honed in a place where the ability to do that meant your life.

For a while we got suspicious of this Jamaican guy who was always coming and going from an apartment off the lobby. In our world, our friends weren't even really friends, and everyone else was automatically an enemy. Over months of watching him, we sensed he was a big player in the game. We called him Dread, though he didn't have any. He was discreet, quiet, and killer smooth, part grace and part menace.

Devon was an extrovert, and they were neighbors, so he started talking to Dread first. We were all hoping for a connection of stature, a ladder to the next rung of the game. That payday, that pot of gold, kept us going. We worked corners all hours of the night, all times of the year, to become the next Tony Montana or Nino Brown. It's every street-level dealer's dream. We made dangerous decisions in the hopes that we'd become big enough to rewrite our misery. That was the costly lie we packaged and sold back to ourselves.

Users and peddlers would flood in and out of Dread's apartment daily. I kept my eyes up for an opening, a chance to talk to him, maybe get some work and boost my clientele. One Saturday afternoon I was hanging in the lobby with Fernando when he walked over to ask where Devon was. Dread spoke in this strong patois that gave him a layer of authenticity.

When I told him I didn't know, he looked me up and down. "What about you," he said. "Wanna take a trip?"

Fernando and I exchanged a look. I knew this was a risk. But one errand with Dread might open some real doors for me, get me off the corner for good. It would be an investment. High risk, high reward. Frank had named me Buffett for a reason.

"Sure," I said.

"Okay, wait here," Dread said. He grabbed a Desert Eagle from his apartment, tucked the handgun in his waistband, and waved me over like, *Let's go.* By then I had seen all types of guns but this one popped out at me. The barrel was like a visible threat. A gun like that might have given me a false sense of protection, but it would likely break my wrist.

I jumped in the passenger seat of his two-door red van and we took off like a missile, dipping in and out of traffic. He was the wildest and most erratic driver I've ever seen, and I'd ridden with Devon, who literally didn't know how to drive. But my face remained a rock.

At the entrance to the Brooklyn Bridge, a driver cut us off. Dread sped up and pulled next to the guy, rolled down the window and pointed his Desert Eagle right through. "I will kill your fucking bloodclot!" he kept yelling as he sped up and stopped, sped up and stopped. This was a Jamaican phrase I'd heard before, though I had no idea what it meant. I slunk down just slightly in the passenger seat, fiddling with the radio.

"Don't touch that," Dread said. He pushed my hand away and turned it louder. Buju Banton's "Hills and Valleys" shook the car. Dread sang along freely, soulfully, from a deep place somewhere inside of him. We inched onto the bridge.

He parked in front of an unlabeled warehouse on the west side of Manhattan, took the keys, and exited the van, leaving me in there. My stomach just dropped; I was a squatting duck, trapped and convinced something was going to go down. Twenty minutes later Dread jumped back in the van and dropped a white envelope full of cash on the console. I didn't say a word and he didn't offer any.

As soon as he pulled out he rammed into a car in front of us. Little damage but a clear hit; the other guy got out of his car.

"Fuck," Dread said. "Wait here."

The one thing I could do on the trip was not show fear—it's the value I could bring, what I was being tested on. But that car was a traveling felony: guns, drugs, and cash—and those were the things I knew about. But Dread seemed more annoyed than fazed by the sidetrack. He walked up and gave the driver a strong handshake with a stack of bills in his hand. Then he got back in the van and drove off. We didn't say three words the whole ride back to Brooklyn. He just blasted the reggae and kept his beamed-out eyes straight ahead.

Back on Crown Street, he handed me three hundred dollars. "Thanks, yute," he said. "We haffi link up soon again."

It was both the easiest and hardest money I ever made.

Dread had lured me in because of an almost chemical draw that some street dudes just have. Others carry the exact opposite—the guys you just knew to avoid, all quick tempers and invented slights, showy threats and follow-ups. Ky-Mani was one of those guys, much deeper in the gang life than any of us. I'd give him a dap here and there but that was it.

One night Devon, Fernando, and I were hanging out on the Jewish Steps with friends. I had been shook up all day. That afternoon I had come out of a grocery store on Montgomery Street to see a young guy on his back, bleeding on the sidewalk. When I got a look at his face, I recognized it was my friend Reggie's older brother. I froze, able to tell from his empty eyes that he wasn't there. Blood pooled below him, and the front of his shirt was soaked red. Cops had just pulled up and the ambulance was bringing a stretcher out, but I knew it was too late. From ten feet away I watched him die on the sidewalk. Those kinds of things are hard to walk away from, but that's what you have to do. If you didn't, you'd never move. I was trying to get my mind off it while I was shooting dice on the steps with Devon, Fernando, and others.

Ky-Mani was a skinny and dark-skinned guy who used to walk on his heels—duck-like. That night we saw him coming up the sidewalk under the streetlight, pushing along Lamar, who was in a wheelchair. The two of them were a pair; we'd always see Ky-Mani pushing around Lamar, who'd been paralyzed for years.

Everyone stood. A beef had been brewing between Ky-Mani and Fernando and Devon. As Ky-Mani got closer to the steps, he let go of Lamar's chair and bent down. He reached underneath the wheelchair, pulled out a handgun, and started shooting wildly. Four shots popped around us as we scattered, totally shocked.

Then Ky-Mani took off, pushing Lamar in front of him and rounding the corner. As we caught our breath, I looked down at Fernando's foot and said, "Yo, there's something on your sneakers."

"Shit," he said, wincing.

One of the bullets had hit the steps, ricocheted off the ground, and gone through Fernando's foot. We almost laughed the whole thing off. Once we realized no one was badly hurt, the whole thing became comical: who does a drive-by while pushing a wheelchair? If urban teens in America actually knew how to shoot there'd be none of us left.

At that point we had one communal gun, which rotated among buildings and required approval to use. By the time I got to the gun from Devon's lobby, I already had calmed down, come to my senses, and realized it wasn't worth it. It was just stupid to carry a gun unless you were going to use it—you took the risk without any benefit. After hearing cooler responses from a few older guys, I put it back in a stash spot. The natural waiting period likely saved my life. As younger and younger kids get their own guns, which have become cheaper and more prevalent, that practice is dying out. Along with the generation that's carrying them.

Serge, whom everyone called Jigga, lived in the next building over with his grandmother and his father. He hung out with the Jamaicans on the block, like Kino. Jigga was the one who had said hello to my grandmother in Creole that very first day I arrived on Crown Street, and Kino was the one who tried to stare me down. About a year after that I beat Kino up pretty badly on my corner, banging his head repeatedly on the pay phone. That fight settled the waters between us, though I never let my guard down with him.

But Jigga was reserved and quiet. He never went at me to score points, never tried to show me up to impress others. His was a confidence that came from within and it was genuine. A stocky kid with braids, Jigga had a slow-paced walk with a pronounced lean to his left that let you spot him blocks away. Jigga had the swagger of youth but the money of older dudes like Frank. I was taken by the allure of his Jordans, the brand-name jeans and jackets, the food and alcohol he purchased easily, the attention he received from the ladies. He was knee-deep in the drug business, dealing for a charismatic guy who lived a few floors above me named Javier. But it wasn't Jigga who introduced me to Javier.

A few weeks after my intense ride to Manhattan with Dread, some guy I had never seen before walked up to me on the corner.

"You Buffett?" he asked.

"Maybe. Who's asking?" I said.

He scoffed, like he didn't think I was worth it. He told me to be at Mr. B's candy store that Saturday at four. When I asked why, he just walked away.

But I was there. I knew.

Mr. B's candy store was owned by a half crook in his sixties, Mr. B., who had a Cadillac, a nice house, and a fondness for young women. The store was a hole-in-the-wall and always dark, even in the daytime. We'd been going in there after school for years to buy candy and play arcade games like Street Fighter. There was a back room and a basement, neither of which the kids were allowed in. But we all knew Mr. B ran a drug business out of there.

Addicts would come in, buy loosies up front, and then go into the back room to get high. As kids, we'd be five deep at the arcade game, focused on next game and high scores, but we'd see addicts coming out in a daze, women floating through who were paid for their services. If you just walked in off the street, you wouldn't notice much. But there was a world tucked inside that world. If people he didn't know asked about buying a gun or drugs, Mr. B would tear into them. "What are you talking about?!" he'd yell. "This is a kids' place. Get the fuck outta here!" Mr. B was just being careful, not trusting anyone he didn't know.

That Saturday I was at Mr. B's early, sitting at a table next to the back-room door. As I watched some middle-school kids huddled around the arcade game, I felt like I had graduated. In walked a thin-built guy, a few visible tattoos, probably in his midtwenties: Javier. I recognized him immediately. I was nervous but steady. He sat down across from me, his body tilted toward the door. His eyes were mean, black holes.

"You sure you're up for this?" Javier asked. "This business?"

"Yup," I said.

"This ain't selling to school kids anymore. You know that, right?"

"Yup," I said.

"The risk goes up. The rewards go up. Together," he said.

We discussed the numbers, how much I'd start with, what I would owe him, when and how to pay him. I was a beginner again, and had to prove myself before I could move more weight. "Don't fuck up the money," he kept saying.

Javier was a known quantity and people would not mess with me. But if I got nabbed, he said, I did not know him.

He reached into his jacket and passed me a small pack under the table, but when I reached for it, he held tight.

"Say it," he said.

I hesitated. "I don't know you," I said. Then he nodded, let go, and walked out.

Javier specialized in exotic marijuana like haze and hydro, more potent and expensive than I'd been handling. He was also a heavy crack and cocaine dealer, products I soon moved up to once I saw how much more money was to be made. For me, it was even more lucrative because I would never smoke my supply. It was a line I refused to cross, so there was no temptation. We were schooled on crack, warned what it could do to a person, witnessed it in the drug addicts who lived in the neighborhood. Their bodies were skeletal, their families disowned them, cops took advantage of them, the world seemed to beat them around mercilessly. Plus, our music and movies just reinforced it: hip-hop may have bragged about dealing, but anything besides weed was considered toxic.

The expansion into dealing crack cocaine was riskier: it put me on law enforcement's radar, sometimes right in their sights.

Jigga and I teamed up peddling, splitting the same job, rotating shifts, and sharing customers. The game is competitive but we were the rare breed who looked out for each other. If a customer asked one of us for ten dime bags, we would each sell him five.

The most profitable time for business was 12:00 to 5:00 a.m. Jigga and I would be out all night grabbing naps on car hoods, waiting for waves of customers. The corner evolved as prime real estate for a reason: it's where worlds intersect. Jigga and I would get warm in the phone booth or sit on the Dumpsters to get a bird's view of who was coming. We would burn time at the end of countless blunts, talking hopes and dreams over puffs of smoke in the cold air. We'd fantasize about saving up enough money to buy cars, like the sleek new BMW, with the interior like popcorn butter. Every now and then, if things were slow, we would frequent other blocks to get rid of our work. This came with a higher risk so we wouldn't do it alone or often. Peddling on someone else's territory was like asking to be shot. I know more than a few people who got killed this way.

Cop cars would lope slowly up the block trying to catch us in the act but we had it down to hard science. We never had the product on us and could always clock their arrivals and departures. Cops would roll up, throw us against the wall, and search us—all to no avail. They'd tell us to go home and we'd just walk around the block once and back to our home base.

We called our customers custies or fiends, and most were people I'd known for years before I became their dealer. This was before everyone had cell phones so petty hustlers like me lived on the corners, in front of buildings, and in lobbies muttering, "I got it, got that work . . ." just loud enough for the air to carry my voice. We'd stash the drugs under the heater, in broken mailboxes, or outside in the grass.

Marijuana was just a quick hand-to-hand transaction. Harder substances would only be handed over behind a locked door. In the open we'd drop the product somewhere and once we got paid we'd give the customer instructions about how to pick it up. The older guys told us never to keep crack on us unless we had absolutely no choice; even a small amount of crack is a felony, ten years. The older dealers had a stash house to store everything but Jigga and I didn't have that option. I would stash it in bags in my ass crack most of the time. The cops wouldn't check there and crack addicts didn't care. After it destroys people's health, their finances, and their families, crack cocaine takes their dignity too.

Devon had been dealing since he was a youngster and he had a cell phone before anyone, so he was already successful in the street. The phone brought him a wider net of customers, more conveniently and with much less risk. His older cousin, Lawson, was Crip-seasoned in the street and in and out of jail on a regular basis. People would talk about Lawson like he didn't bleed. He'd been shot a few times and lived to tell about it, gaining even more respect. There were all kinds of stories, like how he disfigured some older guy when he was only thirteen. When Lawson got back home from prison he saw me as a threat, so we had it out a few times and I held my own.

I eventually earned Lawson's respect and started to sell drugs for him on top of what I was dealing for Javier. Lawson was a reckless creature. In the hustling business more money means more drama and a much smaller margin for error. The repercussions for mistakes become heart-attack serious.

Lawson and his boys would clean up in Manhattan, spending nights on West Fourth Street in the Village, selling crack to white customers for four times the price they'd get where we lived. This was an overnight operation so they'd return at sunrise, flush with cash and jacked up, laughing about the lopsided profit. In Manhattan, the risk and reward were always that much greater.

Back in Brooklyn, we copied the tactic, exploiting our white customers' fear and ignorance about marijuana. We were always smoking out front on those Jewish Steps, so they knew to come to us to buy. Most of the time they just wanted to get the transaction over with, paying twice as much just to get out of there.

"Here," they'd say, shoving money into my hands, "I gotta go."

"Wait, I owe you five," I'd say.

"Just keep it!" they'd say into the wind. Sometimes I'd purposely take my time getting their change out, knowing they were itchy. Any angle I could find, I'd take it. It was the only way.

The cops were always around, both visibly and invisibly. Once I was sitting on milk crates in front of Devon's building at three in the morning, hustling, and a young white couple walked by. The guy stopped in front of me and asked, "Yo, you know anybody that has weed?"

My sensors went off. He was too open about it, like he didn't know how to ask, which is how cops talk. A dealer is always alert to certain words or how people choose to speak. If their approach is suspicious, you play dumb and send them away. But there are other times—if business is slow—when you risk it. You rationalize your way in.

That particular night I said, "Sure, I got it," and it turned out the guy was a plant. An undercover cop jumped out and searched me, looking for crack or weapons. When he discovered I had nothing else, he actually gave me my weed back. That happened a couple of times. The cop would find the weed, hand it back, and say, "Get the hell out of here, just go," annoyed I had wasted his time.

We called these cops "T and T's"—Tuesday and Thursdays— because on those two nights detectives would flood the hood specifically looking for guns and hard drugs. There'd be very few blue and whites, but plenty of black Impalas circling the street in the dark.

If we were desperate or dry, we'd take other chances. Jigga and I would cut a piece of soap and put it in a plastic bag, trying to pass it off to custies. Addicts are about the moment and the trade-off had to happen quickly, so they'd walk off without checking the bag. Papi, a custie who lived one block over, was our easiest target. We sold him soap a few times and he might not have even noticed. Sometimes a crack addict comes to buy but they're already so high they don't even know what's going on. And even if they did come back to argue, we could get away with saying it wasn't us who sold it to them.

My survival mechanism relied on other people's destruction, my own community's. I was young and desperate, but I still made the choice to do it. When later I read Malcolm X's autobiography, I was struck by how he viewed drugs in the ghetto: how it makes you "prey upon other human beings like a hawk or a vulture." At fourteen, I was already both.

* * *

Many veteran hustlers worked out of a trap house, a private spot where everything gets sold: drugs, clothes, electronics, women, guns, and more. I had hung out in trap houses before, playing video games or bringing girls over since I didn't have many options. A trap house is always somewhere in the cycle of getting robbed or busted by the police.

One night around 4:00 a.m. Jigga and I went to Javier's trap house to re-up on our supply. I was also looking to buy some Prada shoes for a girl I was seeing. Right as we walked in, I realized we had stumbled onto a robbery in progress. One of the dudes turned his gun to us, and walked us to the back room. He tied Jigga and me up, put us both in a tub, and took the sneakers right off my feet, almost a thousand dollars cash right from my pocket. Then he left with his crew. The whole experience was terrifying—we had no idea who those guys were, how likely they were to shoot, or whether they'd kill us just for seeing their faces. The experience shook me, but it didn't change me at all.

That next week, Ky-Mani and I got into a fight outside Mr. B's in broad daylight and I beat him up. There was this sense of disrespect— he was five years older and a street veteran—as well as unfinished business. But I was too deep into it, and wasn't thinking about him coming back with a gun. He would, but I was lucky enough to be gone by then.

At the end of that summer, Javier and I both got arrested one evening at our regular corner. The hot day was fading, but the daylight was still pronounced. I gave him the money for the re-up on my corner and he gave me a plastic Baggie of crack cocaine, which I quickly slipped in my pocket. But we were being watched. A cop and his partner came out, put me on the wall, and asked me to empty my pockets.

I hesitated, playing dumb, but there was no way out. I pulled some cash and then a rock of crack cocaine wrapped in plastic. In my other pocket was a small bag of marijuana. They found almost a thousand dollars on Javier, and we were arrested on the spot. I was booked, processed, and charged with criminal possession of a controlled substance with intent to distribute. My court dates were set and then they sent me home.

A week later, I got picked up again.

I had recently bought a new bicycle—a green Terra mountain bike—and I thought I was a genius for stashing the drugs underneath the seat. I'd keep a sheet of plastic wrapped around the bottom so the product wouldn't fall through. That Sunday afternoon I had just finished a sale in the alley behind Devon's building. I hopped back onto my bike when an unmarked detective car came screeching the wrong way up Crown Street. They pulled me off the bike and went straight for the seat, taking the drugs, the two hundred and thirteen dollars out of my pocket, and the bike. Then they cuffed me and shoved me into the back of the car.

They said they saw me make the sale, but I doubted it—we were well-hidden and my eyes were always peeled. There was one particular neighbor on the second floor of Devon's building who hated us hustling around there. I think she saw it go down and called them. If someone makes that call, gives a description, and you're already known to cops, they don't send the blue and whites. They send the detectives in the unmarked Impalas, siren on the dash. That's who got me.

Though I was a minor, fifteen years old, I was arrested and booked for a class D felony, which held a maximum of seven years in prison. I had isolated myself so completely that no one in my family would help me out. They wouldn't even come down to the station or to court. That's why it's called burning bridges: no one can cross and no one can get to you. I was another lost kid in the juvenile justice system, on the verge of becoming a statistic with no options and no way out. Except through.

PART II
THE SYSTEM

7

State Property

August 2004

- - - - - - - - - - - - -

When we make mistakes, meander, slip, and sometimes fall, we find means to gather ourselves, reset our compasses, and continue the journey.

—DESMOND TUTU[3]

"I was hoping to never see you again."

I had been staring at the dead brown floor for hours. Then, without a word, a heavy clanging and the door opening. A uniformed staff member, handcuffs dangling from his waist, silently took me into a visiting room. There sat Christine Bella, head tilted, slight smile pushing through. "Hi. Remember me?"

It was a relief; I had just about given up on seeing a kind face.

"What happened?" she asked.

The Spofford Juvenile Center in the Bronx was one of the few lock-up detention facilities in New York for juveniles. Also known as Bridges, it was a notorious intake place for troubled teens. Word was that lots of guys from the area who rose up and became something—Mike Tyson, Fat Joe—went through Spofford. It was a twisted rite of passage for black and Latino teens in New York, but an awful institution. No matter how much credibility it earned you back home.

For juveniles, this place was the real deal: heavy, locked doors; thick cement and cinder block; high walls with barbed wire; stoic staff; group showers. We were constantly being searched: forced to take off our shoes, which staff would bang upside down; our socks turned inside out; our pockets emptied; our collars padded; our pants taken off and shaken. Staff would enter our rooms randomly and turn everything upside down—as if I could've received something to stash, though I hadn't moved.

My room was a small locked box with a metal sink, so I couldn't hurt anyone or myself. A rickety bed was covered with a slice-thin mattress. There was a window up high but the glass was frosted, maybe because they didn't want us to get any thoughts about the outside world. The hours eked out like a slowly dripping faucet. There was nothing to do but go over how I got here and where I'd be going.

I'd had run-ins with the police before and they were routine: a ride to the precinct, maybe fingerprinting, and a call home. But a Class D felony meant I was headed deeper into the system. Maybe too far for any light to shine through. I would have to adapt quickly, hurt anyone who tried to make me a target. I would just go off on the first person to look at me funny. The heavy metal door and thick walls told me I had no choice but to adapt and survive. *Adapt and survive.* It was like a mantra that I repeated to myself. I just had to keep my head above water as the levels rose and the waves came crashing down.

The law treats crack more severely than cocaine. At the time, crack sentencing was literally a hundred times more severe than powder cocaine. The irony is that crack is actually more diluted than powder cocaine; it can be stretched out with baking soda and cooked up, which is what makes it cheap. The harsher penalties reveal racial bias and embedded systemic issues: it's much easier to arrest crack dealers on street corners than suburban kids or Wall Street brokers. It was only a matter of time before I got caught. As far as Brooklyn police were concerned, I was fish in a barrel.

Before Christine showed up, I had been running through everything in my head, alternating between the small and the large: How did the cops find the product so fast? How long were they going to put me away for? Was being sent away actually better for me? Was someone going to take my spot on the corner? What was my father going to say? Does my family even care enough to visit me?

I thought about the day we left for America, four years earlier. Everyone from the neighborhood knew where we were going so they congregated out in front of the house. I met up with my family on the main road and got on the back of the tap tap to the airport. Neighbors were waving good-bye, yelling things like "Don't forget us!" as the tap tap kicked up rocks on the dusty road. I remember carrying only a small bag, which didn't hold much of anything. I had my plane ticket, I had my visa, and I had the clothes on my back. I was so young, I assumed America was going to take care of the rest.

Spofford was the gateway, the first step into the system. There's a reason it's called the system; it's a well-oiled machine that takes in troubled kids and churns out hardened men. I was on my way.

"You're moving up in the world," Christine said jokingly. "Two D felonies." We sat in a sparse room, two wooden chairs and a phone. "What, one wasn't enough?"

"But I didn't do it."

"Really?"

"Really," I said. "I swear."

"Okay, then this will be easy," she said, half-joking.

"It wasn't even my bike—"

"And the drugs?"

"It was like a dime bag of weed—just to smoke. For me."

"And the crack?"

"Not mine," I muttered.

"All right," she said, exhaling as she opened my file.

I couldn't make eye contact with her; I felt like I'd let her down. But even as I avoided the truth and her look, having her there calmed me. The system is cold and faceless, an entity that towers over you and seems to exist to make you feel small. Christine made me feel like me again, even if just during the length of our conversation. She laid out my sentencing options. If I lost the case, she could try to convince the judge that I would benefit from a structured environment.

I was conflicted. Ignoring rules and running wild was the only childhood I'd ever known. From six years old I had been fending for myself for basic needs. In Brooklyn, that expanded. I had a powerful thirst for the streets: the block, my homies, the money, marijuana, and alcohol. Lockup would bring withdrawals—both physical and psychological. It was all toxic but my body needed it to function. I'd also heard horror stories about drug hustlers who got traumatized while incarcerated, beaten up or thrown in solitary or kept way past their release date.

I also knew I'd be guaranteed a meal, a bed, medical care, and, hopefully, adults who had a stake in my welfare. I felt guilty and wanted to give my family some peace of mind. Now at least they'd know where I was.

There was a drop of foresight in me too, a voice saying there had to be another way. I knew that my life back on Crown Street had a short clock and I wouldn't make it out. Even then, I recognized the opportunity brought by my arrest.

But all this didn't even really matter because where I went wasn't up to me. It was a Hobson's choice—the illusion of free will. The truth is I had no choice at all.

Christine always complimented me on being a good listener, but often I couldn't comprehend what she was saying regarding my case. I didn't understand the ins and outs of the juvenile justice system or the various services and options being presented to me. The legal terms were beyond my comprehension. I was polite and nodded a lot; most teenage boys aren't too expressive anyway, so I could hide what I didn't understand. But her level of attention and interest mattered more. She would regularly check back, ask if I understood; even when I pretended I did, she would still go over it again more simply. She was caring like that, not forcing me to reveal how little I understood.

The level of compassion I felt from Christine was more important to me at that moment than any details about the legal process. All that felt abstract. The law has to be more than an intellectual exercise. Being seen as a person in that fragile moment can change a child's life, help him feel a basic sense of security in a terrifying world. I don't know how much attorneys understand this: a child about to lose his freedom is looking at this adult as maybe his only hope.

For our rides out to court, or medical appointments, juvenile offenders were transported like dangerous criminals, searched yet again and marched outside. Staff clinked tight metal cuffs around our wrists and ankles and escorted us single file into a white government van, with "Department of Juvenile Justice" in bold on the side. I accepted that I was state property. But I wasn't afraid to ask questions;

that's always been my way. We were always in the custody of black or Latino males in their late twenties and thirties, many of whom had been in the streets or had kids in the streets. One time while they were preparing to transport me to Family Court I asked one, "You really need to do this? Cuff my arms and legs like I'm a murderer or something?"

As he clicked the ankle cuffs closed he eyed up at me, a visible sneer, like, *Who does this kid think he is?*

"This is my job, man. I didn't make the rules," he said. "You don't like it, don't get locked up. You thought this was Boy Scouts or some shit? You want to get milk and cookies? Get tucked in to bed?"

He laughed as he got into the passenger seat, but I could see his partner, the driver, looking at me through the rearview mirror during the drive. Old-school hip-hop played through the speakers and all the kids in the back were bopping their heads and mouthing the words. Their eyes were unfocused, the music taking them somewhere else. Music was a luxury and the van was the only time we got to hear any. It was like a satellite back to Earth, as far as we were concerned. Inside those vans, rusted white metal gates ran horizontally in rows, separating the driver from the kids and the kids from each other.

"Hey, son, what's your name?" the driver asked over the music. "Hey you, Mister Question Man. What's your name?"

"Me?" I asked. "Jim."

"I been where you at, Jim."

"Yeah?" Just hearing my first name out of his mouth sounded strange because we were rarely called by name like that. It was usually our full name bellowed in some official way—or a docket number.

"Yeah, a few times," he said. "And my boy's going through it now. And you looking at this wrong. What are you, sixteen?"

"Fifteen."

"Well, shit. This'll be over soon. This is like a crystal ball."

"Huh?"

"The future. If you don't leave the street alone, this will be the rest of your life. What you have left of it."

He wasn't trying to scare me. It was more like he was leveling with me. "Yeah," I said, "maybe, but why do you gotta—"

"Yo," a kid yelled from the back. "Shut the fuck up! We're not trying to hear you. Tryn'a hear the radio, man, not your dumb-ass questions."

"Word up," another voice said.

I turned my face into the gate behind me. "Mind your own fucking business, pussy," I yelled at him.

"Fuck out of here!" he said, kicking the seat.

"Hey, hey. Enough! Quiet!" the driver yelled. He killed the radio and we rode in silence the rest of the way to the courthouse. I could feel the kid in the back stewing.

The van pulled up to a separate entrance area behind the Brooklyn courthouse. We were taken out one by one, lined up, and escorted to a back elevator, then into a dark and depressing room. And there we sat, all day among the faded cinder block and hard lighting, on heavy lockdown. There were cheap plastic chairs bound together and then to the wall so nothing could be moved. A thick metal door with a small square window buzzed every thirty seconds as lawyers, social workers, and probation and court officers came in and out. A phone connected to the courtroom let the guard know whose case was up.

There was an old TV in the corner and since we'd be waiting eight hours, the staff would throw in VHS tapes, usually old boring movies that served as a distraction. Sometimes they'd play "smack" DVDs, homemade videos of underground rappers waving guns, boasting about selling drugs and pimping women, showing off their cars and jewelry. Smack DVDs were the purest form of a familiar impulse: showing off what pieces of the pie we were able to get for ourselves. When a lawyer would come in and catch sight of the movie, a staff member would run up and shut it off.

Some of the juvenile justice staff members weren't that far removed from the kids they were watching. Most were from the same neighborhoods and had similar perspectives. It's true they put in those videos because it kept us content and quiet, but looking back, it's disturbing. Why were they showing us these movies? Didn't they just reinforce some of the reasons why we were there?

The kids were only allowed brief communication with each other; if you encountered someone you had an issue with, this wasn't the place to settle it. But we were kids, and fights were inevitable. If a kid already had been sentenced and there were no longer any incentives to behave, something often went down.

They'd bring in boxes of squashed bologna sandwiches at lunch and if anyone complained, they'd get another version of the "this is why your ass shouldn't get locked up" speech. We'd elbow one another and scramble for ketchup, mustard, and mayo packets, squeeze them onto the sandwiches, and devour them, hoping there'd be extras. Sometimes when I sat there scarfing my food, I thought of the lunch line at school. How we didn't want to show our hunger if it meant showing our poverty. In juvie, that equation went right out the window. Everyone was equal, eating as if our life depended on it.

When the phone from the courtroom rang everyone got extremely quiet to hear who was up to see the judge. When a kid's case was called, he'd stand up and take a deep breath; his face would instantly transform from youthful disregard to fear, the tough-guy façade left on that chair. He'd go down the line and everyone would give him a dap, wish him luck: maybe he'd get to go back to the world that led us here in the first place. Since we were all from the same community, we'd also send messages through that kid, things like "Yo, tell my dude Rae I say what's up!" or "Tell B-One I'm holding it down in here." We wanted to send word of ourselves back out there, hoping it would only be a matter of time before we returned too.

Kids who lost their case would be escorted back into that room crying or keeping quietly to themselves, holding in their anger. Others returned beaming, a little bounce in their step, knowing they were getting out soon. And then sometimes a kid didn't come back at all, which meant he got to walk out the door and go home. "Lucky dude," we'd say sometimes. More often we'd say, "He'll be back."

Though it was comforting to see Christine, who always brought a smile and support, my three-minute appearance in front of the judge was just a formality. Most decisions were made before we got there. We were pawns in the larger moves made by invisible hands. It's a strange feeling, having your life decided as if you weren't even there. Most judges wouldn't address us, and prosecutors and defense attorneys talked about us in the third person, and in legal jargon that we didn't have a prayer of understanding. It seemed like we didn't even need to be there. Most kids leave their day in court feeling as unreal and small as they do in the cell.

I got moved from Spofford to a nonsecure detention facility (NSD) on Beach Avenue in the Bronx, right alongside a public housing complex. It was freer, though still far from free. At no time can a kid be alone at an NSD; you are under constant watch, even while you sleep. My room had a lower window, one I could see out of, and even curtains. A thin wooden desk was pushed against the wall with a stool. Security was looser and we could leave our rooms with permission.

Beach Avenue was a blur of faces and forms and questions. Of judges and lawyers, social workers, counselors, probation officers, and psychologists. They packaged me up and reported to the court, trying to find me suitable placement. I told and retold my life story, spilling all my transgressions, hopes, and fears to people who looked nothing like me, and who couldn't possibly understand me.

The strange thing was that I was comfortable being honest with them, since they judged me on a different scale than the one in the streets. They didn't care if I was tough or weak; I could just be me. It was like taking a long breath. The adults I met in lockup were expecting me to project weakness, vulnerability, all the hallmarks of adolescence. Christine went out of her way to let me know that it was okay to show myself, that I wouldn't be attacked if I did.

"How do you feel about selling drugs?"

A psychologist was sitting across from me in a closed room at Beach Avenue, yellow walls and open windows. I could hear free kids running around outside, horns honking. On nice days I felt more stuck than others.

"I feel terrible about it," I said. "Like I'm destroying families and that's wrong."

"Well, that's good," he said, writing it down in his leather notebook.

"But—" I hesitated.

"Go ahead."

"To be honest, at the same time I feel like if I don't do it, someone else will do it, you know?" I said. "I got friends that sell drugs to their mothers and if I don't do it, someone else is gonna do it anyway."

"So you recognize that it's wrong," he said, more a statement than a question.

"Of course. I'm taking food away from children."

"How's that?"

"Because their mother's coming to me to buy drugs."

I was trying to charge through the opening I saw, use my charm to make sure I got access to the resources that were offered. The process was backward—throughout my childhood I needed help, support, and services. But it wasn't until I got arrested that people and services came out of the shadows.

"You've had a hard life," he said, peeking at my files.

"Yes, sir," I said. I recognized that how I spoke was as important as what I said. "I know a lot of people that do. But yes, I did. I do." I didn't say it, but I believed that growing up the way I did, especially in

Haiti, forced me to mature quicker. That experience helped me know what I needed from my new environment.

But I was fifteen, so I had a loose understanding of my motivations. Christine said since I was still a teenager I had an "under-informed brain." I allowed negative influences to exert too much control, and I let impulsive behavior govern my actions. The malleable adolescent brain provided fertile ground for the criminal life. The doctors and social workers thought it was a good sign that I attempted to rationalize why I sold poison to society's most vulnerable.

"How do you feel about being placed somewhere?" a social worker asked. She was a mousy woman with small glasses.

"I don't know. I guess I was sad at first but I know that if I stayed in the community I'd be killed," I said. I was getting good at playing my role, though it was also starting to feel more and more like the truth. "Going to a place that gives me medical care, and where I have to be in school every day. I'm excited to learn, to read, better myself. Get opportunities."

"Do you think you can avoid conflict with your peers?" she asked. "Wherever you go, there will be other kids your age. Some like you." It was like she was lobbing underhanded pitches. I knew what she wanted me to say.

"Oh definitely. I don't really have the heart to hurt someone like for real. No doubt. I haven't fought with anyone here."

The respondent presented a history of markedly poor judgment . . . His capacity for sympathy impressed as intact, but sympathy does not appear to play a significant role in the respondent's decision making . . . it does appear that if he remains in the community, he will continue to encounter considerable danger.

The respondent's strong desires to better himself impressed as genuine, not manipulative. He impressed the examiner as a youth who, in spite of his turbulent history and markedly poor judgment, might seize upon opportunities for self-improvement that are presented to him. These strengths will serve him well in the future.

One night at Beach a staff member came to my room and told me to get my things. I did as I was told but he wouldn't answer any of my questions as I packed my few things. I had no idea where I was going and wasn't even allowed to say good-bye to anyone. I was escorted outside into a black car where a Department of Juvenile Justice supervisor sat at the wheel. I felt like a hostage as we drove into the night.

At the stoplight, the supervisor turned to me, seeing the anxiety on my face. "Don't worry," he said. "You're going to like this place."

I didn't even know what neighborhood I was in or where I was going. I took a deep breath and looked out the car window, watching the lights flash by. It was like we were driving into a black hole.

8

Points

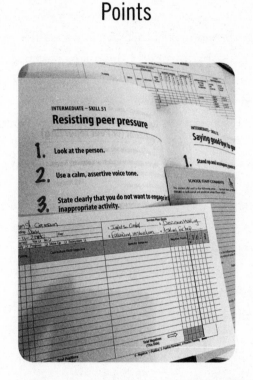

On our life map, he drew a bright circle around twelve through eighteen. This was the abyss here, unguided, black boys were swallowed whole, only to reemerge on corners and prison tiers. Dad was at war with this destiny. He was raising soldiers for all terrain.

—TA-NEHISI COATES, *THE BEAUTIFUL STRUGGLE*[4]

We pulled up in front of a three-story brownstone in a nice neighborhood not far from downtown Brooklyn. I thought it was a mistake: the building didn't look like a facility at all. I was expecting another high-walled place where I waited out my case. I noticed the quiet, the clean streets, the absence of all the typical late-night elements.

The Boys Town NSD was a sunburnt brick townhouse on Dean Street with gated windows of black metal. It was three train stops from my grandmother's apartment on Crown Street—a five-minute ride— but it felt worlds apart. As the Juvenile Justice supervisor brought me inside, the door opened to hallways, rooms converted into offices. On the first floor was a secretary, security monitors, a computer, and file cabinets. I sat down for intake, a routine I knew well by that point. An older white woman fired questions that I answered automatically:

> Jim St. Germain.
> Tenth grade.
> Crown Heights.
> Oh, Beach Avenue NSD.
> Ricot St. Germain, my mom's not around.
> I'll eat anything.
> A couple of shirts, these sneakers.
> No.
> No, my friends are Crip. Were Crip. They're still Crip but I'm not really friends with them anymore.
> No, not me.
> I don't know. Next month?
> My lawyer would know.
> Possession with intent to distribute.
> I don't know.
> No.
> I went through all this at Beach. And Spofford.

These question-and-answer rounds were never about imparting information. Boys Town already had my file. It was about *me*. They wanted to see whom they were dealing with. What hand they were dealt. What a kid like me was like right there in the flesh—not on paper.

A young staff member in a collared shirt knocked as he opened the door to the office. He put a plate in front of me—fried chicken, mashed potatoes. "Here you go, son," he said. I was starving and cleared the plate, ate like I hadn't in a while. I had been eating at long tables with other kids under tight watch and time frames for a few months. It was now hours past dinnertime but the food was hot; they had saved it for me and kept it warm. It was the first indication that this place saw me as more than a case file or money from the state.

After intake, he came back in and sat across from me on my side of the secretary's desk. He was light-skinned and leanly built, two-day beard and a shaved head. He looked right at me and said, "Hello, my name is Charles," corny and formal. Then he shook my hand and said, "It is nice to meet you."

I mumbled my name.

"Okay," he said. "I'm going to walk you through the Boys Town system. First off, you have to introduce yourself the way that I just introduced myself to you."

"Wait. Really?"

"Really. Look at me. Then shake my hand and say, 'Hello my name is Jim.' Maintain eye contact with me as you say, 'It is nice to meet you.'"

We went through this sequence a few times. He modeled it and I copied. He corrected me and I did it again. Charles and I introduced ourselves to each other five or six times. It was forced and awkward and I resisted it. It just seemed phony.

"The purpose here is to retrain your behavior," Charles said, more direct than before. "That's the model." He handed me a thick booklet, bound and laminated.

"We start with the first four basic skills: following instruction, accepting consequences, greeting skills, and reporting whereabouts."

I knew immediately that this place was nothing like Beach or Spofford. This felt like school. School for the outside world. School for after school.

"First, following instructions," he said. "There's steps in there to follow." He took my manual and opened it to a page, then handed it back to me.

I followed along as he recited: *1. Look at the person. 2. Say okay. 3. Repeat the instruction. 4. Complete the task. 5. Check back.*

"We go over these every day, all day," Charles said, "until it's automatic, unconscious. We're going to instill that in your brain," he said, pointing at my head.

He then handed me a wide index card, with boxes and a divider down the middle. One column read "Positive Points," the other "Negative Points." "Jim St. Germain" was already written at the top.

"What's this?"

"That's your point card," he said.

"My what card?"

"Point card. To keep track of your points. You earn positive points for positive behavior, negative points for negative behavior. We're trying to teach you consequences. By the time you leave here, hopefully it'll stick."

"I gotta give this to you anytime I do something bad?"

"No, you keep track. Your life, your card, your points. And it's for positive and negative."

I looked at the card in disbelief. *When in the world was I ever going to use a point card?*

"That card needs to be on you at all times. Think of it as an extension of yourself. Even not having it will get you negative points."

I smiled. "But where you gonna write it down then?"

"That's funny," he said. "You're smart." He flashed a brief smile that quickly got swallowed up by his face. "You always get meals, you always go to school, but a lot else is in your hands. If you accumulate a certain amount of points, you get to play basketball in the back, time to play video games, a later bedtime. Maybe we give you cookies and milk."

"Oh. Okay." I was having trouble processing most of it.

Charles stood up. "Okay, follow me," he said. I grabbed my bag and my new point card, and followed him up the stairs.

On the second floor Charles pointed out the living room, a TV and video game console, a large dining room table, pantries, an almost industrial-size kitchen. The tight hallways had motivational posters framed along the walls. We then went up another flight to where the kids slept—it was after nine so everyone was in bed. The shared bedrooms were college dorm–size with wooden bunk beds and blue-sheeted mattresses. We stopped at one of the rooms with three crumpled figures under blankets, and an empty and made top bunk. Laid out were a clean white T-shirt, boxers, soap, toothbrush, and toothpaste. "This is you," he said. "Now, take a shower. When you're done, store your property for me to lock up." He gestured to a labeled basket. "Wake-up is 6:30."

"Okay," I said.

"Good, that's 750 points."

"Huh," I said, confused.

"Write it down," he said. I patted my pockets and Charles took a pencil from behind his ear and handed it to me. I filled in my card, wondering how long I'd be able to do this.

It was a tight space for four people, with small wooden dressers, one thin closet. On a bulletin board I saw family pictures, a magazine photo of Tupac, a test with "Great job!" in red marker. Most kids lived out of bags, as they were only there a couple of weeks, sometimes less. I didn't know how long I'd be there. All I knew was that this was my new home, my fourth in as many months.

Boys Town was built on structure and routine. That's the heart of the system. We woke up at the same time every day, showered, and brushed our teeth. Everyone made their bed, tidied up their area, did their scheduled house chores, and got checked. Chore checker was a responsibility they'd give to a resident, as were manager and book-keeper. It was about creating a "buy in" culture. New residents see the kids taking responsibility so they fall in line.

After our morning routine, we lined up to go down to the dining room table. Two or three staff members would join the twelve kids for toast and cereal, maybe waffles. The teaching continued through the meal. You couldn't escape it. I was in a constant state of being watched and being taught, down to the most basic things. If I grabbed the milk without asking permission, I'd earn negative points. Someone would correct me and have me redo it. I had to give eye contact and ask respectfully, "May I please have some milk?"

At first it felt oppressive, and repressive. The goal was to teach me behavior, unlearn old habits, and train proper ones: everything from greeting someone to following instructions to accepting criticism. There were steps on how to disagree respectfully, select appropriate clothing, even how to contribute to a conversation.

No matter our crimes or situations we all had the same issue. We hadn't been following the rules: at home, at school, in the world, so there was a precision to everything at Boys Town. The lining up, the constant asking of permission, the overly proper way we had to speak, especially toward authority figures. It was like boot camp for my behavior.

One of my first mornings at Dean Street I had to use the bath-room during breakfast, so I got up from the table and did so. I was almost sixteen years old. It didn't occur to me to ask permission to go to take a piss.

"Hey, Jim," one of the staff, a burly dude we called D Dub, said when I returned. He was round, genial, with a beard and glasses. "Just now you got up and you went to the bathroom." The staff always immediately stated what you just did. Rather than "Hey, what are you doing?" or hitting you upside the head, they immediately identified your behavior. It's like the burn from the hot stove, creating a direct connection between behavior and consequence.

"Yeah. So?" I said.

"And you didn't ask permission and you didn't report your whereabouts. For that you're going to earn a negative two thousand points." D Dub spoke calmly, which was the method there. Staff wanted us to focus on our role. This was new: Teachers threw me out of class, cops cuffed me, and my father smacked me. Boys Town staff clearly stated what I did wrong, what the consequence was, and made sure I accepted it.

That last part was the crossroads moment. If you could control your anger, accept the consequences, and write your points down, you would automatically get half of them back. That day, that's not what I did.

"What?! That's fucking stupid," I said. "I'm not asking permission to piss. You want to hold it too?"

Everyone at the table froze.

"I understand you're upset," D Dub said. "You feel like you didn't do anything wrong, but this is part of the system and you have to accept the consequences."

"That's fucking st—"

"Okay, now that you're not accepting the initial consequence I'm going to assign you another five thousand negative points. Plus, because you're cursing—"

"I don't give a fuck about stupid points!" I snapped back.

A calm exhale. "Okay, I'm going to have to give you another . . ."

I kicked over my chair in protest and started yelling. I was caught in a loop, accumulating more and more negative points, getting further away from my privileges. D Dub stayed locked in on the steps. For all my exploding emotions, he remained even. In order to see if I'd calm down and be willing to accept the consequences, he gave me another instruction—"Please sit down and finish breakfast with us."

That was another chance to end it right there and I took it. Those little opportunities—to earn back points—were hugely valuable. Everyone at that table was paying for a series of bad decisions and consequences going back years. I huffed and sat back down, ten thousand points in the hole for the day. It wasn't even 8:00 a.m.

The Boys Town model makes sure you end on an upswing to show we can always make amends and get redemption, every time. After I accepted and wrote down my points, D Dub role-played it all over again with me. To demonstrate the proper behavior, we tracked back through the incident, which was psychologically powerful. We rewrote the negative incident as a positive one. An erasure. Something about that concept appealed to me.

For the first time in my life I was forced to follow rules, mostly because I had to face accountability on a daily basis. I was also regularly exposed to authority figures invested in my success. Rather than the occasional conversation with Christine or meeting with Dean Walton, this was day in and day out, every little thing I did, from every adult I encountered. But I couldn't always see it for what it was, so I rebelled frequently. It was like I'd been sick for so long that my body rejected the medicine.

After breakfast we lined up for the staff to escort us to the first floor where one by one we'd retrieve our shoes. Every time we entered the brownstone, we'd get searched, and have to take off our shoes and jackets so we'd be less likely to go AWOL, hurt others, or ourselves.

We then lined up again in the front hallway waiting for the blue passenger van to pull up.

Staff transported us one at a time using a grip called manual guidance where they held our arm with one hand, the other on our bicep, and guided us to another staff member at the van door. We were all pre-adjudication, and unlikely to run, but that's how we were transported everywhere. A solid reminder that we were not free. The system's claws were in us.

Behind the wheel of the van was Patrick, Big Pat we called him, one of the morning staff, who treated the van like it was his own. He had a slowly graying beard, glasses, and a gleaming smile. We gave him a hard time because he played only old-school jazz and R&B.

"C'mon, let's hear some hip-hop," I said one time. "You got any Nas in there?"

"That's the problem with you kids—your music is soulless." Big Pat turned back to look at me, then turned the volume up. He pointed at the radio.

"What are you talking about? You been alive like a minute. That's the Commodores. This is the song right here."

She's a brick howwwse. She's mighty mighty, just letting it all hang out.

"Mato mato! What is that?" I said.

"Mighty mighty," he said; then he started singing, dancing in his seat. "She's mighty mighty, just letting it all hang out." The whole van busted up laughing.

"The lady is stacked is what he's saying," Pat explained, drowned out by our laughter. After that anytime that song would come on he'd turn it all the way up and we'd "mato mato" while he waved us off, saying we didn't know anything.

Boys Town had its own school, a small brick building on Willoughby Street downtown, which was part of the larger Passages

Academy, the school system's program for kids in detention. It was the twelve of us at Dean Street, another twelve from the other Boys Town NSD on Bergen Street, along with kids serving longer sentences at the two residential homes—about forty kids total. As NSD kids we wanted to help our cause with the judge by getting a good "adjustment report," so we tended to stay in line. It was like an old schoolhouse where we started at homeroom in the lunchroom, and rotated through English, math, history, and science. An assistant teacher would work with individuals on the side, so as not to expose or embarrass them in front of the class.

The points system carried over to the school. Boys Town staff members would stand by the door, handing out discipline and teaching the model. I had barely gone to school and when I did, I had avoided work as much as possible. But I couldn't disappear in this classroom—the size, structure, and staff made that impossible. The spotlight was on me, and it felt like I couldn't get away with anything.

Ms. Oglio, the history teacher, was a small Italian woman with a fiery personality and a strong New York accent. I couldn't shake a feeling that she singled me out, not telling me the answers that she told others.

I remember a time a month into my time there, when we were reading about world religions. The class was filling out a worksheet on rituals and traditions. I kept raising my hand but Ms. Oglio was ignoring me and instead was helping Alan, an Albanian kid who seemed to already know everything.

"Jim, I can't show you exactly where the answer is," she eventually said. "You have to figure it out for yourself. If I give you the answer, you won't remember it or know how to find it again," she said.

"So I'm stupid?"

She opened her mouth like she was going to say something, but didn't. She just leaned over and went back to Alan.

"That's some racist shit, Ms. O. Fuck you!" I shouted, tossing my book and notebook on the floor.

"Jim. Jim! Step out the room, now," Mario called out from the door. A short and stocky staff member with coolie hair, Mario was earnest but had a black belt and an aura that commanded respect. Sometimes he rode a Harley motorcycle to work and we'd gather around to ask him questions about the bike.

"She's fucking racist!" I shouted as Mario walked me out of the room.

"Stop cursing and calm down," Mario said. He walked me out into the small foyer outside the classroom and I sat on the windowsill. Mario didn't speak a word, waiting for me to breathe it down. I stared into the classroom through the glass of the closed door at Ms. Oglio.

"What happened?" Mario asked.

"That bitch, Ms. Ugly-o, called me stupid," I said. "She's racist, man."

"First of all, don't call her a bitch. And her name is Oglio."

"I don't care, man. She's racist," I said.

"What are you talking about? You're more racist than she is. She cares about you. And she does *not* think you're stupid."

"She *is* racist! You been here so long you can't see it," I said, still staring through the glass.

"Jim, can you calm down?" he asked. "What does racism have to do with this?"

"That racist bitch—"

"Jim, take a deep breath," he suggested. "Do you remember the skill of expressing your feelings appropriately?"

"Yeah," I mumbled.

"Okay, let me hear it."

Once I was revved up, it wasn't easy to bring me down. Reluctantly, I began, "Remain calm and relaxed."

"What else?"

"Look at the person you're talking to, tell them how you feel."

"And?"

"Don't curse, and tell the person you appreciate them hearing you," I said. Just saying the steps aloud helped me follow them, which in turn calmed me down.

"So you just proved to me you're intelligent by telling me these skills. You need to practice what you already know. You need to check yourself and give yourself credit. Can I be real with you?"

"Yeah," I said.

"One of the skills was look at the person you're talking to, right?"

"Yeah," I said, turning to look at Mario for the first time.

"You forgot to take responsibility for how you feel. You feel you're stupid because that is how we describe our struggles of not knowing something. Raising your hand proved you're not stupid. Ms. Oglio's been doing this a long time. Don't project how you feel about yourself onto her. The only thing that's stupid is giving up, like a punk. You a punk?" he asked.

"Hell no. I'm no punk," I said.

"Then fight for your future. You can win only with proper training. We believe in you, but that means nothing if you don't believe in yourself."

I quietly soaked in what he said, but I was all in the moment. I couldn't see the future, even the immediate future. I couldn't see the very next thing, like returning to the classroom.

"Now, straight, that cost you five thousand points and you owe her an apology. She wants you to use your own brain. People cheat on tests but fail to realize that they don't know what they're supposed to know. Would you want a doctor that cheated on his board exams to operate on you?"

"No."

"I'm going to bring you back in there so you can apologize.

Ms. Oglio is gangster. She might look like a little white lady, but don't get it twisted."

After that incident, I cooled down toward Ms. Oglio and she went out of her way to teach me basic things like how to write a sentence. I'd always had an interest in history and politics so I was drawn naturally to what went on in her class. I had an appetite to know what happened before me. I was always asking why, and when there was an answer, it was history that provided it.

Ms. Oglio wouldn't let me hide or slip by. She was tenacious and had a kind of X-ray vision, seeing me as more than my file. She had a habit of touching my shoulder when she was proud, and warmth flowed out of her. Teaching wasn't just about imparting information for her; it was about connection and relationships and love. Ms. Oglio understood there was a brain, an experience, and a soul on the other side of her instruction.

She was a small woman so I became protective toward her and tried to make her job easier. There were authority figures—in school, at Dean Street, back home—whose job I wanted to make harder. Part of acting out was about creating resistance for those I didn't respect, exerting my power and influence. With Ms. Oglio I wanted to do the opposite.

But the truth is that I was nearly illiterate and mostly overwhelmed in those classes. I had been truant for so long, with such a weak foundation, that things were difficult. English was my second language, I lacked basic knowledge of history, and I had a background in a different math system. I either tried to hide what I didn't know or, if put on the spot, made it hard to teach me. I wore the bully cape sometimes, intimidating other kids and initiating conflict with the Boys Town staff and teachers. Survival instincts are like concrete; it takes a long, sustained force for them to crack. Asking questions meant showing my vulnerability and as a kid you never want to do that—you just nod your head and go along with the teacher. Plus, it was all so over-whelming; I didn't even know where to start.

After school we'd return to Dean Street for our prescribed study hours. Then we'd total up our points for the day. If you made your privileges ("privs"), you'd get television time or a sweet snack—another indication we had our feet in two worlds. We were young enough that cookies and milk was a reward yet we were escorted in and out of a van like state property.

Behind a high white fence in back was an enclosed courtyard with a basketball hoop, and thick leaves drooping down. We'd have bar-becues back there in the summertime and play three on three before dinner. Our math teacher let us play chess in class so we got into that for a while. There was also a basketball court on the other side of Dean Street, but we needed permission from the city, state, and Boys Town to go there. Even then we'd get escorted and staff would stand at all exits around the gates.

Lights out was 8:30 unless you were on the highest level, Achieve-ment, and you got to stay up later. That was another psychological and biological wall I hit. I was used to being out on my own, doing what I wanted, staying up late hustling, getting high and drunk, and sleeping in. Now I had to be in bed at 8:30, which was usually before my night even got started. And then I was up with the sun, which I only ever saw on the other side of the night. The point system reset every day, so no one was ever so far in the hole that it was hopeless to climb out. The next day was literally a brand-new day, which spelled something rare: hope.

Boys Town broke me down, forced me to relearn how to behave in the most literal sense. It went against everything I'd ever known. I got tired of early bedtimes, not being able to eat what I wanted, shut off from TV or video games. When I did fall in line, it was often in a superficial way, like I was gaming the system. I got my points, earned my privs, but mostly through tricks.

Once I mastered it, it was easy. Even if I had a horrible day, I knew how to still earn my privs. Before Total Up, I'd ask people if they needed help, every little thing. If someone dropped a pen, I'd rush over and grab it; I'd walk up to a new person and greet him properly. I knew which staff had which sweet spots or weak spots. And I developed keener negotiation skills that allowed me to work myself out of negative consequences. I started to follow the model, but I would not call it buying in at all.

In my heart of hearts, I knew what I was doing. I had turned it into my new hustle.

9

Scars

People pay for what they do, and still more, for what they have allowed themselves to become. And they pay for it very simply: by the lives they lead.

—JAMES BALDWIN

A few weeks into my time at Dean Street, I had a court date where the judge was going to offer me a plea deal. This time Christine was accompanied by a gentleman with shaggy hair. Shaggy for a lawyer. She introduced him as Marty, the deputy attorney in her office.

Marty was older than Christine, early fifties, smart but loose with a silver earring in his left ear. He didn't have that stoic mask worn by so many officers of the court. Before we saw the judge, the three of us sat on wooden benches toward the back of the courtroom.

"So, Jim," Christine began cautiously, "as I mentioned, I'm moving to another job, so I have to hand your case off. Marty is going to take over. He already knows a lot about the case because we work together so anything you can tell me, you can tell him."

"You're leaving?" I didn't hear much else of what she said, panicked that my one life vest was being tossed.

"Yes, but I'm not disappearing," she said. "Marty is just going to take over the case. He's going to do everything he can to keep you out of jail. Get you into the right situation. Placement."

"But I didn't do it," I said.

Christine sighed. She and Marty exchanged a look and then he drilled into me. "First of all," he said, "you have to stop saying that. Seriously." He was direct, without any of the false empathy I was accustomed to. It took me aback: part of me wanted to ask him who the hell he thought he was, but I kept silent. I knew I had no choice but to put my faith in him.

"Now," he said, "the prosecutor is offering you a deal to plead guilty to possession instead of sale, which we think is beneficial. Their evidence against you is compelling." Right off the bat I saw how stern he was, more pressing than Christine ever got.

Marty also spoke in a much more sophisticated style than Christine did. After we became friends, he confessed to me that because my English was good, and he didn't know my background, he thought I was "slow on the uptake." In reality, English was still relatively new to me, so I had to take that extra beat or ask that extra question.

"Look, I can't tell you what to do," he said. "I don't want to manipulate you. I think maybe one of the reasons you're in here is because you're susceptible to that."

I looked at Christine, who kept her eyes on Marty. I started to protest: "But I didn't—"

He put his hand out. "Look, Jim, you have nothing to lose by being honest with me. Remember that acknowledging you did something wrong doesn't mean you have to plead guilty to the judge. Our conversation stays here. I'm your lawyer. Honesty just makes sense for our relationship." Marty was blunt and direct. He knew he was delivering medicine and didn't see the point in pretending otherwise.

I was hesitant. "I don't know. What about going back home?"

"That's not really—" Christine began. Marty put his hand out to interject.

"It's not an option, Jim. That's just not on the table."

I again looked over at Christine, hoping she'd argue for the other side, but it was clear she was with Marty.

"Look, we don't want you to hurt yourself," Christine said.

"Hurt myself?"

"It's straightforward. You're going to lose this trial and you could be locked up for five years. We're not going to let that happen."

"Five years?" The words alone smacked me in the face.

"The evidence they have is unimpeachable," Marty added.

I crumbled after that. They went through the details of the offer, the kind of placement that they would look for. I decided to go along with it. I trusted Christine completely, with my life even, which is what was on the line.

Christine never really left me. She stayed heavily involved in the case, would call Marty for updates, check in on me when she could. But it was a tough adjustment and it took some time for me to get over my feelings of rejection and abandonment. The system itself is a never-ending cycle, but all the players are temporary. Christine had made me feel whole again, provided my main connection to the world, and her leaving hit me hard at a time when I couldn't take many more hits.

Though I'd always had issues with male authority figures, I was lost and confused enough to put my trust in Marty. We had no history, and he had a different style and approach, but I could quickly tell he had a giant heart, and sincerely wanted what was best for me. Marty came from real affluence but, like many others, he had dedicated his life to working for those who couldn't afford justice. He took on America's most forgotten and vulnerable youth. Such a righteous quality erased any assumptions I might have had about him.

Out of habit, at Dean Street I treated every interaction as a battle. My relationships there became as contentious as those on the street and in school, so I was constantly deprived of privileges. Despite markedly better surroundings, things were deteriorating. I was headed in the opposite direction, railing against everyone I encountered on the way.

As I became increasingly angry, isolation became my coping mechanism. I would cry in the confines of my room until my eyes were bloodshot. I would defy adults' instruction and be quick to attack my peers. I worked to alienate those who tried to bring love and normalcy to my life. I had decided that life had to be a battle.

The Boys Town program gives each kid specific skills to work on; one of mine was impulse control. If someone cursed at me or took something from me, I'd black out and overreact. I usually came back down and apologized, realizing how out of balance my reaction was. But soon enough it would happen again. I had trouble stepping out of the moment. Quick, angry responses were laced into my sense of self. It was the demon that was always chasing me.

For this exact reason I never engaged in any play fighting, which was common at Dean Street. I was vocal about not participating. The line between playing and real fighting was way too thin, especially at Boys Town, where every action had a tangible consequence.

LaDanian was a light-skinned kid of about seventeen, heavyset with a low haircut. He had been at Dean Street for a year, which was unusual. He was given a great deal of leeway and almost treated like junior staff. The rest of us would get jealous because LaDanian was on Achievement, the highest level at Boys Town. Even though they explained the levels (Daily, Weekly, Achievement), we still complained about the special treatment. LaDanian was tight with all the staff, especially David, who would horseplay with him regularly.

David was not that tall but a solid two hundred and thirty pounds, shaved head and earrings. The horseplay was never serious but it was always intense and physical. David and LaDanian were play wrestling once and LaDanian's head accidentally cracked on the side of a cabinet, cutting a big gash back there. Everybody froze. David ran downstairs and got a staff member to take LaDanian over to the hospital to get stitched up.

When David returned, he came over to me and two other kids who had been in the rec room. "He all right?" I asked.

"Yeah, he'll be good." David took us out of earshot of the kitchen. "Listen," he said, "it'd be easier if y'all say it was you play fighting with LaDanian, not me."

"Why?" I asked.

"Cause you know, then the boss lady comes into it and it's like a liability issue."

"Sure," one of the kids said.

"No problem," said the other.

I could see them all looking at me. "Uh uh," I said. "Hell no."

David turned to me, almost hurt. "What's the problem, Jim?"

"Nothing. I'm just not saying I did something I didn't do."

"Nah, man. It's not like that," David tried to explain. "Just if they *ask*. I'm not gonna take your privs away. It'll be me and—"

"Nope. Not doing it."

David glanced at the other kids and back at me.

"C'mon man," David said, now annoyed. "Just if Carolyn asks, say you were messing around and he slipped."

"I didn't do anything and I'm not saying I did."

"Oh so, you wanna get me fired?" David asked.

"Nothing to do with that. I don't horseplay, I tell you I don't horseplay, and you can't get me to say I was."

"C'mon Jim, it don't even matter—" one of the kids started.

"Fuck outta here," I snapped.

David's temperature rose, and so did mine—no one understood me. The whole thing was unjust; it didn't sit well and I was stone, unwilling to budge.

We addressed all the women in Boys Town formally: Ms. Lorraine, Ms. Carolyn, but we called the male staff by just their names. It was unconscious, but based on the world we knew: Black males were competition, or people looking to take advantage. It was hard to see them as "Mister." That tension was present no matter what their role. Unaccustomed to positive male images on our block, we put our guard up when we met one.

David was from our neighborhood and lived according to the rules of protecting your own and never snitching. To him, I was breaking that code. "So you're a snitch now," he said.

"I'm not gonna snitch," I said. "I'm just not saying I did anything."

The no-snitching code is like the Bible where I'm from. When someone presents a situation to you under those terms, you often fold; the snitch label is a giant stamp on your forehead. But I didn't see it as snitching. I wasn't involved, wasn't participating, and was only failing to say I was. There was no snitching involved at all. But I paid for my independent streak.

After that, I became a pariah. All the kids teamed up with David, singling me out. "You gonna snitch," they said. "You're not down with us. You're gonna get David fired." Some of the other staff joined them and the whole house turned against me.

Eventually it all spilled out. I got interviewed and I told the truth from my angle. I didn't say what happened; I was just adamant that I wasn't a part of it, that I wasn't going to accept consequences, that I was going to raise hell if they tried. It was frustrating on both ends—the staff and kids thought I was snitching, and the higher-ups could tell I was hiding something. I found a middle ground where I could adhere to my own principles; unfairness had always meant more to me than customs and rules. Even when I was engaged in the criminal life, there were things I just wouldn't do. It's why I stole from Macy's, not local businesses; why I felt the need to protect the other bilingual kids in school; why punching that kid in the face in the elevator sat with me for so long. Bryan Stevenson calls it restoring your "peace quotient"—a need to reset any imbalance that's been created.

That incident—and the fallout from it—spurred my anger, which was always like a beast kept tenuously at bay. I was acting out so often the staff suspected I had psychological issues. They made me talk to a therapist, who tried almost to intimidate me into talking.

"You seem angry," she said. "Why are you so angry?"

I'd been asked this more than a few times. And usually what I thought was: *If you're a young black man in America and you're not angry, there's something wrong with you.* But I didn't say that. Instead I said, "I don't know."

I couldn't even articulate it then. I was born from anger. My dad was an angry person, a strange mix of always around but never there: not for any of our births, not even when my mother was nearly dying in the hospital. His life was in the streets, smoking marijuana, playing poker and dice, getting drunk with his friends. So I had to be self-sufficient from a young age—making money, finding places to sleep, surviving. And when we moved to New York I had to do it all over again. It took its toll. I don't think my dad envisioned that bringing me to America was going to be another war. He was as swayed as I was by the dream of American prosperity.

Once I got locked up, forcing me to stop and take a breath, all
the collective weight of the forces in my life came down hard. It was
crushing me. And I couldn't breathe.

One Saturday afternoon at Dean Street they called me downstairs to
take a phone call. A staff member escorted me into the social worker's
office to receive it, rather than the intake desk, which was the norm.
The social worker was speaking into the phone when I got there. I
sensed something was up. Life in the streets gave me some advantages
and one was picking up vibes before anyone said a word. My survival
depended on it.

"Here he is," she said into the receiver.

I took the phone and was surprised to hear my dad's voice.

"Well, everything happens for a reason, don't it?" he said.

"What do you mean?"

"Your friend you're usually hanging out with?" I knew he meant
Jigga. "Doing your thing with late night?"

"Serge?"

"Yup. Shot and killed last night. Right outside. Right there on the
corner."

My muscles tightened as I processed his words. A chill ran through
my blood, and I went numb; if someone poked me with a needle, I
wouldn't have felt it. I shut down completely. The social worker hur-
ried around from the desk, took the receiver, and helped me sit down
into the chair. I don't remember anything else about the call. Sometime later, I got the full story.

Ky-Mani had shot and killed Jigga. Ky-Mani, whom I had beaten
up a couple of weeks before getting locked up, Ky-Mani who shot
at us while pushing Lamar's wheelchair past the Jewish Steps. The
whole thing hit with the force of concrete: My closest friend was dead.

I'd never see him again. Reuniting with Jigga was one of the main things I looked forward to when I got out; his presence was one of the few things that had kept me going. I'd encountered death before—it swirled around my world and regularly visited my block—but this time I felt it in my bones. It shook me from the inside.

I went back up to my room and lay down on the top bunk, staring at the ceiling as residents and staff came by to offer their support. Ms. Lauren was one of the regular staff who was like a mother figure to me at Dean Street. When I was angry I wouldn't listen to anyone else but her, but now I shut even her out. Everyone's words slid off me as my emotions stayed locked behind a door inside my brain. I was sixteen years old and my best friend was dead; I had every reason and right to openly cry—but my experience wouldn't let me. I had to hold it back until I was alone. When everyone finally left, things started to blur and my eyes opened into a flood. I couldn't catch my breath and my eyes stung with the salt and the heat.

There was the senselessness of it, the coldness. We were all so desensitized to violence that the permanence of it never pushed through. But I couldn't move on. At the time, it felt like I might not ever move on. Like I'd always be frozen in that spot and that moment, with all the horrors of it washing down on me.

Had I been living at home, I would've been out there on that exact corner with Jigga, right next to him, right in the trajectories of those bullets. My dad knew that too; it's why he said "everything happens for a reason." In fact, since I had just beat Ky-Mani up, not only could it have been me, it probably *should've* been me. The guilt was overwhelming. Jigga and I were so close, and our lives were so intertwined, that I experienced his death vicariously. As I tried to process his death, it felt I was also mourning myself.

I was railing inside about the loss, the guilt, my powerlessness at being unable to prevent my friend's murder. The questions looped through the night into the next day: Could I have stopped it? Would I have seen Ky-Mani coming? If I had been there would Jigga still be alive? Why was my friend taken? Why was I saved?

Boys Town provided me with special counseling and I was put on "one-on-one," which meant a designated staff member shadowed me twenty-four hours a day. Even when I was in bed, a staff member was right outside my door. I was put on watch to make sure I didn't hurt myself.

In my sessions with the counselor, I couldn't explain how Jigga's death upended everything in my world, what I thought I was and what I thought I'd be. It was preverbal. I couldn't explain it with any words I knew and had little desire to try with a stranger. I sat across from this older white woman with gentle eyes, her voice floating in from a distant place. With all her years of training and multiple degrees, she couldn't know what I was going through. I just let out one-syllable answers and tried to run out the clock. It didn't seem possible that talking about it could do anything but leave a deeper scar.

Internally, I focused on getting out so I could seek revenge. So when, a few days later, I heard the police had picked Ky-Mani up, I was angry. Cops had nothing to do with our idea of justice; we handled it ourselves. It's not just that I wanted to kill him myself, I was *supposed to* kill him myself. That had always been how it was done.

I remember as a child there was a thief, a stranger from outside La Plaine, who was murdered in broad daylight by some of our neighbors. His body stayed in the street for days and I was afraid to go outside. But it spoke to some sense of self-protection, and justice. No one would take care of us so we had to handle things on our own.

From the moment I had been arrested I treated being in the system as a punishment, something to ride out until I got back home. But things were starting to get blurry. Since the day I was arrested, I was put on a trajectory that had saved my life. Literally, it had prevented me from getting shot by Ky-Mani or going after him. On a larger level, I began to feel something else at work—the people and forces that had been protecting me. Perhaps I was there for a reason.

One afternoon after school, at one of my low points, Charles called me downstairs to the office. I assumed I was in trouble, about to be put on subsystem, a form of probation where you had to earn double points for every privilege.

"Hey, Jim, here you go," he said, handing me a black trash bag.

"What's this?"

"Some new clothes I got that are too small. You want 'em?" Of course I did; I wore the same white T-shirts and single pair of black jeans almost every day. But the generosity was suspicious. "You sure?"

"I gave it to you, didn't I? You want 'em?"

My brain flashed back to roaming the streets of Haiti as a child in search of work, sweeping hair and painting houses in Brooklyn, diving into the criminal life as a teenager. It all came down to something simple: the need not to ask another man for help. My rationale was that anything given could be taken back. My pride had blocked my ability to accept things from others.

"Sure," I said, looking inside the trash bag, the weight of the clothes stretching it low.

"Cool," he said. "I also got these." From behind the desk, Charles brought out a pair of deep blue Iceberg jeans. I rubbed the fine denim texture between my fingers, marveling at the thin white lines in the fabric, the brand's signature. I'd never owned a pair but my favorite hip-hop artists sported them. Charles also gave me a pair of S. Carter Reeboks, Jay-Z's sneaker line, gleaming white with white laces. I had always craved brand-name gear and here Charles was just handing me these sneakers. Not three months earlier, I'd been risking my life to be able to sport them. No doubt Charles knew this and was trying to subtly communicate they were no big deal.

Charles could see my excitement, but he probably didn't understand how tough it was for me to accept those things. I didn't take any of it for granted, treating the jeans and the sneakers like newborn babies. I would religiously scrub the S. Carters with a toothbrush to keep them sparkling white. Perhaps Charles spotted the grief hidden underneath my façade; perhaps he too was once abandoned without the shadow of any hope. What he offered went far beyond mere clothes. It was a kindness and generosity during a time when I was carrying a heavy weight around me like a chain.

For months, I went back and forth from Boys Town to court where first Christine, then Marty, argued my case. They both treated me like someone worth caring about. Attorneys still want to get you home, because constitutionally it's their job to protect your freedom, but for me, there were other things at stake. The fact that my lawyers couldn't win the case was actually a gift. While at Dean Street, waiting for my case to be adjudicated, I interviewed with a handful of long-term placement facilities: Lincoln Hall, Brookwood, then Tryon.

One of the last meetings was with an older white woman, nicely dressed, a pair of glasses on her nose. She was short and heavyset. When I walked in, she stood up to greet me.

"Hi, Jim. I'm Paula. Nice to meet you," she said in a squeaky voice that didn't quite fit her body. "I'm the program director at Boys Town for the residential facility. I want to talk to you a bit, see if you're a good fit for our program. And then I can give you an opportunity to ask questions of me. Okay?" Her manner was stern but also sympathetic, making sure I was following everything.

"Sure," I said, maintaining eye contact. I knew as program director she'd be looking for me to demonstrate the model.

"Good. Do you like it here?"

"Here? Sure."

"Why's that?" she said, acting like she really wanted to know. As I replied, she scribbled some notes without looking down, which I thought was a cool trick.

It was hard to explain that I just liked having somewhere safe to sleep and regular school. "I don't know," I said.

"Is it the people?"

"Yeah, they're okay."

"Can I ask you some questions about your background?"

I nodded.

"What is your relationship with your parents like?"

"Um . . . To be honest, not good. My mom's in Haiti. I didn't see her as much as I wish. My father and I don't get along."

"How so?"

I let my guard down a bit. "He's very physical with me. Mostly because of the trouble I put the family through. Most of my family isn't too happy with me right now."

"What kinds of things make you angry?"

"When people disrespect me, talk bad about my background. When things aren't fair."

"What kinds of things do you do when you're angry?"

"I break things, throw things. Hit people. I don't feel better until I get physical."

"I meant strategies."

"Strategies?" I asked. I wasn't sure of the word.

"To cope. To deal with your anger."

"I don't deal with my anger. I used to drink, get high. But I can't do that anymore."

"Okay. What do you like to do for fun?"

"I don't do much for fun."

"Nothing?"

"I used to play football but I stopped when I broke my wrist."

"How'd you break your wrist?"

"Fell," I lied. I rubbed it unconsciously.

"How about school?"

"Doesn't it tell you right there?" I said, gesturing to her papers.

"I'd like to hear it from you," she said.

"Not great? I'm struggling. I didn't have much schooling at all so it's hard. The math here is different. I do okay in history. I feel like I can't catch up."

"Why do you think that is?" she asked in a way that wasn't condescending but seemed genuinely interested in my answer.

"In Haiti my parents couldn't afford school for me and when I got here I really didn't go, so it's maybe my fault but it's also not, you know?"

"Sure. What about your friends?"

"What about them?"

"Well, how do you know them, what kinds of things do you do, are they in gangs?"

"To be honest, a lot of them are Crip, but I never joined."

"Why's that do you think?"

"Well, I don't like taking orders, plus I don't see the gangs around when my friends got beef and I already do most things they do so, I don't need them."

She pulled out a file from her large handbag and started to flip through it.

"So, Jim, the Boys Town residence is more like a home. With family teachers who live there with you. They're like parents. Do you think you would succeed in that kind of environment?"

"Oh definitely. I think I would."

"Could you expand on that? Why would that be?"

"Well, I never had any structure, so I probably would do good if I had adults like that. Make me behave, go to school."

Reading the situation, I knew exactly how to play it. I was soft-spoken, polite, and offered what people wanted to hear. Despite my issues at Boys Town—I was far from happy—I had no interest in exploring the alternatives.

A few weeks later, David and I got picked up by Big Pat in a mini-van and rode out to the courthouse. It was my day of sentencing. David and I had gotten over our beef by then. I trusted his mix of street smarts and maturity and we had bonded.

At the courthouse, we waited on line to go through the metal detectors, went up to the third floor, and checked in with Department of Juvenile Justice staff. We found space on the hard church benches in an underlit room. The place was a zoo of court staff, DJJ staff, kids at all points of the process awaiting their fate. And we were not supposed to talk. David and I had little to do but stare at daytime television, and wait for the lunch of cheese sandwiches.

I heard more than one person whisper, "There's the Boys Town kids."

In a low tone, David tried to comfort me. "All right, man. I've done this a bunch of times. Be prepared for the worst, maybe you'll get to go home. But be prepared in case."

"Oh, I know what's gonna happen. I'm not going home, I'm getting sentenced."

"Ah shit, sorry man."

"Naw, it's not like that. I'm excited. Getting sentenced to Boys Town."

"What do you mean? You *want* to get sentenced to Boys Town?"

That I seemed not just unworried, but almost happy about the prospect, seemed to confuse him. I was fifteen years old: Why didn't I want to go home?

10

Inside Out

Being broken is what makes us human. . . . Sometimes we're
fractured by the choices we make; sometimes we're shattered by
things we would never have chosen. But our brokenness is also
the source of our common humanity, the basis for our shared
search for comfort, meaning, and healing.

—BRYAN STEVENSON, *JUST MERCY*[5]

I was a stranger in a strange land. In a quiet, upscale block in Park
Slope I shouldered my bag—the sum total of my life at that point—up
the stone steps. Boys Town residential was in a beautiful three-story
brownstone in the middle of one of Brooklyn's nicest neighborhoods:

clean sidewalks, tree-lined blocks, neighbors leashing dogs or driving luxury sedans.

I went inside, dropped my bag on the threshold, and slowly panned my head: a comfortable living room, long white curtains, photographs of kids on the wall, a bulky couch and a big television, a polished wood dining room table, two heavy sliding doors leading to a large kitchen. It wasn't just the space itself that awed me but the aura: that unmistakable sense of a home.

My eyes were drawn to a silver framed group photo on the mantel: Damon and Iza Canada, the family teachers, alongside their two young daughters and six Boys Town teenagers around the perimeter. Everyone was dressed in yellow and peach short sleeves and the faded filter caught a gauzy, relaxed light. Then I braked on one of the faces: *Devon*. His face was frozen in a youthful smile, looking like an alternate version of himself. Though it was a recent picture, he looked years younger. It was a shock; I didn't even know he had been there.

When someone is in the streets and then he's gone, especially as often as Devon was, no one thinks about where he goes. He's just gone. Like taken out of the equation. Putting those two disparate pieces together—*Devon had disappeared for six months and lived here*—shifted my sense of where I was. I had entered another dimension, one running parallel to life on Crown Street.

Devon was already back on the street, Jigga was dead, and I was hovering, my feet not yet grounded. Standing in that quiet family room, I could see a path being formed for me. I was not yet in the mental space to accept it, but I could recognize it for what it was. What I did, and who I would become, had not yet been written.

Soon after my interview with Paula at Dean Street, a bed opened up at the Boys Town residence. Marty emphasized how fortunate I was to land a bed in the home on Brooklyn's Sixth Avenue—he knew how bleak the other options were. Relieved I wasn't in something resembling jail, I was still so bottled up that I ignored my good fortune, blind to the path that God had unfurled before me.

Dean Street had been more of a way station, a purgatory where kids passed through while awaiting their fate. The Park Slope residence was something else: for one thing, Damon and Iza lived there with their two daughters. There were only six residents—all long-term—and no rotating staff. But there was something more there: the walls and roof held something intangible together.

Shuffling up the blue-carpeted stairs, I ran my hand along the polished wood railing. At the top I found the first door, the Daily Room, the bedroom where every resident started. My roommate, a compact and wiry dude whose limbs seemed to operate on their own, hopped off his bed. He was dark-skinned—darker than me—and wore oversize jeans and had waves in his hair. The thick bass line from Cam'ron's "Oh Boy" filled the space, almost shaking the walls.

"What's up?" He came in for a dap, smiling big. "You're Jim, right? Renaldo." He took my hand tight and then brought me in to his body, knocking his closed fist twice on my back.

"That's you," he said, pointing to the twin bed at the far wall. "Laundry is right here"—a white door beside the closet—"and the rec room is through there. Damon sets up his PlayStation in there sometimes. No Grand Theft Auto but he's got Madden."

"Cool. Thanks." I dropped my bag and sat on my bed, already feeling that it had more give, its mattress thicker. The closet had space to hang my few nice outfits. Though I didn't have a lot of clothes—all my nice items came from Charles—I was fastidious, took extra care of my things, and took pride in how I dressed. Since I had so little, each item held more concentrated worth.

"Yo," he said, peeking at the doorway and dropping his voice a bit. "What gang you rep?"

"None. I mean, my friends are all Crip. Not me."

"Yeah, me neither. The gang thing don't fly in here anyway. What you listen to?"

"Jay. 50. Nas."

"I feel that. I got *Illmatic* right here," he said, pointing to his head.

I smiled. Renaldo was funny and quick, reminding me of Kevin Hart.

He gestured to the CD player. "I been using this but we can share it now." It was a smooth black setup with a ten-part EQ and a five-disc changer, legit speakers, even a subwoofer.

"Thanks."

Renaldo couldn't have been there that long—he was in the Daily Room too—but he had a relaxed air in that space. Like it was his. At Dean, just about everyone but LaDanian acted like a visitor. I didn't know if it was Renaldo or the house itself that accounted for his air.

"You got a girl?" he asked, lying casually back on his bed. A few pictures of ballers and rappers were taped up behind him. A *Slam* cover with Allen Iverson in an old-school Sixers jersey—with his trademark scowl and his hair picked out.

"Nah. You?"

"A few. Some from St. John's, the girls' house."

"You see them a lot?"

"We have trips, picnics and shit . . ." his voice drifted out. Then he started counting on his hand. "Felicia and Stephanie live in the same building, a few blocks over; Karla was at St. John's, but she's back in Brownsville now. Ashley's still there. She's in some of my classes. Once I get a home pass I can see some girls from my way."

"Where you from?"

"Harlem."

I must've made a face. He must've seen it.

"Harlem girls are *fiiiine*, dog," he said. "What are you, Brooklyn?"

I nodded. "You know it. Crown Heights."

"Psssshhh."

"What? You think Harlem's got any rappers on BK's level?"

"Shit. Cam'ron, Dipset—"

"Get the fuck outta here!" I said, laughing. "Those guys are broke compared to ours: Nas, Jay, Biggie—"

"Nah, nah. But Harlem's where the real hustlers are from, son. Frank Lucas, Alpo—"

"But the real 50 Cent, the gangster, is from Brooklyn!"

The playful back-and-forth had no real fire. Just two kids getting a sense of each other, volleying a rhythm.

Damon knocked on the doorframe, filling the whole space. He was a sturdily built six feet, a thin beard along his chin and a pronounced bald head. "Good to see you settled, Jim," he said. "Renaldo, show Jim where to wash up for dinner." Then he was gone.

"What's he like?" I mouthed to Renaldo. He waited to answer while Damon climbed the stairs to the next floor.

Renaldo walked to the bathroom outside our door and I followed him. "He's cool. Fair but tough," he said. Then he exhaled. "He expects a lot, yo. Iza'll give you a little more slack. Damon's a good dude, but—" He tucked his voice lower. "—he can get amped up, man." He shook his head like he had dealt with it more than once. "He lets me battle though."

It turned out that Renaldo was a really talented rapper. He would carry a pen and paper around like it was his point card and constantly scribbled during chores, class, conversations. He'd pull out that little pad to write rhymes. I'd wake up in the middle of the night to hear him mumbling and drumming on his leg, a small flashlight piercing the dark.

Renaldo and one of the other residents, Kareem, would have rap battles that Damon supervised. He made sure it didn't get physical and that the lyrics stayed appropriate: no drugs, no sex, no violence, no n-word or any other derogatory phrase. It made it more difficult—rap is about freedom of expression—but Renaldo and Kareem responded to the challenge. It actually forced them to be more creative. In the living room Damon would beatbox or drum as Kareem and Renaldo slapped their back and forth and the rest of us acted as judges.

A day at the residence was similar to Dean Street, but compared to NSDs, the freedom was unparalleled. The trust was more pronounced, the staff wasn't all over us, and we all felt more connected to the home. For breakfast, we could make eggs on our own if we woke early enough. We didn't have to be escorted outside; we'd sweep the front steps, play in the backyard alone, go around the corner to buy a soda if we got permission. In Park Slope we were of the neighborhood, fixtures of the block, embedded into the scenery—to an extent.

If we had our privs, we could walk the twenty minutes to the school on Willoughby Street, which we loved, especially on a nice day. We didn't get out much so that trip down Sixth Avenue was a luxury. We'd laugh, holler at girls who passed, just let loose and be kids again in the open air. For someone living in a facility, that's a big deal. After school we'd come home and do our assigned chores, laid out on a big color chart on a wall in the kitchen. Then we'd gather in the living room for Total Up, where we'd add our points and see who earned their privs that day. Our free time hinged on those numbers.

Residents with the most privs could go to the YMCA a few blocks away or to the park to play ball. Until I got those privs, I'd be in the backyard playing basketball or down in the unfinished basement lifting weights. It was a dusty stone space with a chest press, pull-up bar, and a hefty punching bag dangling from a chain. I'd go down there sometimes to cool off, letting my anger and energy flow out of me through the weights.

Afterward we'd all reconvene for family meeting. It was both a way to keep everyone unified and a forum for speaking our minds. If someone had issues, the Canadas would hear them out. If a conflict was spreading and infecting the house, Damon or Iza would hash it out. There were no cameras in the house, no one was checking up on us, so family meeting was a form of self-government. With ten of us living in that house, with shifting freedoms and contentious relationships, tensions could pile up. I'd seen it happen at my grandmother's apartment: all of us bottling up our issues until the heat made them explode.

Sometimes at family meetings a resident would apply to move up a level—from Daily to Weekly or Weekly to Achievement. He had to make a case for why he had earned the promotion. Damon and Iza would throw out hypotheticals for the resident to answer. "Okay how about this," Damon would say, "you're walking to school and you find a bag of weed on the sidewalk, what do you do?" Or Iza: "Let's say you're in the bathroom getting ready and Travis bumps you at the sink. What's your reaction?" The habits we leaned on to survive back home didn't serve us in public school or outside of our square blocks. They certainly wouldn't serve us in the workplace. As adult members of society, they would be our ruin.

Dinner was an event, something we prepared together: Kids would set the table; sit on stools around the marble island in the kitchen; someone chopping up vegetables for Iza, someone else at the sink cleaning the meat for Damon. It was a communal experience. Over the meal we'd talk about what happened in the school day or any residual issues left over from our family meeting. Damon and Iza would also lead a mandatory conversation about the day's news. Damon challenged all of us to be critical thinkers on things like race, economics, and education. He got heavy into politics, current events, and the world at large. I couldn't follow it all but my interest was piqued. Even the food itself was part of our growth; salad was mandatory and we earned thousands of negative points if we didn't eat it. I complied but always took out the black olives, little eyeball-looking things that I couldn't imagine anyone eating.

Walking to school gave me a sense of the neighborhood, which was its own teaching forum. I was immediately struck by the stable, upper-middle-class community. Residents got up in the morning, dressed professionally, took their children to school, went to work. It was a foreign routine to me, someone who grew up not three miles away. I'd notice books piled on the sidewalk, perfectly good furniture just sitting out on the curb.

As someone who praised, pursued, and was brainwashed by materialistic things, I had a lot to ingest on those blocks. Studying the Benzes and Range Rovers I began to ask questions and piece things together: *Oh, that woman next door drives the Jaguar because she's a judge. She got that job by being a lawyer first, which she became after graduating law school, which you need a bachelor's degree to get into.* Boom, just like that, I was learning. I had scarcely been exposed to people like this, but in Park Slope, they were my neighbors.

And I'd see the children, and picture their futures, all laid out in front of me. I could envision who was going to be the lawyer, the doctor, the Ivy League graduate, the business executive. The tracks were all set down for them, and I started wondering what it would be like to be on one of those paths myself. Those walks were an expansion for me, an opening of possibilities.

But I had to undo a lot of things. The reward system I'd learned on the street was inverted and destructive: the worse you behaved— the more conflict you caused—the more people feared you, the more respect you commanded. Boys Town had to flip those incentives for me, re-create mine from the root. It was an arduous, push-pull process.

Damon was a big proponent of discipline and he signed all the residents up for karate. He and Iza also both understood that aggression, properly channeled, can be lifesaving in our world. The karate place was run by a tough black woman with dreads named Tessa. We'd change into starched all-white karate suits, wrap around belts, and line up on the mats. We'd learn proper punching and roundhouse kicks, hitting the pads while a sparring partner held them. It was a productive release of my anger for a change, a healthy outlet to air out pain. The class was filled with well-to-do Park Slope residents who didn't seem to know or care what world we had come from. They'd ask what positions our parents held, what Broadway plays we'd seen, what books we were reading. They didn't know I couldn't even read a full sentence. The depth of their wealth, knowledge, and culture was a flood we had to swim in.

When Tessa scolded us in front of the rest of the class, things got tense. I became self-conscious, a young black male in a predominately white space. With the exception of Yi, a Chinese resident, we were always late to her class, and a few times showed up high, which makes karate exponentially more difficult.

I didn't let on but I enjoyed the transformation: getting out of my worn street clothes and dressing up in my crisp white uniform. As a child, I adored karate movies. I'd catch fifteen minutes of a Bruce Lee or Van Damme film at a neighbor's house and then we'd all rush outside to re-create the moves on one another. Ten years later karate classes let me relive those fantasies for real. Sometimes Tessa would break out thin pieces of wood for us to chop and I'd pretend I was breaking concrete, yelling like the guys from Mortal Kombat.

One class, after repeated instruction to perform a specific kick I couldn't land, Tessa did a quick kick on my arm. That kind of contact was her style and business, but I responded poorly. Travis and Renaldo rushed over to walk me away before I went Hulk on her. I wanted to drive her through the glass entranceway and if they hadn't intervened, I might have.

But like water seeking an opening, my rebellion found its way in. As we changed in the locker room, I couldn't help noticing something else about Park Slope. One time, I elbowed one of my housemates. "Yo, stay back."

"Why?"

"Just do it," I said, under my breath. Once the room cleared, I gestured to all the pants lying around, the unclosed lockers. "Shit, these white folks just leaving their money out!"

I started to lead a few of the other residents on regular raids: we'd stay back and take any money left lying around in wallets, pockets, and bags. Partly strategically and partly out of guilt, I never took all of someone's money. That felt like poking the beast and it didn't sit well with me. Even at my worst, I had an inkling of fairness and an aversion to greed.

Once people started to complain about missing items and money we were easily fingered and the owner kicked us out. Word got back to the Canadas and the whole house lost our privs. Tessa was so livid that Damon had to convince her not to press charges.

Park Slope had become gentrified but it still had elements of its low-income past on certain blocks—the Puerto Ricans who ran the barbershop, the Hispanics on the corner who sold weed. When we found someone we could relate to, it was like being on another planet and finding someone else from Earth: *You breathe oxygen? I breathe oxygen!*

That wasn't all we breathed. A few of us got high on a regular basis; one of the veteran residents, Dawkins, was always magically pulling blunts out of his pockets. Because of Damon's random room checks, I had to hide mine: under the carpet, inside video game boxes, wrapped inside the toilet tank, in the back of a radio. The brownstone's roof was always open because of the fire escape, so at night, I'd sneak to the roof to smoke weed and sometimes drink if someone had snuck a pocket-size bottle. I'd come down and put my headphones on and escape, completely zoned out. I'd let the music rain down on me like a torrent, washing the pain away.

Iza eventually tracked down the guy who was selling to us and got up in his face. "With all due respect," she said, "I know you have your business and you got that going on but I got *my* business and can't have you interfering. And I need you to stop." And he listened. He wouldn't sell to us anymore. I was moody anyway but when I couldn't get high, I'd be in a funk for long stretches.

"I didn't do nothing to you, fam," Damon once said to me. "Lighten up. For real." It was a late night and he, Kareem, and Travis were playing spades, which Iza had taught the whole house. Damon was getting silly with Kareem, who was a chronic giggler. They were cracking each other up, doing imitations of people around the house. Kareem was rolling around, not breathing from laughing so hard. Damon noticed me on the couch all stoic. I might've been bracing for them to imitate me.

"Yo, real talk, J. I don't get you," Damon said. "You too cool for us? Why don't you loosen up?" I couldn't answer. Any ease or playfulness inside me was just inaccessible, a shackled prisoner I refused to release.

And I was still the consummate aggressor, full tilt if I felt cheated, and ballistic if somebody fought back. We spent a lot of our free time playing Damon's PlayStation in the rec room. Once I was playing Madden NFL against Kareem and we were getting animated in front of the TV, elbows up, thumbs clicking away like madmen.

"You bumping me, man!" he said. "Knocking my controller! Fuck out of my face, man!"

"Now y'all know there's no cursing in this house. I'm issuing you—" Damon said from the other room.

"Get outta my house," I said. "I just broke your wack defense."

"D, he's bumping me!" Kareem yelled out.

"Don't be going to Damon, you pussy!"

"Jim! Kareem! No cursing in this house! Now both of you—"

"Fuck you, pussy!" Kareem said, turning his body to me. Kareem was a true giant, about six feet five, 260 pounds. Linebacker size. I cocked back and punched him hard on the side of his face. He quickly threw one back at me that grazed my head.

I was tunneled in tight on Kareem, on hitting him again, on going after whoever got in my way.

"Jim, Jim! I'm giving you an instruction," Damon said, suddenly appearing and filling up the space in front of me. "What are the four steps to following instructions?"

I wouldn't make eye contact with Damon, but my answer was automatic.

"You look at the person. You say okay. You do the task. You check back."

"Real talk. You asked me why you can't go to the Y?" he said. "If you can't control yourself here, how do I know you won't bust someone up there? That comes back on all of us, fam. For real."

Damon was appealing to my sense of community and justice. He took a breath, remaining his even self. "I appreciate you're frustrated right now. But you punched Kareem in the face. That's a negative two thousand points. Get out your card."

"Two thousand, man? Fuck out of here. He fucking came at me first! Why you giving me negative points?"

"I didn't *give* you anything. You *earned* it," Damon said calmly. "I see you're frustrated but instead of looking at me saying 'okay,' you argued."

All the kids hovered nearby, ready to see the fireworks.

"You have a chance to turn this around," Damon said. "If you can stop right now, take a deep breath, you can earn half those points back."

Working against all the rage bubbling, I sat down on the couch, stared at the floor, and tried to breathe it out.

"Do you accept your consequences?"

Inhale, exhale. Inhale, exhale.

"Jim. Look at me. Do you accept the—"

"Yeah, yeah."

"Good choice. Okay, take out your point card," he said. "Fighting is automatic subsystem." I knew better than to keep protesting.

A conflict like that, if left to fester, infected the whole house. The relationship had to be rebuilt so Damon made Kareem and me clean up the whole kitchen together.

Damon could be fun but he was highly principled, with reserves of self-discipline. He was a Black Muslim, socially conscious, and an avid reader, not just of the Koran but history, politics, and social issues. I admired him but clashes were inevitable. My hostility toward males was second nature. This was common in a community with a high percentage of absent fathers. Even though my mom was the one who left, I shared that sentiment: you don't allow certain things from men. Every heated interaction was like a test of your manhood, even if it wasn't. I read Damon's high standards and expectations as a wall to punch, rather than a ladder to climb.

One of the things Boys Town drilled into us was the law of unintended consequences. "No matter how small you think the situation is," Iza would say, "there's a ripple effect you can't see. Like throwing a rock in a pond." Something small can lead to death or twenty years in prison. It happened all the time.

Iza was half Puerto Rican, half Dominican, and short with long curly hair and a bright smile. She had a nurturing style that I was drawn to. The Canadas lived on the ground floor above the basement, with their two daughters, who were around nine and six at the time. Iza loved all types of music, was a skilled cook, and had as much medical knowledge as a doctor. She transformed that house into a home. From Christine to Ms. Oglio to Iza, I had always gravitated toward maternal figures, especially those in a professional capacity. I became attached to Iza, her mothering responses, her willingness to listen, her nonconfrontational approach. I didn't even know how much I craved that.

"Jim, we need to get you some clothes," she said to me one Sunday afternoon. I was lying on the couch watching football and zoning out. All the other kids were down at the park, but I didn't have my privs so I was glued to the house.

"What's wrong with my clothes?"

"Nothing," she said. "You just been wearing that denim outfit like every day since you got here."

"C'mon, why you knocking my clothes?" I asked jokingly. "Charles gave me this."

"I'm not knocking. You just got to mix it up. Plus you gotta get some pants that fit."

"Nuh uh. No way. This is—"

"You can't be wearing your pants all saggy. Who's going to hire you?"

"What? Hire me? I ain't gonna wear 'em different just cause somebody says."

"Okay, okay. Look at you, all defiant."

She took me out shopping, got me some smaller pants, a couple of button-down shirts, sweat outfits. When we got back to the house she pulled out another bag.

"What's this?"

"It's yours," she said, with a mischievous look. "Open it."

I opened the box and pulled out a nice pair of matching red pajamas. I laughed. Every piece of clothing I owned was blue—Crip colors—and Iza purposely got me Blood colors as a playful shot at my old ways. It was almost like a dare, but I wore them.

I felt like she was looking out for me, maybe even more than the other residents. After one of our family meetings was breaking up, Iza came up to me. She kept her voice low, knowing how embarrassed I could get. "Jim, can I be straight with you about something?"

"Sure."

She waited for everyone else to clear out. "Let me tell you what I see. Tell me if I'm wrong."

"Okay."

"You have way too much pride. You have so much pride, it's like it's blinding you to everything else. Even the good stuff."

Ordinarily I'd react or shut down if someone criticized me like that, but coming from her, it didn't feel like an attack. And she was right: I was too proud to apologize, too proud to admit my errors, too proud to back down. I was a bully who tried to run the house and intimidate the residents. I fed off of physical altercations—it's why I sought them out—and I didn't care about consequences and relationships like the other residents did. On the street, the person with the least to lose always has an advantage. But not here.

When Iza would confront me like that, I would be very defensive at first. After she'd explain things to me in detail, with a rationale that helped me process it, I would calm down and apologize. It made me feel vulnerable to a certain degree, but not as weak as apologizing to men. Usually after I'd disappear to a quiet place alone. But Iza couldn't work with me twenty-four hours a day.

After a fight I had with Travis during a basketball game out back, Iza and Damon sat me down in the living room. They told me the agency was considering moving me to a secure facility, locking me up for a longer term, and notching me one step further into the system. They began to discuss a concrete plan about moving me, "adjusting my treatment," they said.

In response, I became more isolated and radioactive. The other kids had already had enough of my temper, my instigating, my penchant for destroying things around the house. After I punched a hole in the wall in the living room, Damon made me spend one Saturday doing all the spackling and repainting. Even Iza was getting impatient with me—disappointed, she said—which was rare.

It all came to a head one cold Monday night about a year into my time there. I was in the living room watching a football game with Damon, Renaldo, Kareem, and Travis. Iza sat with a thick book on her lap, barely paying us any mind. I had the remote control and my feet were up on the coffee table, like I was "mayor of the house," as Iza used to say. There were about five minutes left in the game when Damon told me I had to go to bed because I hadn't earned my privs.

"What? Fuck no," I said. "I'm not going to bed."

"Jim, I just gave you an instruction and—"

"C'mon D! Everyone else is staying up. Let me watch to—"

"Jim, you didn't follow my instruction," he said, getting up and walking over to me. Not threatening, but assertive, his body blocking my view. "Now you're going to earn five thousand negative points. If—"

"There's like two minutes left!"

"Jim—"

I got up and threw the remote control at the television. Then I flipped the wooden coffee table, knocking everything over, including Iza's tea. "Jim!" she yelled, startled.

"Okay," Damon said, "now you've earned another ten thousand—"

"Shit, man, you always on me! Get the fuck out of my face!"

I turned to go upstairs and as I approached the railing I punched the big glass pane in the center of the front door. My hand went through it and the thick glass shattered everywhere; a loud crashing echoed through the hallway. I watched as thick red blood streamed down my hand. My entire middle finger was severed wide open, and I could see down to the bone, chalky white under the flowing red.

Iza quickly grabbed a washcloth, wrapping it around my finger and pressing down. She put her hand on the back of my neck, seeing I was panicked. Damon made like he was about to speak but Iza gave him a glare, like, *Let it go.* She took me out to her car, holding my other hand as we walked down the street in the freezing night. We drove silently to the emergency room at Methodist Hospital: me with my hand wrapped up, staring out the window; Iza saying nothing. We sat in the waiting room all night. It took them a while to see me and even longer to stitch me up.

When we got home, Iza fixed me a snack in the kitchen. I sat on the stool and she stood across from me. I was relaxed by then, the hours with Iza sending a calm flow through my body. While we were talking she noticed I was wincing when I put my hand down. She came around the island to look at my hand.

"It's fine," I said. "For real. Don't touch it."

"Just let me," she said, wrestling my hand onto the counter. I let her. Something felt wrong.

The bandage was coming off, there was still glass in my hand, and my finger was still bleeding profusely. She brought me back to the hospital, where I saw the doctor again. He opened it back up and then had to leave it open, unstitched. My hand was like a metaphor attached to my body: my rage was hurting no one but myself.

On the drive home with Iza—I could see the sun coming up—I asked her why they didn't sew it up again.

"They couldn't," she said. "The doctor told me he wasn't able to."

"Why not?"

The streets were asleep, silent and empty. I could hear garbage trucks and birds, the quiet hum of our engine.

"That's the way it's gonna heal."

I nodded like I understood, but I didn't really. I stared back out the window.

"It's gotta be open," Iza said. "It's got to heal from the inside out."

11

Light

Kids need to think that you care before they care what you think.

—WES MOORE

There are three flecks of light that poke through the loneliest moments in the system: letters, phone calls, and visits. They're like candles placed outside pitch-black rooms. Yet I remained in darkness. During all my years away from home, contact from my family was scarce. This was partly due to cultural norms: my family subscribed to the idea that if you violated the community rules you had to pay on your own. I had burned my bridges, so it was my sole responsibility to swim alone. That feeling of abandonment cut my insides. I was exposed and raw, and—like a lot of kids do—I acted out.

I'd watch other residents go home on weekend passes, see kids spend holidays with their families, often be the only kid left in the house. The hopelessness was crushing; there was nothing for me to look forward to, which in the system is like a type of death. Even when my behavior improved, and I could've earned a home pass, my family never approved one.

Hindsight allows me to see how lucky I was. I was so vulnerable that had I gone back to Crown Street before I was ready, I would've found trouble or it would've found me. The walls of the system wouldn't let me float back into my comfortable orbit. Being trapped kept saving my life. It was like I was incubating, not to be released into the world until I could breathe on my own.

One Sunday afternoon Marty came by to visit. When he arrived I had just finished another blowout with Damon. Though they had opted not to transfer me out of Boys Town, conflicts were still regular. I had barricaded myself in my room so Marty came upstairs.

"Hey, Jim. What's going on?" he asked. "You okay?"

I must've looked like a demon, wrestling my anger out in the open like that. Marty had never seen me in that mode before.

"Look, I don't know what's going on, but you need to step out of the moment," he said. "You've come a long way. Don't destroy all the progress you've made."

Not only was Marty my attorney, but I also felt duty-bound to him. He and Christine had gone far beyond their professional roles with me. They didn't have to call me, visit me, talk to me the way they did, bring me in the way they did. My well-being was entirely disconnected from their lives. They *chose* to insert themselves.

I just sat on the edge of my bed and nodded my head, sweating and breathing heavily.

"Jim, did you hear me?"

It was like he was behind thick glass. "Sorry. What?"

"I said, I can't pretend I know anything about what you're dealing with."

I looked up. I could feel my heart rate sputter slowly, like a foot dragging across speeding ground.

"You and I have nothing in common," he continued. "Compared to you, I grew up with a silver spoon in my mouth." His blunt honesty struck me. I was always wary when adults said, "I know what you're going through." They almost never did.

I was trapped in a corner and Marty offered an opening. He promised to visit more if Damon gave him a better report about my behavior. It had gotten to the point where there was nothing for me to lose and no one to impress, which is dangerous at that age. Every kid wants someone to impress.

A month or so later, around Christmastime, Marty and Christine followed through and came to visit. I gave them a tour of the house and introduced them around, basking in the fact that important people came to see me. They took me out shopping for clothes and sneakers, then to lunch. Being on the outside, without the other residents, made me feel all the more human. It made me feel normal again, a part of society. That day was like a breather, a break from my life. It was the first time I got to see Marty and Christine outside the barriers of my confinement. Because visits were so rare, it was all the more impactful.

I stayed off subsystem and, as Marty had promised, the visits continued. I had mentioned that Renaldo and I were making music and Marty offered to give me his daughter's electric keyboard. One day he walked me over to his house, a spacious brownstone a few blocks from the residence. Intricate metal railing led up to this majestic wood front door. I thought the Boys Town residence was impressive, but this place was next level—and he lived there all by himself.

As we opened the door a dog darted at us like off a spring. It was a chocolate Lab with floppy ears.

"Hamlet!" Marty yelled. "Down, Hamlet!"

"Hamlet?"

"Yeah. I love Shakespeare," he said.

"Ah," I said.

"If you have a chance, you should read him." Marty's face grew animated. "I've been to London a few times to see productions at the new Globe. It's . . ." He drifted off. "Well, it's something."

I nodded but didn't for the life of me know what he was talking about.

Marty was a literature enthusiast so his house was filled with bookcases raised to the high ceilings in room after room, and books piled up on the coffee table, his nightstand, even the bathroom. It was the first time I ever saw that many books in someone's house; he had his own private library. More than the nice furniture or the square footage, I decided I wanted a house full of books. They spoke to something potent, intoxicating even: the power of knowledge.

"You read all these?" I asked, scanning the spines on one of the large bookcases.

"Some. Some not yet," he said. "You know a book you'd like I think I have around here? *The Human Stain*. It's a Philip Roth book about a black man living as a white man."

"Why'd he do that?"

"He's light-skinned, a professor, and he hides his blackness to assimilate, gain the advantages of the white world. But it backfires on him."

I thought about an old skit where Eddie Murphy dresses up as a white man and rides a city bus. When the last black person gets off, all these formally dressed waiters come out with cocktails and the bus turns into a party.

Marty's house was my first time inside that rarefied part of Park Slope, the one I previously glimpsed only through front windows. Being invited through the door was like stepping into another life.

* * *

"Everyone put their hands together for his first time up here," Ms. Oglio said from the front of the cafeteria. "Student of the Week, Jim St. Germain."

Our school knew how starved we were for awards and recognition, but more important, the system was built on positive reinforcement. They wanted to give us incentives for success. So every Friday there was an awards ceremony in the school lunchroom. At first, I dismissed them, likely as a defense mechanism. Why crave the impossible? But as I noticed my peers accumulating certificates and getting that spotlight moment, I wanted it too. We were not who people thought we were. We might've acted tough and street, but we were just kids. A small piece of paper had a colossal effect.

That moment was literally the first time my name was called for a positive reason—not to see the principal or the judge or a police officer. But I was still not even out of the starting gate in terms of turning around my education. At Boys Town, most of my learning took place back at the residence under Iza's guidance. She taught me the most basic rules of writing and reading and simple math. After school and on the weekend Iza would tutor me alongside her daughters, who were both in elementary school. She would give me a topic to write an essay on and return it to me the next day all red-penned up; then I'd rewrite it. That individual attention—and the fact that she felt that I was *worth* giving that individual attention—was enormous. It was like being carried across deep water.

Just as things were opening up, I got a call one Sunday afternoon from my sister, Geraldine. She and I barely spoke—and she never called me—so my internal alarm went off. I took the phone from Damon and walked into the hallway. She didn't waste any time: my father had kidney failure and was in the ICU at Jamaica Hospital. "From what I can tell," she said matter-of-factly, "I don't know if he'll live any longer." My father had lived such a hard life and had dealt with so many illnesses that it was surprising he had made it this far. No one in the family thought he would live very long.

After I hung up, I sat glued to the steps of the front staircase. The weight of her words paralyzed me. Iza sat down next to me as questions whirled through my head: Was this my fault? Would my father die while I was in the system? What would happen to my family? "Jim, it's okay," Iza said, taking my hand. "Tell me what's going on." She arranged for a staff member to escort me to Queens to see him.

When we got to my father's room, a still form lay in a thin bed, buried under equipment. Somewhere in there, hooked up to tubes, draped in wires, and wearing a breathing mask, was my father. I sat down beside him and let it out, crying over the beeps of the machines. There was no life behind his eyes, though I still talked and asked questions. More for myself than anything.

Despite our toxic relationship—all the carried heaviness between us—I still found myself strangled by the sense that I was losing him. As I got older I accepted that he had done the best he could, operated from what he knew. Family is family. Blood is blood.

When it was time to leave I had to be physically helped out of the room. I had the feeling that once I crossed through the door, it'd be like crossing a threshold: my father would be gone. I walked out under the dull fluorescent light of the hallway, past the whispering nurses and the drone of the PA, preparing for a funeral home and a body. I recognized a new burden: it would be up to me to carry my family. Rarely do turning points feel like ones in the moment, but the world shifting under my feet was palpable that day. Everything banked and shook, and I struggled to keep my balance.

A few weeks later, the ground moved even more. During my years away, my cousin Chrislie, whom we called Breeze, had gone much deeper into the street. Small-time hustlers are all trying to make enough money to hustle "OT," out of town, a more lucrative enterprise. When I was arrested I was on track to go OT, where guys can sell product for four times what they can in New York City. The move is dangerous on two fronts. The law is almost always tougher in these more conservative states. The judges are much harsher, especially on young black men, whom they view as traveling hundreds of miles to poison their community and bring violence into their sleepy town. The local dealers also want to take you out for stomping on their territory. I had first introduced Breeze to the street and when I was away, he starting going OT. He thought he was moving up in his world, and got caught in the crosshairs.

Breeze and his crew started traveling hundreds of miles out to a town in Pennsylvania, the same town that a rival clique a few blocks up was also hustling. Sunny was a tall and dark-skinned dude from Union Street who'd known Breeze most of his life. Sunny had braided hair, which he kept under a do-rag with a backward fitted cap. He had this stiff walk where his upper body would be a beat behind his lower body, and a "buck fifty," a scar from his ear to his jaw. Breeze and Sunny got into a fight out in Pennsylvania, and Breeze broke Sunny's jaw. With no hesitation Sunny shot and killed him.

When I got the news, I couldn't process it. How can a man murder someone he knew as a child? How black is the heart that can fill his body with bullet holes? It ate my insides. No matter what I'd seen in my life, I couldn't shake Breeze's murder. I obsessed about it, and the what-ifs kept snowballing: What if I hadn't gotten close with Breeze? What if I never introduced him to some of my friends? Why was I so lucky to get sentenced when I did? To the place that I did? How come he didn't get the same opportunity?

What made it worse was that Breeze was not a typical street kid at all. He had a certain innocence, a reserved kid who wouldn't even look people in the eyes. Just like Jigga's, Breeze's murder struck me on two fronts: One was my closeness to him, our relationship. The other was his closeness to me: my life and his had been running the same path and my life would've played out the same way. His death was a peek into the alternate future. It haunted me.

"Do you think about hurting yourself? Do you have suicidal ideation?" I was sitting in front of a psychiatrist in Brooklyn Heights, his glasses barely hanging on to his nose and a checklist on his lap.

"What do you mean?"

At the residence the night before I had been throwing pictures and kicking the walls, screaming and crying and not letting anyone near me. Damon couldn't calm me down, and when Iza put her arms around me I pushed her away, which alarmed her. When I started talking about how I didn't want to live anymore, they had no choice but to take me to see a psychiatrist. By law they were required to do so: I was still state property.

"Do you think about killing yourself?" he asked me in a stuffy room with framed diplomas on the wall. "Do you plan how you would do it, if you did it?"

"No. Never."

He seemed suspicious, like I was hiding something. Like he was used to people hiding things from him. I was there, after all, against my own free will. "Well, why do you think the Canadas brought you here?"

Recognizing the severity of the situation, I tried to speak honestly. "Maybe cause I ask 'Why me' a lot," I told him. "I probably said something like 'Why am I living if this is what life is like for me? If this is it I don't want to live anymore.' Something like that."

"Hmm . . . okay," he said, finishing up writing. Then he looked up. "Do you feel that way now?"

I shrugged like I wasn't sure. Intellectually, I didn't believe that. But emotionally it was stone solid true.

"Do you want to tell me why that is?" he asked.

"To be honest? Not really." I didn't have the energy to explain something that seemed so obvious. Any day I might get the call that my father was dead, and I panicked every time the phone rang. Friends of mine were dying, my family didn't want to see me, my only conscious memories were of poverty and hopelessness, and here I was trapped in a system that most kids never recovered from. How was I supposed to react?

My father spent a month in the hospital and then got released to a local clinic. He had ups and downs but somehow slowly recovered. When he was eventually released back to my sister's home, new problems arose because he needed dialysis five times a week and couldn't work. But at least he was alive. And being alive was enough.

Iza's compassion and support carried me through the darkness of that storm. She also taught me something valuable: to use my pain and anger as motivation. Iza enabled me to view myself, and my future, in a positive light. My very first exposure to college—even to the word "college"—was through her.

"What are you always doing schoolwork for?" I asked her once. She was sitting on a stool reading from a textbook and taking notes. Damon was preparing dinner with some of the other residents.

"Well, I'm in college," she said. "You know I'm in college. I have homework every night."

"Yeah I know. I know." I hesitated. "But what's college?"

Damon looked up from the stove. "You never heard of college?" he asked. Iza flashed him a look.

Even if I had heard the word—and it wasn't tossed around on my street—I'd never made sense of it. "Maybe. I'm not sure."

Five-year-olds in Park Slope already knew about college, its significance, that their life's trajectory would pass through there. For them, it was the standard, and the expectations were clear. Here I was, sixteen years old, hearing about it for the first time. The world is only as small or as big as the things we are introduced to.

I began to get curious about the homework Iza was doing along-side us in the house. "I'm writing a paper," she'd say, or "I'm studying for an exam." Damon would explain things too, tell me about classes he took or books he read. Sometimes Iza had to watch a documentary for school.

"You get to watch movies?" I said, dumbfounded.

"Sometimes," she said, smiling.

"Can I watch with you?"

"Of course. But you have to talk to me about it afterward. Help me answer my homework questions."

The dots started to connect for me. My father, if he were to survive, would not be able to take care of the family. There was a huge void there and I needed to step into it.

What really got me excited was Iza telling me that in college you pick your own schedule, go to school when you want, and pick what subjects to study. Freedom. I incessantly peppered her with more questions.

"How do I get there?" I asked her. "What do I have to do?"

"Well, first you have to graduate high school," she said. "Get a diploma."

"Okay. So college is just like school."

"Yes, but it's a school where you can obtain a degree in a special-ized field like social work, business, medicine, politics. Your major."

"What's a major?" I was relentless.

"Like your focus of study. I'm studying human services."

"What's that?"

"Similar to the work I do here with you guys. Like a social worker that helps people."

Out of habit, I tried to find the trap in all this. "Costs money, though, right?"

"Yes, but if you maintain decent grades the government will help with tuition and expenses. You just have to fill out a bunch of forms."

Then she came with the icing on the cake: college was filled with women. "You're going to be outnumbered by the girls," she said. "Like three to one."

I badgered and begged Iza to take me on a visit to her school, the Borough of Manhattan Community College (BMCC). If I had my privs, she eventually agreed, I could accompany her to class.

The next week, I was sitting in the living room area counting up my points when she yelled up from the basement.

"Jim, I'm leaving for class in five minutes if you want to come!"

I rushed up the stairs, threw on my outfit from Charles: clean T-shirt, blue jeans, and Reeboks. We drove over the bridge into Manhattan, to the upscale streets of Tribeca on the west side of downtown. It was the New York that I had no part of, that I felt wasn't designed for someone like me, that I assumed wanted nothing to do with me. That day I saw it through brand-new eyes. Because of Iza, it was almost like I belonged. Or that I *could* belong.

After parking we walked up a small hill past an elaborate playground: clean rubber padding and attentive parents. As we entered the main floor of the school building I spotted a large cafeteria, rows of computers, offices, and a huge glass window overlooking traffic zooming up the West Side Highway and a majestic stretch of the Hudson River.

"Don't wander too far. Stay around here," Iza said as she got on the escalator. "I'll be back in an hour."

I barely heard her; I was entranced. Students dapped each other on the run, bulleting to class. Others sat in the computer lab typing, listening to music on headphones. A pack of them had folding tables set up to recruit for their clubs. Eager dudes were all bottled up in one area scamming on girls, showing off their new Jordans and flirting like high-school kids. The student body was all shades and origins, a melting pot that intrigued my virgin eyes. I absorbed as much of the scene as possible, trying to hold it tight inside of me so I could access it later.

I likely looked deranged, wide-eyed and staring at everyone and everything. The freedom and independence was a palpable thing on the campus. On the footbridge that connected the wings of the building I froze in a haze, absorbing the view of the Hudson. There were boats, high-rises towering over the water, golf driving ranges, and a basketball court so clean that its black looked like rubber. People were jogging, playing pick-up games, walking their dogs, or relaxing with books or headphones. This was it. This place. I wanted to be here.

In what felt like a blink Iza was back.

"You okay?" she asked.

"Yeah. Why?"

"I never seen you smile like that," she said. "Ever. You got like a clown face on."

She playfully shoved me and said, "Let's go."

On the ride home I assaulted her with more questions, making sure it was possible for me to actually go to college. She reassured me that it was in my hands, if I took a different approach to life and learning. "That could be you," she said. "I'll help you, you know. But I can't drag you there. You gotta meet me halfway."

Damon used to say something similar, how you could lead a horse to water but you couldn't make it drink. After that trip, I realized how thirsty I'd been. How ready I was to drink.

Not long after, I was sitting with Damon and Yi in the rec room watching the six o'clock news. I was daydreaming a bit when I caught an image on the screen: faces from the old block. They were handcuffed, and being perp-walked in front of cameras. The NYPD gang squad had rounded up a bunch of dealers and boosters I knew well from my neighborhood. I could've—or would've—been with them, facing football numbers, my future walled off in an instant.

Breeze's murder had been something of an epiphany, a wake-up call. My still-developing maturity compelled me to process it more profoundly: the scarcity of opportunity that led people to the drug game, the tornado of violent culture that swept in and took everything out. I saw his death through a wider lens, one that clarified details and gave context, like a picture coming into clear focus.

Boys Town became what I needed it to be because I let it. Like the planets aligning, enough things shifted into place at the same time that I got the necessary momentum going. I quit smoking weed, exercised more, paid attention in class, and made an effort to be agreeable in the house. I was still at the age where my brain was a clay that could be molded new.

One of my rituals at dinner was removing the black olives from my salad and tossing them in the garbage. "You been throwing those out for years," Iza said to me once. "You ever try one?"

"Nope. Don't need to. They're nasty."

"C'mon. What's gonna happen? Just try it."

Iza hadn't steered me wrong yet so I popped one in my mouth.

After that they had to hide the olives from me. I'd eat them straight out of the metal can for breakfast, lunch, and dinner.

A few weeks after my visit to BMCC, I was rumbling around in the kitchen, opening drawers, looking for a pen for one of Iza's assignments. Inside a drawer I found a beat-up paperback titled *The Pact*, with three young black professionals on the cover. I took it up to my bedroom and started reading—the first time in my life I'd ever done that on my own initiative.

The Pact was the true story of three friends from a poor section of Newark who grew up in troubled homes without fathers. As juveniles they each had run-ins with the law, and one of them came close to doing serious time. As teenagers, realizing where their lives were headed, they made a promise to one another: they would all go to college and become doctors.

In alternating chapters, each talked about the "positive peer pressure" he gave to the others, how it motivated them and forced them to keep up. One of them wrote about a formative experience when he was young. During a dentist appointment he started asking questions about the tools and teeth, and the dentist took the time to teach him the names of things, how the tools worked, even making a game out of it during his appointments. That simple interaction lit a flame inside of him that turned into a fire.

Their story was inspiring. It had an impact because these men were just like me. And they had risen out of the rubble to all become doctors, the most prestigious profession there is. Like the hip-hop lyrics I once absorbed, here again was my story reflected back to me, only this time with hope at its center. So many passages stuck out to me, including this:

> Among boys, particularly, there seems to be some macho code that says to gain respect, you have to prove that you're bad. . . . The wrong friends can lead you to trouble. But even more, they can tear down hopes, dreams, and possibilities. We know, too, that the right friends inspire you, pull you through, rise with you.[6]

I had never encountered myself on the page like that. Some of it was timing; Ms. Oglio had actually given me the book a while back but I wasn't ready for it and left it lying around the house. Or perhaps it was divine grace that had it find me when I was ready to open it. I knew I didn't have other kids to build this pact with, so I decided to make one with myself.

It began with me not wanting to disappoint those who invested in me: Christine and Marty, then the Canadas. Eventually, it turned into me not wanting to disappoint myself. Damon and Iza modeled the type of adult I was interested in being. I was almost seventeen years old and finally open to the idea of becoming one.

12

Astonishing

They tried to bury us. They didn't know we were seeds.

—MEXICAN PROVERB[7]

The will to change doesn't magically wipe the slate clean. I'd been spending nearly half my day in school, and more in tutoring sessions at home, but what actually seeped through was still a slow drip. One morning, Paula, the program director, was observing class through the glass window. She noticed how inattentive I was. "It's like your body is there but your mind isn't," she told me in a meeting afterward. "I could see it in your eyes."

After less than five minutes of watching me she detected a chasm: the gap between what I needed and what I was getting. Besides language barriers and minimal schooling, I was a slow learner and easily distracted. But she didn't get on me about it. Most teachers and administrators placed the burden of pulling myself up solely onto me. Like it was a question of will. Paula had vision: she looked outward and saw an opportunity.

She proposed something unprecedented for Boys Town: the chance to attend a GED program, on my own, outside the school. It would be a smaller classroom, individualized attention, a setting that would give me the opportunity to succeed. "It won't be easy. But it gives you a fighting chance," Paula said. "How does that sound?"

It was another Hobson's choice; it's not like I had other options. I literally had nothing to lose.

In order to be accepted in the GED program, I had to go through a battery of evaluations. They discovered I had significant learning disabilities, including ADHD, that made it hard for me to concentrate on work and to focus in class. My body could not stay still for tests and my attention was all over the place.

Teachers had always attributed my failing in schools to lack of motivation, and I have to admit that was part of it. Still, there was a physiological explanation for my academic troubles, one that went beyond my external conditions. Looking back, I can't help but notice the irony: recognizing and naming my deficiencies were precisely what gave me strength. Nowadays I don't put too much stock in such diagnoses, but back then I was in no position to reject the accommodations that came with it.

On school mornings, when everyone walked down to Willoughby Street, I'd take the subway alone out to Kings County Hospital, where there was a wing that housed the GED program. That subway stop also happened to be walking distance to Crown Street. At first I exploited the freedom, stopping by to see my homeboys, catching up on hood politics, sometimes falling back into smoking weed. I soon realized that this was basically spitting in Paula and the Canadas' faces, and I wised up. So each morning after that I made the decision to turn left toward the GED school instead of right toward Crown.

Right next door to the hospital was Wingate High School, and an ambulance station, and across the street was the office of the chief medical examiner of New York City. Those buildings told a story that you could follow with your eyes, one that I'd heard too many times. That one-block radius contained the institutions that shadowed just about everyone I knew. The GED program there was like a final exit, our last chance before society threw up its hands and left us to the elements.

A counselor in the GED program contacted the Brooklyn Learning Center and convinced them to see me for free. On my first day there after school, I met my tutor, Joanna, a beautiful young white woman with long brown hair and a blinding smile. Her cheeks would rise and her front teeth would take up half her face. There was something innocent about her appearance, but when she spoke I was disabused of that assumption. She got angry about the right things: injustice, bias, inequality, exploitation.

At our first session she sat across from me at a small round table, a thick manila folder containing the sum total of my printed life in front of her. She casually let me know that I wasn't the normal kid on her roster.

"So, where should we start?" she asked.

"What do you mean?"

"The GED test is in June. What do you want to work on?"

I laughed. "How much time you got?"

"Well, what do you want help with?"

"Everything," I said. To her credit, she was not fazed.

"Okay, let's dig in then," Joanna said, opening a math book. "This is a shitload of material to cover," she said.

"Yeah?"

"Just because it's an alternate track, doesn't mean it's easy. The average high school graduate can't pass the GED test."

"Good I'm not average then, right?" I said, trying to play it off.

She exhaled deeply, but teased right along. "Let's hope not."

When we started working together Joanna spoke of this enormous balloon of information hanging over my head, representing everything I had not yet learned. We both tried to ignore it—all it did was overwhelm us—but it floated there in our presence, just like she described.

Like putting my shoulder into something heavy, I felt the world offer a little more give. There was a link, a cause and effect between what I did and what I got, which appealed to me. I could control more aspects of my life and started to respond to that sense of ownership. As the pressure released, I found room to move and space to breathe. It became clear to me that life is a series of choices.

With the privileges came freedom, so I was out of the house on my own more often, regularly going to the YMCA or playing basketball at one of the parks down the street. Park Slope was like an oasis in Brooklyn, located between some of the borough's roughest neighborhoods. But things bled over boundaries. A few blocks from the Boys Town residence was a large faded brick elementary school, William Alexander Middle School 51. In the back was a high-gated metal fence, surrounding black pavement of basketball hoops with fresh white nets. On the weekends, the park was a mix of higher-income white kids and black kids from the nearby public housing.

One Saturday afternoon I was alone at the courts waiting up against the fence for the next game. Another dude came wandering through the court. He had sleepy eyes and wore a Yankees hat, Jay-Z style—clean, its brim a flat line. Short and thin, he carried himself as if he had a Napoleon complex, preemptively on offense. He was looking down at his phone, swaggering around like it was his backyard, making comments about the game.

"I'm on next," I said to him, leaning back on the fence.

He ignored me, but started shaking his head and laughing. I was allowed out only for an hour so my time was precious.

"I called next," I said. "You gotta wait, man. You weren't even here."

"You talking, man?" he said.

"Fuck yeah," I said, putting my weight back onto my feet.

"What you say? What?" he said.

"I said I got next."

He waved me off and circled a little around the park, talking to someone on his phone.

When the game ended, he wandered back onto the court, grabbed the ball, and started shooting. I had about six inches on him, had quit drinking and smoking, and had been lifting weights; it wasn't even a contest. Though I always found it unfair to fight smaller guys, I hated reckless mouths.

"Yo, gimme the ball," I said. "I'm next."

"Fuck out of here," he said, still shooting.

"You gonna give me that ball or we got a problem."

"Yeah, motherfucker? What's gonna happen?" he said, about to take another shot.

"Keep shooting your bricks and find out."

He stopped for a second, like I cut him. Shaking his head, he mumbled under his breath. He hung still a moment, waiting. Then he fired a chest pass at me and walked off. "A'ight," he said, just floating it there. "A'ight."

About thirty minutes later he was back with one of his friends, a guy about my height with a rippled chest, tattoos up his forearms.

"What now, pussy?" he was saying, but I wasn't looking at him. Now Yankees Hat had a .38 revolver pointed right in my face. I dropped the ball and backed up to the fence.

It wasn't the first time I'd had a gun pulled on me but it's something you never get used to. Pulling a gun is like signing a contract; if someone pulls a gun on you he better use it. And if he doesn't, you have to get yours and use it.

"What's good, pussy?" they were shouting over each other, shouting and weaving an alternating rhythm between them.

"What's all that shit you was talking?"

"You think we're pussy out here?"

"Who's pussy now!"

A gun in your eyeline washes the world away. Everything blurs and fades. There's just the gleaming black and the thump in your chest. As I was cornered back to the fence, I gradually sidestepped to the entrance and then backed out of the park. "Yeah, pussy! That's what I thought," they yelled after me. I could hear they weren't chasing me because their voices remained distant and I heard no footsteps. "What's up now, motherfucker!" I just kept running up to Sixth Avenue.

My ability to retaliate was limited, but that doesn't mean I wasn't thinking about it. But I had no phone, no quick access to my old neighborhood, no way to round up anyone. The program saved my life again that day. And I felt like I passed some kind of test.

There was a trade-off, though. I was impressed at how I reacted but annoyed that it had happened at all. I had let my guard down, didn't even have an antenna up when the guy took off after we first had words. I forgot that the safety in Boys Town didn't transfer out into the world. Reading body language, sniffing out potential danger, are life-or-death skills and mine had gone rusty. I had lost what I had already earned the hard way, and it almost cost me my life.

* * *

"How did you get here?" Joanna asked.

"I ran," I said, trying to catch my breath.

I was late for our session because someone at the house had stolen my MetroCard right off my dresser. Joanna helped me with writing, with math, with everything on the GED test. But she also had an intuitive grasp of the big picture—that I was living in a world where things like that would happen all the time. In my experience, schools didn't seem to care what happened to me before 8:00 a.m. and after 3:00 p.m. But those things are as important as what's going on between first and last bell.

Some days when I was overwhelmed, Joanna helped me move the goalposts. She taught me that the final result is not the measure that counts; people can't be viewed in a vacuum. What matters is the distance between where you were and where you end up. How do we grow relative to ourselves? That giant balloon floating over my head was over everyone's head, so it's meaningless. I loved her for making me see that.

It got to the point where Joanna and I would get so sidetracked talking that she started to schedule me as her last student. She had an amazing grasp of language that inspired me, even when she was just talking. I'd end up staying for hours talking politics, race relations, family dynamics. I'd show up with fast food from McDonald's and we'd get into a thirty-minute conversation about how corporations exploit impoverished communities. Tutoring would bleed into therapy or larger discussions of the world. Any one thing might trigger it. She would eventually return to the algebra or history lesson, but it ended up seeming small in comparison.

It was important to me that reciprocity was a part of the learning process. Eventually, I got the sense that I was teaching her as much as she was teaching me. She'd ask in-depth questions about my life and her curiosity would peak when I went into detail. It made me feel like the hardships I endured were a thing of value.

I once read that for a child to grow, he needs roots and wings, a comfortable home base, and the self-confidence to fly on his own. Boys Town gave me both. First, it gave me my childhood back. I'd led a life of self-sufficiency since I was six years old; the residence gave me a respite from that. The second thing it gave me was the room and support to mature. A few weeks into my GED program, I made my case at the family meeting and earned a bed in the Achievement room. I tried to make the place my own: I hung up basketball and football posters, family pictures, a Nerf plastic hoop over the door. It was the biggest room on the top floor, with a couch and its own bathroom. The room had slanted ceiling beams, skylights, and windows onto the street where I would sit and watch the world go by.

Achievement was designed to function as a bridge back into society, so there was no longer a card or point system. All the consequences became natural: normal parenting things like getting positive praise or being forced to stay in your room. There was a self-directed component too because the family teachers couldn't keep track of everything you were doing at that level. Your independence is kind of the point. One of the things I used my free time for was something I had never done before: read. Reading was a new outlet, a way to seek solitude and sanctuary that I never knew existed.

Just as I became open to a different kind of role model, two perfect ones appeared, almost divinely. First, Damon handed me a copy of *The Autobiography of Malcolm X*. He preached so passionately about his hero that I cracked the book immediately. Malcolm rose from nothing to become one of the most powerful and influential men of the twentieth century. As a young boy, Malcolm's father was killed, likely by white supremacists. The stress on his mother triggered a nervous breakdown and the state confined her to a mental institution.

Seeing my own story through his was powerful. We both had been through troubled homes and the juvenile justice system. By sheer force of will, and education, he rose like a phoenix. He would debate kids from Oxford and Harvard and embarrass them. He blew through the library catalog and read the dictionary cover to cover. The first time I saw the word "astonishing" was in Malcolm's autobiography; I looked it up and started using it, arming myself to converse with a different class.

I connected fiercely with Malcolm's passion for justice. Though I hadn't even thought about it in those terms, that feeling was always in me. "They cripple the bird's wing," he once said, "then condemn it for not flying as fast as they." I could relate to the mix of activism and the street that Malcolm embodied—to his aggression, his purpose, and his power.

Malcolm was a credible messenger to me. He grew up in a single-parent home, in poverty; had done and sold the drugs, had been in the streets and in prison. So when he told me to leave the streets alone, clean up my act, and focus my fight, I listened. He didn't lecture on personal responsibility from a perch; he had been down in the hole. His message was *I am you and you are me and we can do this.*

I learned about the forces of white supremacy, the need for our people to control our own destiny, and the level of brutality blacks have endured in this country. Though these issues obviously affected me, I had never really put much thought into them. In fact, my interaction with white people had been mostly positive across the board: Christine, Marty, Joanna, Ms. Oglio. Opening Malcolm's book and learning history through his eyes was like being thrown in the deep end of the pool. He never stopped sounding the drumbeat against institutional racism in America. That book was one long awakening.

He was such an imposing and powerful presence—even on the page; the only person I knew like that was Dean Walton back from my junior high school, who could move crowds off a simple word or action. Malcolm was in control, unafraid, and unapologetic. He was the pure embodiment of righteousness and justice. He loved his people so much that he made the ultimate sacrifice for the cause. I'd been a fighter my whole life, but not always for the right reasons. Malcolm was interested in love and unity; he was about channeling the fight toward the systems that oppress us. In reading his book, I was full of energy, anger, and love for people that I hadn't even met.

Malcolm's pursuit of knowledge was a huge inspiration and aspiration for me. Through him, I recognized that books are the gatekeepers to many of the answers we seek. Malcolm led me into African American history, which I'd had little to no exposure to. Haiti's history of early independence, its routing of its colonial masters, and the heroism of L'Ouverture and Dessalines are some of the first things we learned at a young age. But in America, if you miss a couple of days of school in February, you won't encounter African American history at all. Malcolm taught me about the larger world and helped me understand the context of who I was.

The other book I read up on the couch in the Achievement room was *Dreams from My Father*, a memoir by a then-rising politician named Barack Obama. I felt a kinship with this mixed-race senator with a foreign background, a funny name, and the gall to think he could change the world. I identified with Obama's feeling like a foreigner in America, and then a stranger in Africa. His visit to Kenya to meet his family there affected him profoundly, allowing him to pull back the lens on his own identity. I thought of Haiti, how I'm both fully separate but entirely connected to its people and its land, how it contributed to the person I am.

Obama was the future and he introduced me to what things might be. He was political and polished, but still a child of Malcolm's. In the forty years between the two of them, progress had been made in society and their ascensions reflected that progression. Malcolm was the consummate outsider, the revolutionary shaking the gates open; Barack was the chosen one who would walk through, rising to the top of the establishment while always remaining himself. These men are giants, and their very existence gave me a sense of who I wanted to be. They were so far ahead in the distance, of course, but at least I knew which direction to face.

As the end of my two-year sentence approached, I made a decision that most reflected how far I had come: I chose to stay at Boys Town for an additional year. Being away from the street and from my home for so long gave me perspective. I was standing above something and seeing things I couldn't see while down in it. Like how insidious an influence my old world had been. My few visits home on the way to the GED school were a stark reminder. Park Slope and Boys Town were so much more conducive to my new lifestyle, which was still shaky and precarious. Though I stood more firmly inside my new self, the street had a magnetic pull that I still couldn't trust myself to be around.

With Joanna's perpetual support and help I passed the GED test and immediately enrolled in BMCC, which Boys Town helped me pay for. No one in my family had ever attended college, and the burden of that actually felt good. With college on the horizon, I wanted to put myself in the best position to succeed. I wasn't going to get anywhere unless I stayed exactly where I was.

College blew my world wide open. I had only just learned it existed a few years before and then I was there, as hungry and motivated as any student on campus. To someone who had been at the mercy of others for so long, college was liberating. I could pick my own classes, which were up to me to attend, and I was surrounded by a diverse group of students with years of schooling on me. And the *women*: smart, sophisticated, beautiful women with no interest in tough guys or clowns. I'd be lying to say they weren't an extra motivation. Iza, Joanna, and my professors all helped me with the workload. They saw the student I could be, rather than just the deficits I walked in with. There were all these things college students had prepared for their entire lives—the intricacies of applications, schedules, financial aid forms, computer use, and independent learning. I entered with none of it.

But just thinking about my future turned into me looking forward to it, which itself was turned into something almost magical.

I'd always assumed you had to have all the advantages to succeed, but I learned it's not true. Ambition and passion count for more, and they carried me through. I embraced my new role as a college student and used it to describe myself any chance I got. "I'm a college student," I'd say, loving the sound of it, the new stature it conferred. I had been saved, and on that campus, I finally felt worth saving.

I worked a series of jobs while at BMCC, most of which were set up by the Canadas. But one of my early jobs came about by chance. An optometrist who lived on my street saw me sweeping the steps out front one day. We got talking and she asked if I was looking for work and soon I was handing out flyers for her. Just living on a block where people owned businesses—and the opportunity that afforded—gave me an advantage I hadn't ever had.

As I was working, in school, and on the Achievement level up in my own room, a perceptible distance grew between me and the rest of the house. Sometime during the semester, that distance turned into resentment. I began to rebel against a system that I felt was crushing me, not letting me move or breathe. I was pressing against the sides of a box I had outgrown.

There's the ideal time to leave everything; it's a bell curve with a sweet spot in the middle and a steep decline if you miss that window.

I was eighteen and had mastered the entire program, but still asking permission to use the bathroom or get up from the table. I was still getting constantly punished over infractions, sent to my room, even put back on subsystem, back to the card and the points, which felt like an insult. "You guys fucking know me!" I'd yell at the Canadas. They'd send me upstairs and I'd stew on that couch: *I don't need this shit anymore.* I was the grizzled veteran, mature and bitter and dying to get out. Close to thirty kids had passed through the system and gone home since the day I walked in that house. I had grown out of BT. But I remained, the fixture larger than the space.

I met with Iza and Damon and then spoke to Marty and Christine. I talked to Joanna. Everyone agreed that the best thing to do was leave Boys Town at the end of my first college semester. No one wanted me to lose ground: we'd all done too much work to get me where I was.

Though I avoided it by delaying my release, the monster was still facing me. I had to leave the place that allowed me to be a kid, a place that let me be a wrecking ball without having to pay enormously for it. That level of forgiveness wouldn't exist past the front door on Sixth Avenue. The real world didn't care where I'd been, what I'd been through. There would be no safety net to catch me as I dropped through the air.

"What are you afraid of?" Joanna asked me.

"I don't know. Like what if nothing has changed," I said. "I *know* things haven't changed back there."

"Well, you can't worry about that, Jim," she said. "You can only worry about what you can control. You've changed just in the short time I've known you. I can't imagine how far you've come from the day of your arrest. It can't even be measured in time."

Joanna tried, but she didn't really know the world I grew up in. The orbit of poverty, the one I'd be returning to, isn't just one thing.

It's an infection that seeps into every area of your life: shelter, clothes, meals, health, family dynamics, fear, crime, and constant violence. And the exhaustion and distress of every day being a constant fight.

I knew my grandma's apartment hadn't changed. Nor had my block. Nor had just about everyone I knew. Those three years were like decades to me, but to everyone else, it was just three years. Some of them were doing exactly the same things in the exact same spots. People I knew might be a bit taller, have a little bit more money or a new hairstyle, but they were all essentially the same.

Two days before my release I was in the car with Iza coming back from the bank. I had accumulated $987 in allowance through the years and Iza helped me set up my first account. That plastic card was power to me, an intoxicating thing that represented privilege. I kept pulling it out during the ride and pretending like I had real money on it. Iza and I were joking how no one needed to know.

She parked the car in front of the residence. As I undid my seat belt and was about to open the door, my muscles braced. Then a flood washed over me. I started crying and crying, had never cried like that before, especially in front of another person. Iza was the only mother figure that I ever had. And now I was losing her. The safety she embodied would vanish. As would my home, my family, my support network.

"It's going to be all right," she said. "You will always be part of our family. Of our life."

I didn't see how that was true. And I couldn't stop crying.

"You're welcome to come back to the house whenever you want. We'll be here." Then her voice caught and she started crying too. It was strange: Iza was always nurturing, but rarely so emotional. Working with all of us had given her a tough exterior that she kept wrapped tight. It was painful for us both to let go like that, but it was cleansing. We needed to do it.

The unknown was terrifying. The Jim I had become had never

been out in the world. I went straight to my room and lay on top of my clothes, my eyes focused on the bare ceiling. I had no idea what life after Boys Town would be like. Would it look like this? Like my childhood? Something I couldn't even conceive of?

A real fear was coursing through my mind and body. I had no frame of reference to know if I'd actually changed. Was it this place or was it me? What if I didn't like the answer?

PART III

OUT

13

Re-Entry

February 2007

All the truly living, at least once, are born again.

—TA-NEHISI COATES, *THE BEAUTIFUL STRUGGLE*

When a young person is dropped back into the world where he first learned how to behave and assert himself, he can't just shut it all off or out. It's embedded in his responses, and in his identity. It's connected to his very being. It's not just that he was in the streets; the streets are in him.

When I walked out of Boys Town at eighteen years old with a semester of college under my belt, I returned to the push and pulls of the old neighborhood. Part of me looked forward to heading back there, to the place that taught me about resilience and community, to the streets that formed so much of my identity and sense of self. I had a complicated relationship with my home and my family—but despite that, they still made me who I was.

But the shift was more difficult than I had imagined it would be. I was back in my grandmother's cramped apartment on Crown Street where everyone struggled for their own bit of space. Sleeping in the same room with my father and my younger brother, Roothchild, felt like a giant step backward. My foldout bed was out in the middle of the living room, and everyone had to walk past it all hours of the day. I didn't have a closet or any space for my clothes and few possessions. I had this twisted feeling that my freedom was back in the system, that I had given things up by being released.

Although back there I had been state property and constrained by the rules, I come from an impoverished community. I was home and I was free, but I was just back in the hood with nothing. I'd wake up in the middle of the night and forget what year it was, what I was doing. Then I realized I was back. All those years had passed and I hadn't moved an inch. I hated it in my bones.

My father had been in and out of the hospital for years. By the time I was back home he was living with my grandmother again, having lost both of his kidneys. He'd hole up in a chair next to his bed watching basketball or Catholic services on TV, shut off from the world. He'd rarely leave except to go to church on Sunday or to get dialysis. With no education and no English he was only qualified to be on his feet in an assembly line for eight dollars an hour, and even that he couldn't do. My dad has always been strangely militant with me while playing fast and loose with himself, his prospects, and his health. I suspect he was hard on me when I was growing up so that I didn't turn into him.

Even though he couldn't work he was not eligible for government benefits or social security because he didn't speak enough English to pass the citizen test. Dad never embraced America the way I did—or the way his own father did. My father was a grown man when we arrived, set in his ways. A big part of finding your place in a new land is being able to speak and understand the language. So my dad was here but not here. He was like a ghost, his existence not even recognized by his own country.

The walls had closed in even tighter over those three years. There were eleven of us total: My aunt and her boyfriend lived in a bedroom on the other side of the apartment with their own bathroom. The rest of us shared a tiny one off the entryway. My younger cousins were in a smaller bedroom, as was my aging grandmother and my sister Geraldine, who had been looking after my father. Wilfred and his wife still rented the narrow room by the kitchen.

My older brother, Colin, would sometimes drop in under the influence and stay in different rooms; other times he'd be off finding trouble, crashing wherever, dealing with the demons a hard life brings. There was always tension in that house—the kind that comes from not knowing people at all and the kind that comes from knowing people way too long.

My mind-set was so different than before. My focus now was on my education, working, exercising—smoothing out all those rough edges. But things escalated quickly between Colin and me. It was peaceful when we weren't there, so a common solution was to lock people out, especially late at night.

Colin was taller than me but skinny and wiry, with a squeaky voice and thicker accent. He actually did go back to Haiti that time my father tried to send us and I hid out to avoid getting on the plane. Sometimes I'd look at Colin and see the version of me I never wanted to be. He wasn't street smart, just a loudmouth whom I always had to protect.

We'd go at each other like monsters, like gladiators, the way only brothers can. Once I was in the house late at night, doing push-ups during a break from studying. The house was asleep and Colin started to bang on the front door.

Boom, boom, boom.

I didn't move.

"Open this door! Fuck!" he said.

I kept my eyes on the floor and held the tension in my muscles.

Boom, boom, boom.

This went on for over ten minutes. It reached the point that I knew if I let him in, things were going to fly. So I kept ignoring it, finished my reps, and broke the book back open. I thought maybe he'd give up and sleep it off somewhere else. But he kept knocking and ringing the bell. My dad and Roothchild woke up.

"You gonna let him in?" Roothchild asked, groggy.

"Nah," I said. I kept my eyes on my reading, willing Colin to go away.

Then he started to kick at the door—thwack, thwack. "I know you're up, Jim! Let me in!"

Thwack! Thwack! Thwack!

"Open this fucking door! Open the *door*, Jim!" Colin boomed in the hallway. "I'm gonna fuck you up!"

Roothchild pounced up from the floor and opened the door. Like a windup toy, Colin turned the corner at the hallway and flew for me.

I was bigger and stronger than him, sober and in shape. I picked up Colin's whole body like a sack and slammed him onto the floor in the hallway. Then I pulled him down to where he couldn't even get his arms up.

"Get off me! Get off, yo!" Colin said.

I put my mass on top of him, just to subdue him. The whites of his eyes were crackly and red.

"Let me go, yo! Get off!" He made like he was going to spit at me. "Shit!"

When I started to walk away, he sprung from the ground and came at me again. I turned quick and punched him in the jaw, knocking him back down.

"Fuck!" Colin yelled. He sat on the ground for a few seconds. Then he gathered up again and darted to the kitchen. He grabbed a bread knife—a long one, sharp and serrated—and came back at me full speed.

"Colin! Fuck, man!" Roothchild yelled.

"Enough!" I heard my dad yell. He was up now, standing in the doorway.

As I saw the knife coming at me I instinctively grabbed a hammer from the hall closet. He started to swing the knife sloppy, just hitting air. Then he charged at me. I took his momentum and carried him into the wall, his head and the hammer making holes in the plaster. The noise shook the whole floor and the knife dropped.

My dad picked it up and then stood in between us, hands out on both our chests. He wasn't big but when he wanted to be, my dad was a giant. He'd get that growl in his eyes that could shut anything down.

"Both of you! Enough!" he yelled. "Out of your fucking minds."

The cops came knocking about ten minutes later. It was like a routine call for them; they had been coming semiregularly by that point. I knew how to speak to the police. Working and being in college gave me the upper hand once they arrived.

The cops mostly focused on Colin. He was the problem: they could see it in his red-shot eyes, in his slurred curses and rah-rah nonsense. Colin never did himself any favors.

"Fuck y'all!" he was screaming from a chair in the kitchen. My dad and one of the cops were standing over him. "You can't fucking come in here trying to arrest me." Colin was banging on the kitchen table on each word. "I. Don't. Give. A. Fuck." The table rattled under his slapped palm. "I don't give a *fuck*. I'll go to jail. You think I'm afraid of *jail*, I'm not afraid of jail. I'm not afraid of *dying*! I don't give a fuck."

In the spaces between his rants, I stayed measured and calm. "Officer," I said, maintaining eye contact, "my brother came in to the house drunk; he started screaming and waking everyone up. I—"

"You can arrest me, I don't give a *fuck*." Colin was still raging. A scared kid hiding behind a giant mouth.

"I have class in the morning," I continued. "I'm a college student studying human services. He started to bang on the door. We got into a verbal altercation, which led to a physical altercation, then he came at me with a kitchen knife. I grabbed a hammer to protect myself."

"You know I'd fuck you up!" Colin was yelling. "You should arrest me! Better arrest me or I'm gonna fucking kill him!" Colin was asking for it that night. The cops ended up giving him a warning, but they made sure he left for the night. The hectic energy lingered in the apartment for a while until we all just went to bed.

My grandmother was a strong, beautiful woman with fine gray hair and soft caramel skin. All over her face was written the beautiful struggle. She was quiet and respectful, a churchgoing woman of God. She brought us here and took us into *her* place, even though there wasn't much room. Over the years, the toxic environment in that house caused her too much stress. My grandfather had died while I was in Boys Town, so by this point, she was also a widow.

Eight months after I returned home she got ill, was hospitalized overnight, and died soon after. It was like a huge part of me was cut out, and I felt responsible. At her age she needed to relax and be taken care of. She didn't need to live with all the adrenaline and noise of youth. She and my grandfather had been sending us whatever they could since we were babies, had brought us to America, had given me *my life*, and our presence made things that much harder for them. It was a huge sacrifice, more than I can ever fathom or repay.

Damon and I had ended on bad terms, an accumulated heaviness that comes with that kind of tight experience. But as was his way, he set me up for success, arranging an interview with the Park Slope Key Food supermarket. The interview was succinct and straight to the point. The manager, Eddy, was a tall, heavyset, dark-skinned gentleman with a bald head.

"Wassup baby, so you want this job or you want to waste my time?"

"I need this job," I said.

He fired back. "Well, I got a business to run. If you're here to play games I'll fire your ass in a heartbeat."

"I don't have much of an option. This isn't about the six bucks an hour or whatever. It's lifesaving. A real opportunity."

Eddy eyed me for a few seconds, wondering if I was for real. Then he tossed an apron at my feet, summoning me to work on the spot.

Eddy was a refined and experienced chameleon, able to switch back and forth depending on his audience. No one was as eloquent when attending to a customer and no one was as blunt with the kids who staffed the back rooms. He was a grandiose dude, but I learned a lot from him. And during a vulnerable point in my life he stuck out his neck for me, even though he didn't have to.

So in between classes and studying I stocked shelves, unloaded trucks, cleaned floors, and helped customers. It was mindless work but structurally vital. Having my own money, having to be at work at certain hours, it all saved me from going down the wrong path. Damon knew all this, as did Eddy. Being unemployed is a slippery slope, leaving you one bad choice away from falling back into hustling. The job was like a levee, a type of protection against relapsing.

That first year back home, I saw how relentlessly my past would chase me down. A few friends invited me to go with them to Wet Fete, an outdoor Caribbean party held once a year in Brooklyn. I went with Trini, a skinny dude with braids I worked with at Key Food; and Fernando, my friend from hustling days whose foot had been hit by Ky-Mani's bullet ricocheting off the Jewish Steps. He had been in and out of trouble with the law while I was away, most of it gang-related.

That afternoon Trini picked Fernando and me up in his Mitsubishi, which he had hooked up like the Batmobile. His car had one of those deafening mufflers like a jet engine buzzing you, the sound carrying for blocks. Trini thought he was some kind of street racer and drove like a maniac. I avoided getting in the car with him when I could. But he had the tickets to the party and had fronted the money, so we rode with him the fifteen minutes down Nostrand Avenue. I sat in the backseat all juiced up: I had been clean and straight since returning home. That afternoon was really my first break, my first chance to unload a bit like a normal nineteen-year-old.

Wet Fete was held in an outdoor yard between buildings in East Flatbush, one of the toughest parts of Brooklyn. Tables, booths, tents, and stages are set up in a fenced-in space. I was wearing shorts, a tank top, and the slip-on Crocs I had been rocking since Park Slope, gear that I didn't mind being soaked in all day. We came through the gates and headed inside into the madness: Live artists performing reggae on stages, and DJs on platforms spinning soca music. Water hoses sprayed the crowd; shirtless guys, and women in barely hanging bikinis, all letting loose and dancing, their eyes turned back like they were under a trance. The strong scent of marijuana blanketed the air, blunts flowing freely. The sensory memory was fierce.

"I can't believe I never heard about this!" I yelled to Trini over the music. "Shit, I'm coming every year!"

Trini gave a creeping smile. "That's what I been telling you, man," he said. Trini's eyes were scanning the crowd of women lost in the rhythm.

"Shit, I need a drink!" Fernando yelled out over the music.

"Damn right," Trini said.

The three of us were weaving through the crowd when we bumped into a clique from the neighborhood. Among them was Dexter, a cold-looking dude I had had a scuffle with before I went away. While Fernando chatted with them, Dexter stared just past me, almost off my shoulder. He didn't want to show fear but he didn't want to meet my eyes either.

It's strange how you can be completely changed on the inside but the outside world has no idea. I gave Dexter a nod, just to let him know it was all good. He nodded back.

Fernando, Trini, and I reached a tent to get a drink, vodkas on ice in big red plastic cups, then braided our way toward the center of the party to scout out the girls and dance. At Caribbean parties like this, the men bump and grind on the women and then the women return the favor. It's called dubbing—as in you get a "dub" from a woman. The woman moves her backside on your privates and grinds on you to the music, and then you switch. I found a sexy dark-skinned girl in a pink bikini and we went at it.

It's like a competition. Fernando, Trini, and a few others crowded in, circling around me and hyping me up, calling out "Oh!" "Yo!" "Damn!", their hands covering their mouths. The girls' side had women doing the same thing. The hoses were showering the crowd every few seconds, spraying us while we traded dubs. I took my shirt off, showing off my lifting work, the one thing people could see.

* * *

About an hour or so in, I looked up and noticed Fernando and Trini were gone. Realizing I was alone in this chaotic space, I instinctively stopped dancing, a trace of panic rumbling up my nerves. With the pounding beat, the crowd hollering, the spraying water, it was impossible to spot my friends.

As I turned to watch one of the reggae bands, I felt something hit my chest—sharp and quick, like a tap. I didn't even notice what it was. Adrenaline was rushing through my body and I was soaking wet. Then I felt warm liquid trickling down toward my stomach. Looking down, I saw my chest cut open. The white meat of my flesh was poking out and blood was gushing from the hole.

It took a beat for my brain to catch up to what had happened.

Then I spotted it: a broken shard of a Hennessy bottle in the shiny grass at my feet. Someone in the crowd had stabbed me and taken off, blending in with the crowd. *This is it*, I thought. *I'm dead*. I couldn't believe I had come so far only to be killed at some party by a ghost. Then my brain shifted into crisis mode: *Get out of there*. I didn't make a scene, I didn't show emotion; I just walked straight for the exit. Time was precious and in a crowd that size any scene would've made it worse.

I covered my chest with my tank top, pressing it down over the wound. *Just get to the hospital*, I thought. *Just get out and to the hospital*. I tried to stay calm, weaving through the crowd toward the exit. At the gate up ahead I spotted a security guard. As I walked up to him, a beefy guy with a walkie-talkie, we locked eyes.

"What's up?" he yelled over the noise.

I didn't say a word; I just pulled my shirt away and showed him my chest, cut open and pooling out blood. The shirt was a deep, dark red. His eyes popped and he snatched me by the arm, pulling me through the crowd and the gate. He rushed me over to a medic, who took me into one of the ambulances parked out front. They loaded me into the back, taped a thick patch over my chest, and sped off to Kings County Hospital.

As the sirens blared, I lay my head back on the gurney. My breathing was forced and I tried to still my pumping heart.

I didn't spend too much time or energy trying to figure out why. It could have been retaliation for something from years back, I could've been mistaken for someone else, or it could've just been a random act. Knowing wasn't going to solve anything. All it would've done was loop me backward, plant the thirst for revenge in my mind. It was a rabbit hole I wanted nothing to do with.

The medics rushed me into the emergency room at Kings County and everything was scary fast, triple-timed and hectic. My vision was blurry and everything was fragmented and confusing. I was like an emergency object. I got wheeled into a tight room crammed with boxy equipment. A doctor, a light-skinned back woman, began talking in a clipped tone.

"Okay, tell me what happened," she said. Faceless doctors in green scrubs scattered around, wheeling beeping machines, flinging curtains open and closed. Like a slab, I was moved onto a steel table.

I went through what I remembered. "Not sure . . . I was dancing . . . then I felt something like tap me." I felt the thin paper sheet rubbing against my back, the cold metal underneath. I started to jerk upward.

"Don't get up," the doctor said. She put a firm hand on my shoulder, guiding me back down. The doctor's eyes were focused but I could tell she had trains running inside that head. "Something sharp? Did you see what it was?"

"A bottle, I think? Like glass?" Talking required more air than I had.

"You got stabbed," she said.

"I think so." My voice felt far away, like someone else's.

"Oh, you did. The wound is right below your heart," she said. "You're lucky."

I must've looked up at her like she was crazy. "Yeah?" I said.

"If this thing had gone a few inches deeper, it could have punctured it."

They put sixteen stitches in my chest. It all took less than an hour. When the doctors were done, they rolled me into the hallway with the rest of Brooklyn's wounded all parked on top of one another. I was weak and woozy from the blood loss. I tried to stand but my vision was blurry; I made out patches of white and whirling blue and green.

Then they released me. That's how they have to do things there. Kings County Hospital was the first Level I trauma center in the United States: through those doors come a lot of gunshots and stabbings, a lot of blood and gruesome wounds. And that's how they're seen—as injuries, not as people who have them. It's the only way for doctors and nurses to keep going. They need to clear the beds, so they patch you up and send you back out—like in a war zone.

When I walked into my apartment, stitched up in gauze and bandages, my dad, aunt, and Roothchild went crazy. My aunt started screaming about Jesus, and Roothchild cupped me under my arm and helped me inside. I mentioned Wet Fete, getting stabbed, the hospital. My dad just stared at me. He waited a beat, then began ranting in Creole.

"You don't listen!" he yelled. "You never listen!"

"Dad—" Roothchild interrupted.

"What the hell you going to a place like that?" Dad's temper was unraveling.

My brother brought me a glass of water. "Dad, just let him—"

"Of course that's what happens!" Dad yelled. "What do you expect? So stupid!"

My father's words started to drift and float. The stitches were coming apart and I was still bleeding through the seams. The blood had soaked through the gauze and was leaking down my stomach, onto my shorts, onto the floor. The walls started to close in and I got out just enough breath to say "ambulance" before fainting on the hallway floor.

Paramedics careened me back to Kings County where the doctors patched me up again. They still sent me home again at about four in the morning. I begged the nurses to hold me there, but there was no space. They were in battle, after all, and I could stand up.

I made a hard rule after that: No more outdoor parties, no more house parties, no more scenes where things are loose and off the rails. Some people go to those parties just to take it off the rails. Some people get a rush from it. I know because I used to be like that.

Now I had a physical reminder of what could happen: a three-inch scar just below my heart. It was there when I looked in the mirror, when I got dressed in the morning, when I got with a girl. It told me my past wasn't behind me: it was still hovering, ready to strike if I slowed or let my guard down.

14

Through

If the situation or the context where you make the decisions don't change, then second chances don't mean much.

—*THE OTHER WES MOORE*[8]

Society doesn't accept young black men—formerly incarcerated ones, especially—with open arms and the resistance goes both ways. Reentry is slow and brutal; it's obvious to me why so many people don't make it. It's work, from the moment you wake to the moment you go to bed. You're still in that constant state of alertness demanded by your environment, compounded by an extra level of self-protection. You're keeping your eyes fixed forward and blocking out all the forces hell-bent on taking you off track.

In the movie version of my life, getting out of Boys Town and into college would have been the happy ending. But there's more than one kind of wall in this world.

I had to transition on my own into something new, but I wasn't a typical college kid who could blend in with the others. I had just been released from the system and perceptions form based on that first interaction. No matter what I did, I felt like that's who I was to them. It was where I drew my strength from—but it also felt like a cross to bear.

My outside world was colliding with my inside world. I had a foot in each, but wasn't planted in either, so I floated in a kind of purgatory. The disconnect was heavy. In one of my English classes we read a Robert Frost poem and one line cut me close: *The best way out is always through.*

It came down to an issue of time, how I spent it; and space, where I went. The solution was simple. Eighteen or so waking hours in a day and I'd compact and condense my time on Crown Street down to the necessities—sleep hours—where it could cause no trouble. I started going to the gym on the BMCC campus, some days traveling out there hours before class or when I had no class at all. When I had reading to do or papers to write, I'd stay in the computer lab, go to the school library, or work in different coffee shops in downtown Manhattan.

Some of these places were like Mars to me: mostly young white people meeting up or with laptops and headphones, spending hours at small tables. When I sat down I often feared that they'd ask me to leave, just by virtue of standing out so much. But I felt no compunction about taking a seat. I had just as much right—if not more—to intrude on these spaces of ten-dollar words and five-dollar coffees. My struggle was actually a strength. I was not a victim of my background, I was *armed* with it. I wasn't supposed to be there at all; as far as I was concerned, I was playing with house money. So I felt free to make mistakes and embarrass myself. As long as there was a chance for growth, I had no fear from judgment. That felt like the most effective weapon in my arsenal.

I would wander alone around downtown Manhattan, or head uptown to Central Park or to the museums the Canadas introduced me to. I'd roam the Guggenheim or the Met, taking in the art, the bronze-plaqued history, the echoed footsteps on wood floors. I liked the silence, the air-conditioned calm, the vast open space of those buildings. But walking those streets brought its own loneliness and depression. Coping was even harder because I had sworn off marijuana and alcohol, the outlets I once used to numb the pain.

As the stitches in my chest reminded me, I may have changed but the neighborhood hadn't: the drugs, violence, hopelessness, and death all continued, a raging current sweeping up people in its path. Every morning I woke up to the place where I once was a street kid. Every night I had to pass old friends who still were in the same places talking about the same things. Dudes who didn't know any other way because they had never seen any other way.

When my boys first saw me back, they crowded around me, psyched to tell me what the game was like, what the new hustles were, what drugs were selling where, who was dead, who was locked up, where the new hangouts were. I ran into Devon, eighteen years old and driving a brand-new Lexus LS 600h. He had picked up speed in the game since his stint on Sixth Avenue and showed no signs of slowing. He and I were like passing ships in the night.

"Yo, Buff, why don't you come by my new crib?" he asked me.

"Where at?"

"I got this place up the way, on President." I knew it was a trap house, a place he hustled out of. A place I wanted nothing to do with. But I couldn't say that.

I knew I could go in there for five minutes for a quick conversation and the cops could barge in, or a stick-up kid could hit the place. The possibilities unspooled in my head as I thought of new ways to say no every time I saw him. The line is very thin, almost invisible. One small decision can have ripple effects, as Iza always emphasized to me. Even talking to Devon out in the open, I was vulnerable—cops or shooters don't care that we're passing ships.

"C'mon by, man, we'll be chillin'."

"All right, we'll see," I'd say, until the next time we passed.

In our own little world, going into the system is honorable, like a rite of passage. It's like you graduated from college and returned home with a degree. "My boy just went to gladiator school!" my old friends would brag, announcing to anyone in earshot, raising my arm up like a boxer. They all put a cloak of respect on me that I didn't really ask to wear.

It soon became obvious to my friends that I'd gone through a transformation. I can't remember a single explicit conversation I had with anyone. It was all in the subtext, and in the signs. My clothing changed a little bit, and my hours shifted. They'd see me waking up early for school, carrying books, or coming home late from work. I'd spend less time chatting with them, carrying the vibe of someone who had somewhere to be. They let me be, though. They wouldn't have cared or even understood that being in the system had changed my life. That kind of transformation was rare.

The pulls came to a head during the Labor Day parade at the end of that first summer. I was making my way through the crowd with Trini when I spotted an unmistakable face. I skidded up short on the pavement.

"What's up?" Trini asked.

The face carried the same sneer below that same flat-brimmed Yankees hat. It was definitely him. The dude who pulled a gun on me at the basketball courts in Park Slope. We met eyes, his non-reaction telling me he couldn't place my face. But his was seared on my brain.

"Buff, all good?" Trini asked again.

Lying on the couch in the Achievement room, I had often thought of this guy, picturing taking him out if I ever saw him again. Now his reappearance, a phantom in a huge anonymous crowd, was a gift. The universe had lined up in my favor.

The choice to walk away wasn't easy. I thought about getting someone else to take him out but my better judgment prevailed. Even though it was the right decision, it still nagged at me for months. Old habits are resilient enough that they'll take you down with them.

My old crew might've been cool with my turnaround, but the streets do not care if you've changed. The streets don't even *know* that you changed. It wasn't a physical prison, but it was a social one, defined by broken institutions, joblessness, and poverty. It all swirled around me and I was vulnerable to getting caught in the crosswinds. People talk about "just saying no" as if it were a onetime thing. But to really break free, you are saying no constantly, in the actions and choices you make, over and over again, in a million different ways. You have to re-create a new identity; one that shuts out parts of your old self and your familiar world, that takes what you have left and wraps it tight in protective armor. I said no to everything and everyone I knew.

Then I got arrested for saying hello to them.

One night after work, around midnight, I came up the subway steps from the 2 train at the corner of President Street and Nostrand Avenue. Standing there were some of my old crew. These were once my friends—some of them like family—so I stopped to say hello. A few handshakes, a few pounds, some bullshitting and then I'd be out. I was exhausted from a double shift and ready to hit my mattress.

Not a minute after I got there, an unmarked detective car screeched up President Street in the blackness. We froze in the blazing lights. It didn't matter who was hustling and who was coming home from work. We all blended into one. That's how they get you.

Two uniformed cops popped out, and immediately got physical with us. Amped up, they asked for our IDs, and searched everybody. They lined us up along the metal gate with our backs to them, kicking our legs to spread them out. Our palms lay flat on the gate as they patted us up and down. I tried to let them know they made an honest mistake.

"No, it's all good," I said. One of the cops was crouched down patting at my legs.

He looked at me—registering that I spoke, but not responding. A bulky guy with a square head, he had a dead face, not reacting at all.

"I'm just coming home from work," I said. "I'm heading home." I pointed up the street, as if I could will myself that last block and up through my window. He worked his way back up to my waist.

"I can show you my college ID," I said. "I'm over at BMCC," I continued, flashing a brief smile. "I'm a college student."

"Yeah?" he said, light-years away. He'd heard shit like that a thousand times that day. It was like I wasn't even talking. We were all one thing: young black guys out at night. As the cop was feeling me up, he came to the bulge in my front pocket: my box cutter. A stock worker depends on these. But the cop didn't care why I had it, nor that it was legal.

"That's for work," I said. "I'm a stock boy. I need that for work." He held the knife up to show his partner, almost like, *Jackpot.* They exchanged a look. "I literally open boxes all day," I explained. I made a downward cutting motion with my hand.

"Turn around," he said. He snapped the cuffs on me, the cold metal bracing my skin, and walked me over to the car, guiding my head as he put me in the backseat. Sitting there already was one of the other guys who had a warrant out. As we rode to the precinct, I wouldn't shut up:

"That's for my job. It's not a weapon. I'm a college student. I was just coming home from work. I'm not in the streets! You can call my job and ask them. You can ask this guy. C'mon, man, you can ask anybody!"

Unsurprisingly, they ignored me. I might as well have been behind glass. Police officers in New York City are often measured on how many arrests they chalk up. That's how they're evaluated, how they get overtime, and how they get promoted. There's no reward for giving a college student a break. I was wasting my energy. The other kid looked at me like I was crazy, talking to two walls like that. *What the hell you doing, man?* his eyes were saying. *What's the point?*

At the precinct I was fingerprinted, photographed, and processed. Then I was transferred downtown to Central Booking, my first taste of the adult system. The Bookings is where everyone goes before the judge decides who's going home and who's going to Rikers. It's a drunk tank and death row and everything in between.

I spent a long night in that sprawling cell: dirty yellow walls with a concrete floor, stainless steel benches, a small metal toilet up against the center wall. Over a hundred grown men lying down or puttering in circles. Across from us was another identical cell—like a giant mirror. The only sounds that first night were the hollow clank of the cell doors, some addict trying to jimmy the bars open with his bare hands, random scuffles between guys over two feet of bench, and the occasional deathly scream. It would all echo across that space, as I sat there and stewed.

The Bookings is like a factory. It's the most literal example of the system being a machine designed to treat people as objects. You start at the first-level floor and eventually you are herded up with others attached to a long chain to see your court-appointed lawyer, who is buried in cases he or she can't keep straight and has about three minutes to walk you through yours. Through a thick window, my lawyer read off to me what I was charged with and what I was looking at. Then she presented me to the judge, who told me to stay out of trouble for six months and then they'd wipe it. *What do you think I've been doing?* I wanted to say. But I knew enough to keep my mouth shut.

Just *being* there is an issue. I look like them. I was them. *I am them.* Black and brown teens do not get any margin for error. That net comes down and drops on all of us the same.

15

Exposure

It struck me perhaps the defining feature of being drafted into the black race was the inescapable robbery of time, because the moments we spent readying the mask, or readying ourselves to accept half as much, could not be recovered. The robbery of time is not measured in lifespans but in moments . . . It is the raft of second chances for them, and twenty-three-hour days for us.

—TA-NEHISI COATES, *BETWEEN THE WORLD AND ME*

My arrest was due to a confluence of factors—racial, geographical, and socioeconomic—but it still felt like a setback. In response, I constructed a thicker wall. My behavior had once been based on the fact that I had nothing to lose. Now I was getting an education, with an honest dollar in my pocket and hope for the future. I grew hard the other way. I had things worth protecting, not the least of which was my freedom. What happens when "wrong place, wrong time" means your own community? When heading home after work becomes sufficient grounds for arrest?

I developed a habit of giving a wave to my old friends from across the street—like a politician—and just keep moving.

"Hey, Buffett!" they'd yell. "Yo, Buff!"

I'd have headphones or a hood covering my head to block my periphery.

"Yo, Buffett!" they'd yell out. "Where you headed?"

"Sorry man!" I'd say. "Late for class. I'll holla later, man!" I'd dart down into the subway station.

"Okay, I'll holla!" I'd hear as the words were overtaken by the whoosh and rattle of the train. I'd get on the 2 train and crack the spine of a book, zeroing in as we flew into Manhattan, to streets that left you alone, to a place where the bars weren't so visible.

Coming up the subway steps on the Manhattan side felt like a kind of rebirth, washing me in the bright sights and sounds. Even a year in, I still felt like a visitor at BMCC. The picturesque views, the upscale neighborhood, the confidence of kids who knew where they were headed—it was hard to shake the feeling that I didn't belong. After class I'd go to those pristine courts and play ball with the mostly white crowd. The differences from the hood were stark: rims with bright white nets, trash talk without fighting, the comfort of play without threats. Those guys were always inclusive, but only as much as they could be. I felt like they had extended out as far as they would go with me.

I wasn't immune to the envy and anger that came with it: Why couldn't my situation resemble theirs? Why couldn't I come home to a decent living environment? Why did I have to still look over my shoulder because bullets had no names on them? When it got to be too much, I would walk over to the Hudson and find a bench to sit on. Overlooking the river flowing into the ocean, my tears would run down my face and I would hold out hope for better days.

One time I was leaving Marty's house and as we were saying good-bye on his steps, I noticed a stack of thick books, with MCAT written on the side, on the curb.

"Those yours?" I asked.

"What, those? Nope. Med school was not for me."

"Is that what it's for?"

"The MCAT? Yeah, it's the standardized test you take for medical school. The LSAT is the one for law school. It's a beast."

To a kid from Brownsville or Bed Stuy—where there are *never* any books on the sidewalk—those things are like a portal. An inquisitive five-year-old walking by might ask his mother "What's MCAT?" Then her answer potentially sets the kid's mind going. That right there is schooling, an education from just walking down that street.

Once a month I took the subway out to Park Slope to visit the Sixth Avenue residence. It was strange sitting down with Iza or Damon in that living room, feeling no longer in it but still a product of it. I'd scan the faces of young boys coming through, all testosterone and immaturity and false swagger. Those visits were about seeing Iza and Damon, whom I considered family, but also about them seeing me: letting them know that their hard work hadn't been in vain. I had a duty to hold up my end of the bargain. Gratitude has nothing to do with words; it's a potent and resilient force that binds you to someone.

Marty and Christine continued to extend their hands and allowed me into their personal lives. They too took me in like family, educated me, let me educate them. I would hone my skills debating with them on race, politics, and criminal justice issues. And our dynamic shifted. It was no longer them looking out for a young client; it became a mutual relationship.

They invited me to their homes to have dinner with their families and get to know their children. Christine brought me out to Long Island for Thanksgiving dinners at her mom's house. Marty took me to strange plays in Greenwich Village that thrilled me with their audacity and the newness of the experience. He trusted me to dog-sit Hamlet in his brownstone, where I'd kick back on his plush couch and watch his giant television. *I'm gonna get me one of these*, I'd think, fingering some piece of art or fancy leather-bound book. He had a line of pressed Brooks Brothers suits in his closet like they were the most normal thing in the world. It was something I'd only seen once before, in Mr. Walton's closet.

But it wasn't about the experiences or the things, it was about the people. Marty and Christine both taught me how wide and open the word "family" can be.

One time I was leaving Marty's after dog-sitting and heading to the subway when I heard someone yelling my name, which was unsettling. I was used to hearing "Buffett!" but never my actual name.

"Jim! Jim St. Germain!"

I turned around to see a statuesque man, nice dark suit gleaming in the sun, and did a double take. It had been about seven or eight years but the figure was unmistakable: Dean Walton.

"Mr. Walton, how are you, sir?" I said, heading back toward him.

"Good, good. It's Carlos now. You're not in eighth grade anymore, big son." That's what he called all of us.

"Right," I said. We stood there on the corner. He looked the same, a bit more filled out, but I could see through his eyes how different I looked. They focused on me, conveying a mix of concern and disbelief.

"How are things? I thought I heard you were arrested?" he said, almost hoping it hadn't been true.

"Yeah, yeah," I said. "That was—it doesn't matter. I'm out now."

"Good. That's good. Seriously. You got plans?"

"Some. Yeah. I'm working and I have one semester left at BMCC."

His eyes popped. "Phenomenal, Jim. That's great, son. I heard what happened to Serge and—" I could tell he didn't want to say what he was thinking. He knew Jigga and I were tight.

"And you thought I'd be next?"

He laughed. "Well, I wouldn't put it that way. But, it's just good to see you. Glad you're moving forward." It felt genuine. The last time I saw him I was a troubled kid, staring down a short and tumultuous life. He pulled me close and gave me one of those long hugs where you can feel another person's love as a physical fact, the energy from one body communicating without words. Mr. Walton knew me better than I knew myself. We exchanged numbers and kept in touch after that day. He became something of a friend, something of a mentor.

Mr. Walton told me after I had disappeared from school, he would drive through Crown Street and see me on the block hustling, but I wouldn't see him. He'd look at me and want to reach through that car window out to me, stop and show me love. He was afraid that if something terrible happened to me that he'd not be able to live with himself. But he also felt like as long as I was in that world, he had to draw a line. Mr. Walton was poetic about it. He told me that if you love a bird that's learning to fly you must allow it to do so. He was unsure if I'd vanish like Jigga, which bothered his conscience during the years I was away. But if the bird returns, he said, you know it's here to stay.

Joan Margolis, founder of the Brooklyn Learning Center, allowed me to stay on for tutoring, and Joanna continued to be my life vest in turbulent waters. I struggled mightily during my time at BMCC, particularly with math, which always felt like a giant ocean I couldn't traverse. I was also fortunate to find professors who understood my background and challenges, and went out of their way to help. After class I'd pick their brains about the subject, the college experience, the world of Tribeca, the divisions of New York at large. I was a sponge and eager to learn anything from anyone; each person had something to offer. I continued to try to build myself through them all. After my political science class, I'd follow Professor Ron Hayduk like a puppy to pepper him with questions about the Constitution, the Electoral College, our representative democracy, the branches of government.

Two years after filling out financial aid forms on Iza's dining room table, I stood in a blue gown on a hot day and heard my name called. I was still miles away from fulfilling my purpose, but the idea that I even had one energized me.

After the graduation ceremony, Marty, Christine, Mr. Walton, and Joanna and I went out to a big family-style Italian dinner to celebrate. It was fascinating seeing so many of my mentors together in one place, observing how they interacted and where they intersected. I felt like the nucleus of something special. Watching their faces, I realized that any failure would no longer be mine alone.

I had been talking to Christine for a while about visiting relatives back in Haiti, and she kept bringing up the fact that I wasn't a US citizen. She was motherly about it, worried that if I went I might run into immigration problems upon my return. She set me up with a colleague at Legal Aid and I applied for citizenship, partly as a result of her badgering.

The day I became a citizen Marty joined me at the federal courthouse to watch me get sworn in with other new citizens. In that courtroom, I felt like things were falling into place for me. I felt freer, accomplished, carrying one less burden. There was a sense of safety too, like I belonged and therefore had the same rights as the next person. I felt a piece of a puzzle, surrounded by immigrants of all colors and homelands, all of whom had come here for a better life. I thought about my grandfather and grandmother, my father, my eventual children. One of the things I love about New York City is that you're constantly reminded that you are part of a much larger story.

Marty came up to me afterward in tears and hugged me. His face showed this change in color, like he had been sideswiped. "That was something," he said, unable to elaborate. "That was really something."

A few weeks after graduation I was hanging out at the local barbershop where one of my friends worked, right around the corner from my apartment. While we were talking, I noticed my friend Shawn out front and heard some muffled yelling coming from behind him. I peeped through the window and saw Shawn walking ahead of his girl, who was turned around and screaming back down the block. "I'll fuck you up!" she yelled to someone in the distance. I stepped out to check on Shawn.

I grew up with Shawn, though he was a bit older than me, in his late twenties at the time. We used to play basketball together and throw dice. He was short and dark-skinned with earrings and a goatee. He was wearing his trademark red do-rag that day, walking around in flip-flops.

"What's good?" I gave him a fist pound. "You all right?"

"What up, Buffett. Yeah, I'm good," Shawn said. He looked distracted more than concerned. But he kept an eye down the street while we spoke. A pair of girls were farther back behind Shawn's girl, screaming and threatening her.

"You better shut the fuck up!"

"Keep walking, girl! I'll fuck you up!"

The two other girls were coming toward us up Nostrand Avenue, past the car wash, in front of the church. They kept at it, yelling at Shawn's girl.

She turned around to scream back. "Fuck out of here! I'll fuck *both* of you up!"

Their voices were carrying down the block, but Shawn seemed separate from it and wouldn't engage. This kind of raucous scene wasn't atypical.

"All cool?" I asked. "You good?"

"Yeah, I'm a'ight," he said. "Some bitches just tryn'a front on my shorty." It wasn't my business, and Shawn seemed fine. I said goodbye and went back inside to the barbershop, thinking nothing of it.

When things happen in the street, you can sense it long before you see or hear anything. There's an invisible shift in the air. The energy outside flows in one direction and then people begin to follow it. You see them all headed one way, then you hear the noise, the sirens, windows opening up (or slamming shut) and voices from all directions. About fifteen minutes after Shawn passed the barbershop, I felt it. Through the window I saw people heading up Nostrand.

I stepped outside to head up the sidewalk, along with the flow of people walking toward Carroll Street.

When I reached the intersection, the crowd had formed in a circle, a familiar ritual. "What happened?" I asked one of my neighbors.

"Someone just popped Shawn."

"Wait, what? Shawn *Jackson*?" The name felt foreign on my tongue.

"Yep. Fucked up, man."

An ambulance was just taking off, its white door shut and silent. Yellow tape cut across the street between lampposts. A few cop cars were blocking the intersection and as I pushed my way through I caught sight of thick blood pooling on the pavement.

The crowd was mumbling about what they saw, what they heard, what they heard that someone else saw. Everyone had the same version: Some guy had pulled up in his car and put four bullets in Shawn's back, killing him right there.

All murders are senseless, but this felt even more so. It wasn't even Shawn's argument. One of the two screaming girls had called her boyfriend—a known shooter in the neighborhood—and put a target on him. She might've already called him when I was talking to Shawn. His murder was a click on the clock, minutes ahead, a point in front of us already set into motion. There was a train barreling right at him—and he had no idea.

I watched the ambulance drive off, Shawn's lifeless body behind those doors. The sound of my neighbors' whispering pulled away into the air. I stared at the dark pool in the street already blending into the asphalt, some of it making its way to the storm drain. The rest would be gone by nighttime.

The crowd dispersed, but I was frozen in place: *killed just for being there*. Another young black man vanished, the streets to be wiped clean before the next one. I have known sixteen people who were killed this way. I stayed there until the last bystander wandered away, like as long as I didn't leave, Shawn was somehow still alive.

I thought of Jigga, then Breeze, then Breeze's mother—who lost her sense and then her grip on reality after her son died. If I could, I'd carry her pain as my own. She became unemployed; she lost her apartment, lost custody of her other son, who ended up in the child welfare system. The momentum of the falling dominoes unstoppable. I would run into her on the streets, and she had dropped all this weight and seemed completely gone; she didn't recognize me at all. She talked to herself, slept in train stations, and wandered the streets like a ghost.

16

Outward

Souls are like athletes, that need opponents worthy of them, if
they are to be tried and extended and pushed to the full use of
their powers, and rewarded according to their capacity.

—THOMAS MERTON, THE SEVEN STOREY MOUNTAIN[9]

In its mission statement the John Jay College of Criminal Justice pro-
claims its goal is to "educate fierce advocates for justice." Packed into
that one phrase was so much that captured my young mind and fired

up my imagination. Those words gave me a sense of what force I wanted to embody in the world. I'd be a warrior, freedom fighter, and soldier in this larger battle that touched so many communities like my own. Immediately after completing BMCC I enrolled at John Jay as an undergraduate, majoring in political science. I couldn't waste any more time. "When you're starting behind in the race of life," Dean Walton once told me, "you have to run twice as hard." BMCC was like getting out of the starting block. With John Jay, I kicked into gear and picked up speed. In those classrooms I discovered a passion for public service.

Matter can't be created or destroyed; only its state can change. That's exactly how it was with my anger. I never really lost it; I just learned to channel it in a different way. My anger transformed from a chain holding me back to an engine, an igniter of passion in myself and others. It would become a tool, a motivator, and the well I tapped into to make a difference. On the John Jay campus I developed a clear-eyed focus, and a plan of how to turn my pain into a force that could move mountains.

I had always had an ingrained sense of justice. Whether as a little kid not letting myself be exploited in exchange for food or a couple of dollars, to my time in Brooklyn protecting my siblings and bilingual peers. As a member of an underprivileged group I had built a path forward, largely through the efforts of others. I felt like I had no choice but to pay it all back, become a voice for the downtrodden, a vessel for others as so many had been for me.

My mind was first set on becoming a lawyer. I'd grown up seeing the law as that authoritative force—the eyes watching, the hands ready to grab, the legs ready to jump. But so many people in my life proved that the law could be something else: a tool to shape and bend systems, to help people avoid dead-end alleys or jail pipelines. Role models like Nelson Mandela and Barack Obama and mentors like Christine and Marty all had law degrees. The law has historically been a weapon used to bring others down. But armed with it, you can make that power work in your favor. You can uplift and empower those same people who have been oppressed by it.

In one of my college classes we read a book by Annette Lareau titled *Unequal Childhoods.* Its central thesis is that middle-class (usually white) families believe that systems were created explicitly for them. Consequently, these parents teach their kids to question systems and make demands on the machinery. The parents are constantly involved in their children's schooling and organized activities in an effort to steer, influence, and change them. By contrast, poor families, often black or Latino, view systems as their nemesis, forces that oppose them. They don't trust institutions and they don't make use of them. Their experience tells them that institutions and systems are adversarial or apathetic to their plight. Consequently, their kids' advocacy skills are hindered from a young age. It's a feedback loop that they can't escape.

I responded viscerally to this framing of inequalities. When I discussed it with Dean Walton, he agreed. That's why as he got educated and powerful he made a point to demand more from the larger systems and institutions. I heeded his advice, grabbing what was available and making it work for me.

All of my professors at John Jay were impressive, but the one who had the most profound impact was Danny Shaw. He reframed so much of my understanding of myself, of the issues I faced, and of the world and its battles. Tall, slim, and muscular, with a bright smile and shaved head, he didn't look like any teacher I knew. He had the thick New York accent of a cop on television. On that first day of his Race and Ethnicity in America class he laid out his singular approach to teaching. "One of the most important things for me is that everybody feels free to express themselves," he told us. "I don't care what angle you are coming from. Feel free to disagree, critique and oppose my views and teaching style. That's your right." As someone with a unique perspective and a nontraditional track, I responded to this invitation. It revealed that Shaw was an open person in the way the best teachers are.

An Irishman with New England roots, Shaw grew up in New York City around blacks and Latinos, and attended Columbia on scholarship. He had traveled all over the world, putting his mind and body where his mouth was. He was constantly organizing or joining protests, hitting the streets for a cause, rounding up people and uniting their voices. Shaw was the real deal: a chieftain of justice.

He hit us from all sides, assigning books about global poverty and screening Spike Lee movies. He gave us an article by Leon Trotsky about how cursing was a direct consequence of oppression and urged us to connect the reading to the use of the n-word in our communities. He peppered his lectures with Spanish, Portuguese, and Creole, which he spoke better than me. It wasn't just his wisdom that impressed me but the width and depth of his compassion. He had inserted himself into the issues and had become a fighter in the truest sense of the word.

One day after class, Shaw and I were discussing the latest reading, something about the exploitation of least-developed countries. Then he paused and looked at me with a gleam of fire behind his eyes. "I see a lot of anger in you," he told me in his thick outer-borough accent.

"Yeah?" I said, lightly. I wasn't sure what he meant.

"Absolutely. And it's good."

"Why's that?"

"Because it's fuel," he said, like it was the most obvious thing in the world. "And I'll tell you what."

"What?"

"I'm going to use that passion to turn you into a real revolutionary."

He stoked that fire by turning me on to documentaries about Fox News, the Koch brothers, the Latin Kings and Queens, and Ronald Reagan, which taught me about the larger injustices that divide into all the little injustices I saw in my day to day. The ghetto was not a natural phenomenon; it was engineered by history, by law, and by policy. We didn't create these neighborhoods and we didn't bring the drugs here. It was brought about by forces much larger than us, and presidents from Nixon to Reagan demonized and exploited us for their own purposes.

Shaw and I started to spend time together outside class. He had been a Golden Gloves boxer, even fighting twice in Madison Square Garden for the New York City heavyweight championship. He took me to a gym in the South Bronx, which happened to be across the street from Horizon Juvenile Center. We were taking turns hitting the heavy bag when I mentioned that when I was at Beach Avenue, we were taken there for medical issues. He popped a couple of jabs into the bag and stopped. Then he just went off, like an uncoiled spring.

"How long?"

"What?" I asked.

"How long were you at Beach?"

"A week? I don't remember."

"How old were you?"

"Fifteen."

"What for?"

"Some bullshit. Dealing off my bike."

"All those fucking places are like cauldrons," he said, his anger building. "A perfect storm of white supremacy, exploitation economics, and private enterprise feeding into a police state. The fucking worst. They should burn it to the fucking ground."

Shaw laid the groundwork for me to embark on an intellectual journey beyond the classroom. I was consumed by the idea that I needed to take in as much as possible. Some people are comfortable with their level of knowledge. They fit perfectly in their space, and carry no compunctions about what they're missing. I was not one of those people. The gap between what I knew and what I wanted to know was pronounced, so I was never satisfied. The hunger to fill up that space became insatiable. The more you know, the more you learn about what you don't know. So the space never gets filled.

Christine was always looking out for opportunities—paid work, volunteer openings, community platforms. She connected me to a workgroup called the Youth Experience, through the Mental Health Association of New York, which assembled youngsters and picked their brains around issues impacting at-risk youth. Twice a week I traveled to an office in midtown Manhattan with large windows over-looking the city alongside fifteen to twenty kids from all backgrounds in the five boroughs. Over pizza and orange juice, we offered our perspectives on drug use, homelessness, mental health, employment, education, and juvenile justice. Once they gave me a platform to re-lease all that I had absorbed, they couldn't shut me up. Luckily, they wanted to hear all of it.

The Mental Health Association offered me an internship and then a job as a youth advocate in Queens. My main duty was to help young people who were battling mental health issues and advocate for them in various capacities: school discipline, obtaining services, mediating family issues, or encouraging pro-social activities.

On Friday afternoons, I would get together with all my kids and hold group conversations around issues that affected their lives: gangs, violence, drugs, and peer pressure. I was never condescending and never assumed that their problems weren't pervasive. It was all about connecting to them at their level. To decompress and just to let them be kids, we would then take them to the movies, the park, or museums.

These adolescents were already special, sitting on untapped and unrecognized potential. They were as talented, gifted, and resilient as anyone else—society had just convinced them otherwise. My main duty was to help them locate and utilize their God-given abilities.

When I introduced myself to the adolescents and their families, I'd emphasize my two-sided nature: I was a counselor who could help them navigate the system, but I was also one of them. I could speak to the magnetic pull of peer pressure, my dependence on weed and alcohol, fighting, losing friends to violence, quitting school, and doing time in the system. I would also emphasize, despite all of this, that I carried a sense of optimism. Fortunately, a group of individuals saw something special in me that I couldn't see myself. Now I would dedicate my life to helping others discover those things in themselves.

I did my best to cut through. To counteract what experience had taught them. They understood systems as things that beat them down, ignored them, left them exhausted and fed up. I wanted to break through that, step forward as someone who would lay myself down and become the bridge that would help them move forward, just as others had for me.

17

The Circle

If the young are not initiated into the village, they'll burn it down
just to feel the warmth.

—AFRICAN PROVERB

One night, after a shift at Key Food, I descended the steps into the
train station and froze in my tracks. I noticed my friend Edwin, whom
I hadn't seen in five or six years. The alarming thing was that he was
in uniform. I'm sure my face dropped in disbelief. Edwin had become
a police officer! I couldn't believe it. Where I'm from, it's very rare for
people to become police officers. Unheard of.

Edwin had always been a cautious dude and he spotted me coming his way, with that surprised look on my face.

"Yo! What's up, Ed?" I said, noticing a beefy white dude next to him, also in uniform.

Quickly and under his breath, Edwin just started saying "*Pale'w Kreyol. Pale'w Kreyol*"—which means "speak Creole." He'd always been a very careful guy; he didn't know what I had turned into and didn't want me to blow him up in front of his partner. As far as he knew, Buffett was coming over to talk shop about the game. Once I told him I was in school, interested in public service, he looked relieved and also surprised. We exchanged numbers and began keeping in touch, venting about the specific challenges we were each going through—something almost no one else could understand.

I began to get invited for speaking engagements with different organizations that focused on juvenile justice, education, and at-risk youth issues. Whether I volunteered for such a role or it fell to me was irrelevant. I embraced it because nothing in my life—negative or positive—happened in a vacuum. I was the product of a much larger story.

The first time I addressed a crowd was at a fund-raiser for Boys Town, which has a huge gala every year—tuxedos and hors d'oeuvres, white tablecloths and champagne. The crowd was overwhelmingly rich and white, with a large contingent of Wall Street donors and wealthy liberals. The smell of money pervaded that room and I took to the stage like a prizefighter, focused on winning them over. They had shown up, so they were ripe to give, but I needed to drive home how much they mattered.

I explained that I didn't wake up one day and decide to start selling drugs. Every day of my life had led to that choice. It came from a life of wanting, one I inherited at birth. I spoke to the rarity of my left turn: I was built up instead of torn down because of the people who did the work with me. The system itself doesn't churn out college graduates. It takes a special place, people, and circumstance for that to happen.

I hammered home that Boys Town was an enormous force for good, one that brought me onto the stage that night. That there were millions of kids like me, some a couple blocks away, who *deserved* a chance. That this crowd could *be* their door, their window, their path to a life these kids never even considered they were allowed to have. That helping those kids would create a ripple effect in their families, communities, and beyond. That when we talk about changing the world, this is what we're talking about. *It happens in rooms exactly like this one.*

I told them that when they looked back on their lives, what they will remember—and what people will remember about them—would be their generosity of spirit. "I can almost guarantee you," I concluded, "that the only thing that will be on your mind is how you gave back and how many lives you have helped change for the better."

The response was electrifying. The crowd rocketed up from their plush seats and remained standing long after I left the podium. As I shook hands I could see wide smiles and tears across strangers' faces. For the first time I saw that my story could do more than just exist as something to carry. It could work outward, be a shoulder and a sword and a symbol and a message. A lot of people opened up their wallets after that speech, and calls flooded in for me to speak to crowds: Family Court, public schools, local politicians, media panels, advocate training, youth justice forums, press conferences, school functions, Department of Probation crowds, and high-school graduations.

My new role began to take shape. I would be a servant leader, one who could speak with both authority and humility, sincerity and realness. Push from below, help from above. Occupying both spaces for kids and families who have nothing to latch onto.

It was all about communal uplift. Individual achievement meant nothing in the pool of collective failure. If I didn't become part of the solution I'd forever be part of the problem. There would be no middle ground, and no sitting it out. The stakes were towering.

When a job opened up at the Boys Town NSD on Bergen Street, Marty put in a good word for me, and the brass hired me on as a residential care advisor. This would be the ground floor, the front lines, and an emotional return to a world still fresh in my memory. Standing on the other side, with my scars and memories still crisp, was a powerful reversal.

Working at Boys Town drove home that there was no distance between the kids and myself. I was them, and they were me. I had been exactly where they were sitting, intimately knew the fear that kept them awake at night, the anger that rose from their stomachs, the survival instincts that kept them looking over their shoulders. I could hear it in their voices and read it in their eyes: they felt the walls closing in on them.

The only thing that lifted me out was the connections I made. It was my obligation to offer that same connection. I was hard on the kids, but it came from a place of love. I knew what high standards could do because I was a product of them. Damon saw things in me that I didn't see myself and brought them out through force: by challenging me, by making me push up against the limits of myself. Iza kept me going, but it was Damon who lifted me up. The staff members who allowed you to do what you wanted were not the ones who changed you. It was the ones you raged against who made you who you were.

The job at Boys Town sucked just about everything out of me. I'd come home exhausted and drained. I felt everything far too much and wanted to make everything right for each kid, a daunting task. I have no moderate setting, and have never been able to put just one foot in. Working at Boys Town was so personal for me that anything less than my all would've been an insult.

During my time in the system, holidays were always tough. It magnified how alone I felt. I'd watch other families reuniting, parents taking their kids out for the day or home to see other relatives. My first Thanksgiving working at Boys Town was a fresh reminder that I had to hold on to my memories of that pain and abandonment. In fact, they weren't even memories—they were present and real. They weren't scars but rather open wounds.

We held an early dinner that evening for all the residents' families. A large group was sitting around the big dining room table, reminiscing, and enjoying a breather from the troubled water running through their lives. But this tall, shy kid named Jamal, who had no visitors, sat by himself on the couch the whole time. His body was slumped and there was a far-off look in his eyes.

I noticed out of the corner of my eye that he grabbed the remote and flipped on the football game. I was in the middle of a conversation with a parent, but I had to cut it short. "Excuse me for a second," I said, making my way to the living room.

"Jamal, do you understand that you're not allowed to watch television?" He didn't even turn his head. "You didn't ask permission."

He looked up as if seeing me for the first time.

I continued, "Now I'm going to give you an instruction to shut it off and if you do—"

"Suck my d——," he said under his breath.

I should've taken a step back right there. I should've questioned what would make a normally polite kid say that to me but I didn't. I stepped to him, taking up the space in front of him, a more aggressive reaction than necessary.

"I understand you're upset," I said.

"I said suck. My—" he started to say.

"—Jamal, you earned yourself ten thousand negative points for—"

"Fuck you, man!" he said, standing up and pressing his nose right into mine. His arms were electric, swinging beside his body like independent limbs.

The wires in my brain got crossed. The Boys Town model ran full speed into my old response mechanisms. I was pulled between competing forces: a need to de-escalate the situation, and the instinct to not back down. I made it worse by challenging Jamal in front of everyone, which did nothing but raise the stakes and the tension.

I'd forgotten what I knew about picking my battles and not pouring gasoline on the fire. I could've let the television thing go, worked to calm everything after his outburst, but I was subsumed in my own pain, which had been lying low until that moment.

"Jamal, you are *not* going to—"

"Get out of my face, pussy!" he yelled, spitting the words as he spoke. He threw the remote control across the room and it broke against the wall, the batteries popping out. Jamal started tossing books and smacking plastic cups off the coffee table. "Fuck you, you not telling me what to do! I don't give a shit and you can't say shit!"

We stared each other down, the tension filling up the tight space between us. We were mirrors of each other, feeling the exact same emotion, but we couldn't see each other at all. We were blind to the connection that bonded us. We were the same. The only difference was that I had a duty to his well-being.

Then I took off, started to walk to the staircase and called to a staff member, "Hey, Ant, I'm going downstairs." I took the stairs two at a time down to one of the staff offices. I sat alone on a chair among file cabinets and winter coats and tried to slow my breath. Then a wave of tears rushed through and overtook me, seemingly out of nowhere. They were not tears of anger at Jamal but deep disappointment at myself for missing an opportunity to be an Iza for Jamal. This was the position I had fought so hard to be in, but I had internal battles of my own that weren't finished. And I couldn't pour from an empty cup.

My supervisor came down and asked me if I wanted to go home for the day. "Yes," I said.

Later that night I realized that I was crying because I had failed the very same person that I had committed to be a vessel for. I was battling my own demons and too caught up in them to see the big picture: No one visited Jamal on the one day that even the loneliest kids got a taste of normalcy. The pain was painted on his face, but I couldn't identify it. I was blind to the pain, loneliness, and *hopelessness* inside him. I had forgotten the reason I was even there: I was Jamal. I knew his situation intimately, I *lived* it, but I couldn't recognize it because I was burdened by my own painful memories. If I couldn't empathize with Jamal—and the thousands like him—then who on earth was going to? It was like I proved that he had no chance. What became clear to me was something I once heard: hurt people hurt people.

About a year later, a kid at Boys Town named Amir came back from a nighttime phone call in a fiery mood. All the other residents were lined up when I saw him come into the bedroom. "Amir, line up."

"Fuck you," he said.

"Whoa," a kid blurted out.

"Damn," another kid said.

"Self monitor," I said to them, turning back to Amir. "I understand you're upset but you still need to follow this simple instruction. You earned a negative five thousand points."

"What, you deaf? I said *fuck* you, I'm not going to listen to no—"

"Amir, think about what you're doing right now. You're just making it worse—"

Amir was well over two hundred pounds, a Mack truck with cara-mel skin, wild curly hair down to his shoulders, and a wide baby face. Despite his size, this was not his normal behavior. It was like a force had taken him over.

As I tried to stay with the model, Amir became enraged. His curses and names morphed into physical threats, pushing me on defense. "I can make a phone call and have my people wait outside here for when you get off work," he said to me. My instinct was to switch to offense, and I could feel my muscles moving in that direction. Once a threat like that was launched, you never knew: there might be a ticking clock on you, so you better act.

Amir's eyes were inflamed, his facial muscles tensed. "I can have my boys be here in ten minutes to get at you!" he yelled.

I'd been hit with roundhouse punches, spat on, and screamed at, but Amir's threats broke through a new barrier. Compassion and pro-fessionalism were almost overtaken by self-preservation. Fortunately, my cooler self won out.

I felt relieved when he dropped it, but an anger lingered in my chest. It was a different kind of anger, though, the kind that gnaws at you and troubles your soul. I couldn't be sure how I would've reacted if things escalated. I could've lost control, thrown away all I had worked for simply to help those like Amir. He literally didn't have anyone else.

I went through the motions until my shift ended that night. I transitioned the logbook over to the overnight staff without saying much and made my way down the stairs. As I walked past Amir's room, I heard him say, "Yo, Jim."

I reluctantly peeked in his room. "What's up?"

He handed me a piece of paper. "Here," he said. "But don't read it now."

I put it in my back pocket and left, anxious to get out of there. It wasn't Amir I was escaping, but the version of myself I had worked so hard to leave behind.

Losing your temper at someone whom you don't care for is understandable and part of being human. But losing it on a younger version of yourself is incredibly painful.

The walk to the subway was elongated, with one block feeling like twenty and my knees aching with each step. When I got inside the station I sat down on a bench, took a deep breath, and opened Amir's note.

> Jim, I'm very sorry for what I did tonight.
> I allowed my anger to control me and I didn't mean to.

The directness, the bravery, and the honesty of his words struck me deeply. Amir went on to explain where he was coming from. His mother had been raising him and his two brothers on her own. Part of her income was from a nanny job, and part of it was from an SSI check she got for him. When Amir started getting into trouble with the law his mother had to take days off from work to be with him in Family Court, which led to her losing her job. To compound the family's difficulties, after he got sentenced and went into the system, the SSI checks stopped coming. He felt responsible that her whole world had unraveled. Part of the unintended consequences of the juvenile justice system is that a small thing leads to big things, which then can run rampant over people's lives. A minor teenage indiscretion spills outward and causes a flood.

That night Amir's mother had called to tell him that she and his brothers had gotten kicked out their home. They were now homeless, struggling to find a place to lay their heads at night, and Amir had to carry the guilt. All the ripples and consequences, the domino effect, of his actions hit him when he hung up the phone. He had to carry the extra burden of knowing that he would be in the system that much longer since he couldn't return home. Then, a simple nighttime routine became a platform for him to express his grief and pain.

His anger was borne of a guilt that had been chewing at him until it finally tore through him. I had walked in his shoes just three years earlier and now I was the target of that anger. As the train whooshed into the station, kicking up dust and carrying the wind, my anger was replaced by profound sadness. I had to double down on my commitment. Forgetting where these kids were coming from was like not seeing them at all.

18

The Bridge

It is easier to build strong children than to repair broken men.

—FREDERICK DOUGLASS

As seeds were being planted I felt they had to sprout beyond my personal plot of land. The collective stakes were too high, and I needed a seat at the table; I knew the old adage that if you weren't at the table then you were on the menu. Politicians were finally recognizing that any real reform to the juvenile justice system required the input of community members and those who had been impacted by that system, voices of people who had been silently kept in the shadows.

Years ago the federal government along with the Legal Aid Society sued New York State because numerous adolescents were severely injured—and a few killed—due to harmful restraining practices in state facilities. New York State settled and accepted many of the reform measures from the federal government. When Governor Andrew Cuomo took office in 2011, he had to put in place many of these reforms to the juvenile justice system. He reached out to collaborate with New York City mayor Michael Bloomberg's administration, and the "Close to Home" initiative was born.

For decades, juvenile detention facilities in upstate New York were overflowing with inner-city poor kids of color. Most families had no cars and could not travel the hundreds of miles to visit their children, denying these youths their rights to be rehabilitated with family participation, not to mention their love and support. The correction staff consisted mostly of white, rural men who had no experience with the populations whose lives they controlled. It was a toxic mix, so many kids were permanently damaged by their time upstate. Unsurprisingly, the recidivism rate for these juveniles within three years of their releases was over 80 percent.[10] Youths leaving upstate facilities were soon readmitted to local city facilities, and this time, they went to adult prisons. The original decision to send them upstate had permanently detrimental effects. It's not just that their needs weren't being met and their rights weren't being upheld. Their futures were unfairly being predetermined. Self-fulfilling prophecies were playing out across New York City to the sounds of sirens wailing, gavels banging, and cell doors clanging shut.

The Close to Home initiative looked to tackle a root problem. Its goal was to keep juvenile offenders close to their community while providing them with the services they needed to rehabilitate. The proximity to their family and to staff who understood their issues would be enormously beneficial, possibly cycle-breaking. Close to Home also focused on the types of facilities juveniles were sent to, expanding places like Boys Town that created a proper environment. It wasn't the system itself that helped me rise up and out; it was the type of place I was sent to. Despite its possible benefits, the model had yet to be widely accepted or embraced.

Though close to home, kids would ideally be placed in similar brownstones throughout the city with no bars, no staff members acting like prison guards, and no treating nonviolent teenagers like hardened criminals. Instead they were given an opportunity to rehabilitate and the environment to do so: backyards, family dinners, a quiet place to do their schoolwork, a support system invested in their success. Close to Home would aim to recognize that a juvenile is not a convict, though he can became one through the neglect and abuse of a cruel and arbitrary system.

Mayor Bloomberg's administration contacted me and invited me to speak at a press conference announcing the initiative at Passages Academy in East New York. I was just entering John Jay at the time so the prospect of meeting with the mayor was exciting. I was studying politics and then—boom—I was shaking its hand.

I was introduced to Bloomberg in an empty classroom, where we had time to talk briefly beforehand. He joked about how everyone is always taller than him.

I smiled. "Well, you're the man that makes things happen in this city," I said.

His face turned earnest. "Not really," he said, his unique cadence and schoolteacher intonation pushing through. "One thing you'll learn is that surrounding yourself with brilliant minds"—he pointed to his staff—"who actually know something, makes you appear smarter."

We discussed role models in urban America and the way the justice system treats juveniles. We talked about our respective backgrounds— which couldn't have been more disparate—and he mentioned his time at Harvard Business School.

I shook my head and said, "I'm still dreaming about Harvard—"

"Well, you should . . ."

"Maybe. But I think I'll keep my head above water in the CUNY system for now."

Mayor Bloomberg was not the classic politician. He had a straightforward approach that seemed to transcend things like poll numbers and news coverage. A bold approach, that many did not agree with, was unique for modern-day politics. I learned that he and fellow billionaire George Soros were privately funding a $30 million program called the Young Men's Initiative to tackle inequalities among minorities in the city, the ultimate "money where your mouth is" situation.

The mayor and I walked down the hall of the school and into another classroom that had been prepped for our arrival. Various teenagers who were incarcerated in the juvenile justice system awaited us. He started speaking casually and then asked the students how they had become involved with the law. After listening to some of their stories, he assured them they could make it out if they stayed focused and worked hard. Then he pointed to me. "Look at Jim, here," he said, and they all did. "Jim is a perfect example of what can occur if you take advantage of the services and the people here." I could see them all checking me out, curious. Some looked surprised when the mayor said I had been sitting where they were just a few short years ago and was now a college graduate.

"You're old enough to be responsible for your future," he told them. "You can't blame the system, or your parents. It's up to you now. Jim is a real-world example of someone who made the decision, went through the tough times, and is coming out the other side."

We walked out of the classroom to the front of the school where a podium and the press were waiting. He announced the Close to Home initiative, detailed its goals, and mentioned how "it's in everybody's interest . . . to stop this vicious cycle of going in and out of the criminal justice system. What happens as they get older, the next cycle is they go to Rikers, the prison system, and then a slab in the morgue." I appreciated his big-picture approach and the strength of the words he chose, refusing to sugarcoat what was at stake.

The mayor then introduced me. "This young man will probably make a fortune," he said, offhandedly joking, "and for all I know, be the next mayor." I stood up in front of that crowd, cameras whirring, eyes on me. I took a deep breath and rubbed my palms together. Then I launched into my story.

At that press conference I began to form and shape what would continually be my argument. It was the one I made to the people with the purse strings and to average citizens wondering why they should care.

"It's really easy to give up on our kids," I said, "but it's hard to actually do something for them, help them become productive members of society, have them pay taxes and go to school." We are mutually bound by the well-being of those who may seem as others. We create productive citizens and taxpayers that way. Among these kids could be the next Steve Jobs or Bryan Stevenson, a Supreme Court justice or disease-curing scientist.

The whole event was a perfect distillation of what I was aiming to do. I felt like I actually had the ears of both sides—the men with the power to change things and the kids whose futures depend on it.

While I was working at Boys Town, there was still something missing. It was like I was cutting grass with scissors. Appearing with the mayor and working on Close to Home—and then being invited to speak with legislators from other states about adopting it—gave me a taste of the behind-the-scenes mechanisms that determined so much of kids' lives. I would come back from meetings with high-powered people and sit with youngsters and get frustrated by the disconnect. So many influential and high-level decisions were being made against their interest in rooms miles away. The frustration built over my three years at Boys Town until it felt like I was running in place at full speed.

The sad fact is that many decisions about juvenile issues aren't made because they're good for the kids. They're made through a combination of self-interests: politics, fear of negative press, a need to maintain the power structure, and an inertia that favors the status quo. Decision makers are out of touch, immune to the ferocity and urgency of these problems. The overwhelming majority aren't from the same environment or socioeconomic status as the group they're making decisions for. They speak, and judge, and rule from a distance—physical, socioeconomic, and, by extension, emotional. Even the well-intentioned can go home at the end of the day to their safe neighborhood and detach themselves, blocking out their workday. I can't: That's me ten years ago, my son ten years from now. I still see them when I'm in the facilities, getting off the train, in the park, in the schools, and on the streets. They're an inseparable part of my life.

I still wanted to be a presence in kids' lives, but I also wanted to help change the circumstances they were in. I wanted to absorb who they were and bring that back to the boardrooms and conference tables where their futures were determined.

When an opportunity presented itself to work within a New York City department that is responsible for youth in the juvenile justice system, I availed myself of the idea of working within a bureaucracy as an agent of change. It would help me give direct care to the kids and direct influence on policy decisions. I'd be working with troubled kids one-on-one and in groups, visiting the facilities and the schools to hear their concerns. But I would also sit on committees where the policies and rules were written, acting as a conduit.

Our purview covered a wide swath: physical abuse, visitation, education, allowance, medical and mental health, employment, recreation, and more. In a bureaucracy of thousands of employees and a

$3 billion budget, getting my kids' voices in became a challenge. No matter what the issue or case, I tried to insert the point of view of the single kid who needed us to do right by him or her. He or she wasn't there physically but still sitting there in that room with us.

There are two things I love about young people. The first is that they're brutally direct; they'll tell you what you need to hear, whether you like it or not. The value they put in authenticity is pronounced and it keeps me honest. The second thing is they're masterful at picking up on things and have a sixth sense about whether you care or not. The only way to break through to them is with some kind of heart. They tune you out if you condescend and they'll lash out if you make assumptions about who they are. They've been talked down to their entire lives by parents, neighbors, teachers, principals, and cops. It is the unassailable fact of their lives.

My experience gave me an automatic in that others did not have. One time I was at a school and a teenager I had never met before came up to me. "Mr. Jim," he said, "you've been to prison before, right?"

I smiled. "Well, I've been in the system, yeah. How'd you know?"

He pointed to my head. "The waves, man." He knew because of the way my hair was brushed. It's something that young men usually work on while they're locked up. He had a brush to his hair, doing the same thing,

"Good looking," I said, giving him a dap.

The ones I deal with are already embarrassed, so I try to assess their strengths and build them up. I make a point to stay calm with them, sometimes affectionate, which is something they're not used to. They understand masculinity as toughness and power. It's like a bomb they throw as a defense mechanism. If I come off as a threat then we're working backward, falling into old patterns and dynamics.

The first time a man said "I love you" to me was Mr. Walton, and I remember how uncomfortable that felt. I froze and I don't think I responded. In most worlds, but especially mine, men just don't say such words toward other men. The sentiment is so prevalent in how I feel, but the words are so hard to muster. I'm trying to bridge the gap.

I was twenty-three years old and getting a hold on my purpose, but my personal life was experiencing a major shift. I began dating a young woman named Angelina who worked as a juvenile justice behavior counselor within the school system. We had first met when I came to the school for career day. She gave me her number, but I never called her. When I returned to the school six months later for work she came up to me all sly.

"Hey, you," she said playfully. "Sorry, I didn't call you back but I've been really busy."

I was thrown off-balance. "Oh yeah, uh . . . sorry about that. Things have been crazy with—"

"Don't bother lying. You're terrible at it. Don't ever become a lawyer."

I smiled, because there was nothing I could say.

"I texted you," she said, "but you never got me back."

"What? I didn't get a text."

"Uh yeah—look." She took out her phone and scrolled up to this long text she'd sent. I scanned it, saw the word "mature" maybe three or four times, and then I noticed it was to the wrong number. We laughed for a bit about some random person getting chewed out.

Her mix of boldness and lightness drew me in. Angelina had an easy smile and deep brown eyes. We began seeing each other casually. I was too young and it was too early to be any more than that. Then fate—maybe God—intervened.

About three months in, she broke it off. We were in a car outside her apartment when she said she "didn't want to deal with me anymore." When I pushed her on it, she broke down and cried into her hands. "I'm pregnant," she said.

I was stunned. I wasn't prepared for the revelation, nor was I mature enough to see anything except myself. We sat parked there for hours, me defending why she couldn't keep the child, her arguing why she couldn't terminate the pregnancy. We talked past each other for over an hour.

"Look, you gotta—"

"I can't."

"I'm just . . . Look, I'm not ready to be a father right now," I said. "Not even close."

"Listen to you. This isn't about you! You're not—"

"Exactly! The child would be—"

"You don't care about anyone but yourself!" she yelled.

"What?! How can that be true? I—"

"Fuck you, Jim. You are not—"

"Look, I'm not financially where I need to be. I'm in no position to care for this child."

She cried through most of the conversation, when she wasn't screaming at me. I was overtaken by an all-encompassing fear. Fear that I would be powerless to protect this unborn child. Fear that I couldn't prevent the hardships that plagued my own life. Fear that this child would never know the innocence afforded other children—the very definition of childhood, which I never got. Fear that no matter what I did, I wouldn't be able to erase or shield or protect enough.

That fear made me cold and I regret it.

By the time Angelina got out of the car, I thought it was settled. She agreed she was going to terminate the pregnancy.

But she couldn't go through with it.

Though I understood, I still brought resentment to every interaction with her. I was in my own head too much, concerned with how this affected me, how this child was going to throw me off course.

It's strange but the two biggest and best decisions ever made in my life were made by other people. It was my attorneys who got me into Boys Town, and it was Angelina who decided to have my child.

My father wasn't present for any of our births. He didn't accompany my mother to the hospital, figuring that his presence there wouldn't matter. I almost made the same mistake. Angelina thought I was naturally careless, but my thinking evolved from my upbringing. Right around her due date I traveled to Tennessee with the Children's Defense Fund. Fortunately, the CDF's youth director, Beth Powers, got me the earliest flight back to New York and I was able to watch my son be born. As any parent can tell you, it's a magical, mysterious, and awe-inspiring few seconds. He wasn't there and then—he was.

Watching Caleb enter the world washed away every doubt I had had about Angelina's pregnancy, fears about what a child would do to my life, even thoughts about myself as an independent person. Everything was split into a before and after. Without him and with him. His life was mine to protect; I had to help push the world to be more accepting, more just. As I cradled him in my arms, this football of a person, chubby-thighed and cream-colored, I was also struck by a profound sadness. This pure boy, no bigger than my forearm, would be inheriting so many things that he didn't know about and couldn't understand.

I saw what he couldn't see. The steep mountains. The thick walls. The closed doors. I knew he was going to have to deal head-on with the inequalities, oppression, and injustice that are part of being a black male in America. It echoed back long before him, before me, before my father and his father and into history. He was already chained down by nothing more than the circumstances of his birth and, by extension, my birth.

I knew that no matter how much love his mother and I gave him, we could not erase the collective history. When Edwin, my old friend who had become a cop, arrived at the hospital that day and held him, I found some solace. I began thinking about all the great human beings who would be there in his life, all of whom were an extension of me.

"Black people love their children with a kind of obsession," Ta-Nehisi Coates wrote. "You are all we have, and you come to us endangered."[11] As I grew, I began to see my father's behavior as a way of trying to show how much he feared for me, his version of love. Though I repudiate my father's physicality, I carry those same fears for my son. For the world that might reject him because of his skin color, for police officers that will invariably see him as a threat, for teachers that might suspect he doesn't want to learn. Once a child became the center of my world, I was washed in these thoughts day and night.

My father never said "I love you"; even to this day, he hasn't said it. It's partly cultural: I didn't hear it from mothers or fathers growing up, and I don't hear it much in Brooklyn. But I tell my son I love him all the time. It seems so natural that it just spills out of me. I'll grab him and hug him and say it over and over again. And he'll let me.

19

Thousands of Kalief Browders

You can be a fierce fighter and still be a tender person.

—REV. ALFONSO WYATT [12]

The tragic story of Kalief Browder was like a missile exploding on the public consciousness. It struck the black community, the juvenile justice world, the offices of advocacy, and New York City at large. When Kalief's death was reported in the press in 2014, news outlets called it a suicide, but all he really did was finish off what the system had done to him.

At the age of sixteen Kalief, an African American kid from the Bronx, was arrested for allegedly stealing a backpack. He was never charged, and ending up spending an inexplicable *three* years in Rikers Island. Two-thirds of his time was spent in solitary confinement—twenty-three hours a day locked away from all human contact. He was physically beaten, psychologically tortured, and more than likely sexually abused. He was left to languish in a system that had forgotten about him or never even cared. The harrowing experience led Browder to try to commit suicide multiple times both in and out of prison. Unfortunately even after he was released, got his high school equivalency diploma, and was trying to put the experience behind him, the trauma caught up to him. He hanged himself at his parents' home. He was twenty-two.

As it did to many, Browder's story shook me to my core, leaving me trembling in a fit of anger and sadness. I couldn't believe it, but of course, I could. Once again, I was left to question the moral compass of our country. Kalief was deprived of his basic rights as a human being, and granted less due process than a war criminal. Browder might have left Rikers, but the prison never left him; it haunted his nightmares and invaded his thoughts—and he couldn't shut it out. His story made headlines, viewed as a cautionary tale for the way that the criminal justice system can brutalize young men. That wasn't nearly enough. It should have done far more than that: it should've been a blaring alarm and wake-up call that yielded significant changes, starting with the idea that he was put in an adult prison at all.

New York State and North Carolina are the only two states that automatically try sixteen-year-olds as adults, even for nonviolent crimes. (Seven other states try seventeen-year-olds as adults.) As someone who narrowly avoided adult prison by a few months, I'm particularly struck by the cruelty and randomness of the law. When we're dealing with people's lives, we can't ever be so blindly arbitrary. By the luck of the calendar, I ended up in Boys Town instead of Rikers. A stint in Rikers would have sent me deeper in, taken away my youth, my support system, and my hope—the things they took from Kalief Browder in those long three years.

Recognizing the need to change such a draconian and inhumane policy, I got involved with several organizations, such as the Children's Defense Fund founded by Marian Wright Edelman and the Correctional Association of New York. These organizations were advocating to raise the age of criminal responsibility to over eighteen years old in New York State, a bill first proposed by Assemblyman Joseph R. Lentol several years prior to my involvement in the effort to raise the age. Not only did Assemblyman Lentol propose Raise the Age, but he also advocated a progressive reform of the criminal justice system in all aspects. Under the auspices of the "Raise the Age" campaign, I spoke at press conferences, appeared on television, and met with policy makers and other interest groups to help get this passed into law. It's an economic issue because an inability to pay for bail or proper representation is pure injustice. It's a racial issue because of the bias inherent in arrests and sentencing. Drug offenses and other economic-related infractions make up the majority of nonviolent crimes, and blacks are incarcerated for drug crimes at a rate *ten times* that of whites, though research shows that whites use drugs at five times the rate of blacks.[13]

Society draws the line at eighteen for just about every conception of adulthood: voting, smoking, jury duty, and military service. Yet for the single most consequential thing—prison—that cutoff is sixteen in New York. It defies logic, common sense, and basic understanding.

Late on a Sunday night I received a call from Melanie Hartzog, then the executive director at the Children's Defense Fund of New York. I had met her during the press conference with Mayor Bloomberg, and she had been appointed by Governor Cuomo to the task force for Raise the Age, a commission charged with researching its future viability and impact. After months of traveling across the country speaking to advocates, juveniles, experts, and prison officials, the commission reported its findings.

On a crisp and clear Martin Luther King holiday, I traveled to Albany with Melanie to attend the press conference with the commission and Governor Cuomo. The governor talked candidly about the various benefits of the proposed legislation: economic, social, safety, crime, and, of course, the human cost.

I sat in the front row and when the governor finally opened the floor up for questions from the press I unabashedly raised my hand. All eyes were fixated on me. I could feel the looks and hear the murmurs of reporters wondering, *Who's this guy?* I have no compunctions about speaking my mind, no matter the context. The voices of our young people must be heard by those in power. The fact is I was once made silent and I can never know if that time will come again.

I rose from my seat. "Thank you, Governor, for taking on an issue so close to my heart." The room was suddenly quiet and I felt the hot light hovering over me. I introduced myself and told an abridged version of my story, focusing on how I was saved by the sheer randomness of the calendar. I talked about working toward my master's degree and my work with city kids who needed it the most.

Mr. Cuomo thanked me and reminded the room of why this policy was morally correct. "There you have it," he said. "The young man just gave you a real-life example of what we have the power to do here. Literally transform lives."

In the years that followed that initial press conference, I practically moved to Albany to put as much capital behind what I deemed to be one of New York State's modern civil rights moments. Every time I was there, I attempted to bring the circumstances that I inherited as a child to life, using my life as evidence of the initiatives' worth: Here's how I grew up, where I came from, and here's where I am now—a taxpaying citizen making a difference. What kind of society willingly gives up on its most vulnerable population?

Raise the Age was something that Governor Cuomo appeared to be behind for three years. It was built into the state budget for 2015, virtually guaranteeing its funding as an attempt to tie Raise the Age to the New York budget—a bold move that would force members of the legislatures who were on the fence to pick a side. Advocates and the Democratic Assembly vigorously championed and invested in it as a priority. The reality was something else.

One day I got a call from the governor's office informing me that Raise the Age was taken off the budget. When I tried to inquire why, I was given no direct explanation. What I learned were the actual reasons and, of course, they were political: The Democratic Assembly, comprising mostly members representing the New York City area, is lead by Speaker Carl Heastie. Heastie supported Assemblyman Joseph R. Lentol's comprehensive piece of legislation, which was simultaneously introduced in the Senate by Valmanette Montgomery, to raise the age of criminal responsibility in New York State with the hope of providing resources to families and children seeking to lead productive lives and avoid the vicious cycle of incarceration. The political makeup of the state senate, where certain Democrats known as the IDC work in conjunction with Republicans to essentially form a majority, stymied this progressive vison for the state's most vulnerable. As the negotiations developed, politics over shadowed what was morally right, and the inflammatory rhetoric of the opposition and a lack of political capital hindered the assembly's ability to bargain. Other issues, such as a funding freeze for charter schools and the 421—a tax exemption program that would enable developers to build on vacant land if they included affordable housing—were now thrust into the quagmire that had become the cornerstone of Albany politics.

As the budget deadline approached, these hotly contested issues threatened and eventually derailed the legislature and Governor Cuomo's plan for delivering an on-time budget; but none was as contentious as Raise the Age. Republicans cast this noble bill as a gang recruitment tool, utilizing the same tough-on-crime talking points politicians have used for years. Leaders from both sides proceeded over details, but negotiations stalled and Republicans in the Senate walked away. Several days past the budget deadline, Governor Cuomo, Speaker Heastie, and leaders from the opposition struck a deal that included Raise the Age. The comprehensive legislation first introduced by Mr. Lentol and Senator Montgomery wasn't what emerged following all the compromises; however, Raise the Age remains a positive first step for us to build on as we continue this fight to treat children as children.

I know people still cling to the false narrative that prison is a deterrent for young people, that the experience of prison "scares them straight." I'm on the front lines and the ground floor and I know this is nonsense, pure dangerous fiction. Prison doesn't do anything but scare them into self-protection and traumatize them for life. Just like it did to Kalief Browder.

In 2014, Bobby Scott, a congressman from Virginia, and Connecticut senator Chris Murphy, both Democrats, cosponsored a bill called the Better Options for Kids Act, along with Congressman Hakeem Jeffries, who represents Crown Heights. Jeffries had been an assemblyman I'd become friends with back when I was stocking shelves at Key Food.

The Better Options for Kids Act was a bill focused on diverting money out of the $80 billion our country spends yearly on incarceration to community-based programs, job training, and extracurricular activities for at-risk youth. I had spoken to all three men extensively on poverty, employment, juvenile and criminal justice, education, and the racial disparity that weaves through all of these issues. In June, when the bill was in Congress, they asked me to travel to Washington and testify before several congressional committees in support of it.

One of my professors at John Jay, Andrew Sidman, used to emphasize the cold reality that politics was more about harm reduction and people's wallets than actually serving the less fortunate. Though this claim has some truth to it, I refuse to buy into this notion. Whether I don't believe it or I don't *want* to believe it, I'm not sure.

As I made my way through the gleaming hallways of the Dirksen Senate Office Building, I was overwhelmed with how efficiently it all ran: elevators dinging, a blur of freshly pressed suits, notepads passing hands, congressional aides running, the click-clack of their shoes on the marble floor, everyone's BlackBerries dinging and ringing and making a beautiful wall of white noise.

I found the subcommittee's assigned room, and entered: it felt like I had stepped inside an oil painting. The room displayed a rare aesthetic, both old and new at the same time. A heavy brown wooden door, thick green marble trim. Mocha leather chairs, fine-grained mahogany wood tables polished to a high shine. On the walls, brass lamps lit up like torches. Flowing green curtains covered impossibly stretched windows. The United States seal carved into the wall and centered where a clock would be; in the corner, a stoic American flag. A raised dais with thin microphones poking out. And on a table next to a wood podium, a placard: "Jim St. Germain." I paused, trying to permanently absorb the moment: How am I even in this room?

The senators and congressmen and -women filed in, followed by their aides, the seats filled in with lobbyists, advocates, and reporters. Then all the awe washed away and I focused on the business at hand. Before I spoke in support of the bill, a Juvenile Court judge named Steve Teske, who was working for alternatives to incarcerating youth, testified, noting, "It's not just a legal obligation, it is a moral obligation. These are our children." I echoed this in my testimony, hammering on the idea that youth incarceration was "not just a juvenile problem, this is America's problem." Addressing it would help keep communities thriving, bring our families together, and make our country live up to its promise. Only when we take this issue on as part of all our lives will our country get anywhere.

We call them marginalized kids but they're not actually on the margins at all. That perception is the problem. They are a living, breathing part of society. Their hopelessness, their poverty, their violence, their lack of education lands on all our doorsteps. They are our children, and their choices—or lack of choices—affect us, whether we want them to or not. Our hearts need to be open to them, and their pain needs to be ours.

In front of the panel, as always, I felt obligated to openly share all of my story, regardless of how vulnerable it made me feel. Politicians are motivated when a story moves them, when a face and a voice are attached to an issue, when they can picture their own loved ones in similar predicaments. Otherwise it's abstract and dead, existing only in briefing papers and statistics. I aimed to be a vessel, a channel, a personification of what passes across their desks.

It seems like I'm not angry when I speak, though of course I am— and that anger is justified. I just know that white America miscon-strues anger because it plays into their fears. That anger gives them an excuse, an easy out, not to do right by our children. So I don't give them that opening. I come at them with logic and humanity and compassion for all children, not just their own.

After my testimony, I was invited to eat lunch in the Senate Din-ing Room, an imposing and stately room overflowing with members of Congress, lobbyists, congressional aides, and interns. The patrons were nearly exclusively white and mostly male. The food-service workers and custodians were almost uniformly black. It was a troubling division, es-pecially in our nation's capital. I thought about freshman senator Obama sitting in this same space. Did he notice the janitors and waiters and did it bother him? As a young boy, could he have envisioned that he'd be eating in this room? Could he possibly have imagined that a family that looked like his would occupy the White House, a place built by their ancestors exclusively for men who once owned them as property? The thoughts swirled into a thick fog so that when they brought me my giant bowl of soup, and I caught my reflection in the giant spoon, I felt dizzy.

*   *   *

I know those closest to the problems are closest to its solutions. I try to carry my understanding of each world back over the barrier into the other. Splitting these worlds, I experience what I call the chameleon effect: adapting to the world of suits and stakeholders during some days, and the hood and street corners others. Often it's the same day. The drop-off—the shift—is disorienting, like a change in altitude. It pains me. How can the world be so separated? How can one be so blind to the other? How can one profit from the other's failures?

I've returned to Washington, DC, several times over the years, to testify and meet with policy makers. I've reflected at the lit-up Capitol dome quiet and resplendent, watched our elected representatives debate a bill on the Senate floor, marveled at the stately rotunda and the busy halls of Congress. I visited the Martin Luther King monument, a stone sculpture of the man, arms solemnly folded, a rolled-up speech in one hand. He is emerging out of a mountain three stories high, evoking his famous phrase: "Out of the mountain of despair, a stone of hope." I lingered over his words carved into the monument, tried to absorb each one with as much dignity and purpose as they had been spoken. Across the water, in the distance, I glimpsed the Jefferson Memorial, and it got me thinking about the man who spoke about freedom and the man who actually helped achieve it. The difference—and the centuries—between those two things.

I thought about others, like Thurgood Marshall and John Lewis, forcing America to make good on its promises, about Senator Ted Kennedy making it easier for families like mine to come to America. I thought about my former congresswoman Shirley Chisholm, whose parents too came from islands in the Caribbean, the first African American woman elected to Congress, the first African American and second woman to seek a major party nomination at a time when that just wasn't done.

And every time I do, I feel this thing in my body. It's electric but it also stills me. It's my past rising up from a buried place; it's my future leaking in from the blurry margins.

Then something bites at my heels. I sense it, then it grows, and then—with little warning—it's on me. I think about the struggle to keep my childhood apartment because of the gentrification that's flooding neighborhoods like mine, pushing us farther away. I'm haunted by the stories—far too many—of kids I work with being murdered before they have the chance to be anything. I think about generations of us growing up learning fear—fear of exposure and fear of experience.

Seven minutes north of the White House, homelessness is rampant; I also spotted it on a walk out to the run-down neighborhoods near Howard University. I notice it on the cab ride home from JFK Airport that takes me through parts of East New York and Brownsville that have never seen the light of a new day. I notice it in front of my apartment building, where young kids are out on the stoop late at night because no one is telling them to come inside. And I notice it in the eyes of my son, scared awake by the pop of gunshots and the whir of sirens.

I remember reading that in order to train an elephant, men would chain it so tight for a period of time that the pain of movement would echo and resurface long after the chains were gone. I refuse to put a chain on my son—but the world has other ideas.

Then everything from our nation's capital seems like a fever dream, impossible and distant. It still seems inconceivable to me that these two worlds exist, right on top of each other.

The black community is under no illusions that the system was built for us. But each fresh outrage to our people—from Trayvon Martin to Eric Garner to Michael Brown—brings us closer to the unfortunate reality of how low the price of a black life really is. We did not riot when Rodney King was beaten—even the angriest among us recognized that it was the despicable act of four people. The riots came when the system itself was the perpetrator, letting those four men walk free. We can't prevent every hateful act, but we need to be able to trust the system that is designed to hold people accountable. Once we lose that, we are deprived of our humanity in the eyes of the law.

On December 18, 2014, President Obama signed an executive order creating a task force to study and improve the relationship between the police and these communities. The next month I received a formal invitation from the White House to give testimony before the President's Task Force on 21st Century Policing.

As a young black man with a black son, I saw nothing abstract about this issue. It went far beyond indignation at some recent case of police brutality, or the checkered history of police abuses. It was about my body, my life, and that of the most precious gift God has given me, my son. To know that I could do everything possible to keep him safe and yet a public servant, paid by my tax dollars, might murder him in broad daylight with no consequence? It causes a thick and deep well of pain to collect in my heart. My emotions careen from powerlessness to shame to a feeling of inhumanity and, then, invisibility. Like your country doesn't even count you as human or know that you exist at all.

I had been to all the protests but it felt like shouting into the void: what were we really accomplishing? But an invitation from the president to share recommendations was something I could buy into. I'm not naive and I know that America doesn't always keep its promises to us, but I couldn't ignore the hand reaching out. I had to hold up my part of the bargain to protect my son, my community, and every single black and brown child whose parents carry this fear like a giant rock strapped to their backs.

As part of my invitation, I was asked to submit written suggestions for the task force that would be passed on to the president and the Justice Department. I spent weeks on those, wanting to make sure each of my words counted, struck their target, and had maximum potential to effect change. Ms. Oglio helped me put the recommendations together, which included banning the quota system and "stop and frisk," placing qualified minorities in key positions, and race-theory training that could help extinguish profiling. I also reached out to Edwin, and to my mentor Oliver Pu-Folkes, a high-ranking official with the NYPD, for input.

When I testified, I was respectful of the difficulties that the police face, but open about my own firsthand experience. The fractured relationship between the police and the minority community strikes me as one of the most damaging elements of American society.

One of my heroes, Bryan Stevenson, was on the task force, and we spoke afterward. Stevenson is an activist, advocate, and lawyer who founded the Equal Justice Initiative, which provides legal counsel to those who can't afford it and are condemned to die in prison. He carries himself with such humility and dignity that it would be easy to forget what an enormous force for good he is.

Two months later, after the task force had completed their work, I picked up a copy of the *New York Times*. There was a front-page article about the task force's recommendations to President Obama. Next to the article was a large photo of President Obama in the Roosevelt Room, next to Philadelphia police chief Charles Ramsey and across from Attorney General Eric Holder, holding the task force's recommendations. I know how much work there is still to be done, but I took a moment to revel in the hope and optimism that I felt looking at that photograph.

As the saying goes, politics is the art of compromise. It's an endurance test, a constant game of push and pull, steps forward and back, and the accompanying frustrations. There's the snail's pace of progress and the deboned versions of programs that do make it through. You have to have elephant skin to endure the process. But I have to suppress the anger, or at least not let it ground me in one place. The mountain moves, whether we feel it or not. "The arc of the moral universe is long," Dr. King said, "but it bends toward justice."

20

Fences and Billboards

No matter what the professional talkers tell you, I never met a
black boy who wanted to fail.

—TA-NEHISI COATES[14]

One weekend last summer I rented a car because I was seeing a girl
who lived out in Queens. Returning from her place late one night, I
stopped off at the McDonald's drive-through a block over from the
Empire roller rink, the same place where I'd once spent every Friday
night, the same street where I once was stomped on the sidewalk. The

McDonald's is near Ebbets Field, where the Brooklyn Dodgers' stadium used to be. It's now public housing with a large gang presence.

I was on a long car line at the drive-through, inching forward and blasting rap music. As I pulled up to the delivery window, I felt a loud thump hit the back of the car. I checked my rearview and then turned around, but didn't see a thing. It felt like something hit my car, but it was dark and I wasn't sure. A few minutes later a whirling ambulance and police car lit up the night. Two uniformed cops pulled up right next to me and popped out of the car. One of the cops rap-rapped his knuckles on my window, signaling me to roll it down.

"You see what happened?" he asked.

"Uh no, Officer, I didn't see but—"

"Did you hear anything?" he asked impatiently.

"I felt something bang the back of my car but I didn't see anything."

I could now see in the rearview that two paramedics were working behind the trunk of my car, setting up a gurney.

"Well there's a young man shot on the ground behind you. . . ."

I can't say I was stunned, though the proximity of it was alarming. The cop was talking into the walkie-talkie pinned to the breast of his shirt. Then he leaned back down to talk to me. "Looks like he was shot a block away—" he pointed toward Ebbets "—kept running and then collapsed on your car."

I chose not to get out of the car, not wanting to see the body, the blood, the whole scene laid out six feet away. The officer asked a few questions, and for my ID, and as part of procedure, I couldn't go anywhere. The back of my car was part of the crime scene. I sat until about four in the morning as they taped off the scene and interviewed the bystanders. I admit I was struck with a sense of relief that it had nothing to do with me. But of course, it had everything to do with me. This is what inescapable means.

Getting out of the hood is an oft-portrayed notion in American culture. It's a subset of the American dream, one where the picket fence isn't about money or status, but safety. We all have the natural desire to escape the line of fire, literally and symbolically. We never know when it may find us. As I begin to provide for myself and my son, and that desire propels me forward, an equally powerful force pulls me back. I want to raise my son where he'll be safe and have access to more resources, but I know my presence here is valuable. If every decent person who gets an education and some means gets out of the hood, then what's left? Young black men suffer from a dearth of role models, and I feel a duty to stay. I'm intentional about reversing the trend, not just bemoaning it.

Angelina is an incredible person, generous and giving of herself, and she deserves enormous credit in her role as Caleb's mother. We didn't stay together but I dove into fatherhood with as much love as I could possibly give. My son's presence has been a light, but every moment of joy is coupled with a grappling of fears for him. They're inseparable.

In the evening, around dinnertime, the street penetrates my apartment, the same place I've lived in since the day I arrived here. Through my window, a familiar scene plays out: two teenagers pull out guns and start firing in each other's direction. Bullet holes riddle the cars parked in front, the same spot that Caleb and I pull up to every weekend. At the sounds of the guns, the shouts, and then the sirens, my son lifts his head to the window. I pull him away, already trying to cut the world up into little pieces for him. How do you shut a kid's eyes to things without blocking out the rest of the world?

Running the streets now are a new generation, kids who were infants when I first stepped onto Crown. Their growth has been accelerated; they're expecting and desiring for more sooner, able to access what they want, when they want. I fear for them, but I refuse to fear them. It'd be like being afraid of my own shadow. We are the product of the same world, products of the same code.

Friends poke fun at me, saying I overdress, but I know I'm like a walking billboard when I do. Those clothes I wear transmit a message. One morning I got off the train on the way to a meeting at New Lots Avenue in East New York, one of most economically depressed neighborhoods in the city. Walking by a row of apartment buildings, I saw a circle of young men sitting at the fire hydrant, smoking and listening to music. As I passed, one of them turned to me, dramatic. "Damn bro, you fly as shit," he said.

He smiled and went to give me a pound.

"Good lookin'," I said, returning it. "I appreciate it."

"You going to work?"

"Yep, on my way. Have a good one."

Typically I would stop and engage, go into teaching mode with them. But anything more would've killed the message that was implicit in our exchange. We know one another; my walk, talk, and manner tells them we are the same. But they're thrown off by the suit, or the briefcase, or the book. There's a disconnect that makes them stop and think. I'm partly distant and partly *right there*. Inside that gap, that space, is where I see my opening.

I get far too many e-mails or calls about youngsters I know being killed, and each one tears at my heart. Most recently was Cedric, a seventeen-year-old with whom I worked and had a great relationship. He was shot and killed one night in Brooklyn, an accident, though there's really no such thing. I have a photograph of him smiling with a towel on his head, opening a Christmas pair of sneakers we gave him, his joy frozen in time.

The toughest part is hugging mothers going through the nightmare of burying their kids. They will never be made whole again, not even close. And for me, each one of these losses is like a piece of flesh cut from my side. All I can do is carry their pain as my own, try to turn it into something valuable. I think of all those families, broken, but carrying on—alive but somehow transparent. I think of Breeze's mother wandering the streets, unsure where things start and where they end.

The night before my graduation from John Jay I experienced a new level of insomnia, which gnawed at me through the night. I was up at dawn, watching the sun rise above Crown Street's storefronts and brick buildings, the flight of pigeons dotting the sky.

I had been wandering in lower Manhattan the day before, looking for something to wear under my gown. In a tucked-away clothing store, I convinced an African gentleman to sell me a nice black suit and shirt for a hundred dollars.

That morning I exited my building into the bright sunshine, cap and gown covering my new suit. As Nostrand Avenue veered into President Street and the subway steps, I was caught in the poetry of it: compelled to walk through my past while heading to my future. My story unfurled before me on that sidewalk: where I sold poison to my people, where gunshots flew past me, where I was arrested for things I did and didn't do, where I was cuffed and slammed on a police cruiser, where my friend's mother shouted at me that I wouldn't make it to see my eighteenth birthday, where Ky-Mani left Jigga's body with bullet holes, where Shawn was gunned down in broad daylight. I had absorbed all of it and I was required to pass through it that day.

I thought about the days when food was a distant idea that my mouth struggled to remember, the days I scouted in the dirt for anything salvageable to eat, the days my father seemed on the verge of succumbing to the heaviness that had defined his life, the days that the empty space where a mother was supposed to be spread wide and deep in my soul, the days school was a distant luxury afforded to the lucky, the days I questioned God—at eight years old—if suffering was our sole purpose, which left me wondering what he made me for.

* * *

Edwin and I used to have these long and winding conversations in his living room: How do we change our neighborhood? How do we mentor kids? What can we put into place? Where would we start and what would it look like?

One of our talks was running through my head when I came home after a frustrating day working inside the city's bureaucracy. Things were too slow, or misdirected; we weren't making enough of a dent in these kids' lives and every moment we wasted, we were losing more. It takes constant force to change course and we just didn't have the necessary momentum. I started to think bigger and then back to those state-of-the-neighborhood conversations with Edwin.

I got Christine on the phone. "Listen," I said, talking at double speed, trying to get the words out as my thoughts bubbled to the surface. "The problems these kids are facing are overwhelming and we just have to do more. I have this idea. I want to create a mentoring program in my neighborhood and bring all these people together." I launched into all these servant leaders I had recently encountered, those who shared a common purpose to invest in the lives of the youth, and how they could participate.

"Jim, Jim," Christine said, finally getting a word in. "I'm in. What do you need?"

In one burst I typed up and fired out a mass e-mail to about twenty people—Marty, Joanna, judges, advocates and legal-aid attorneys, people who'd handed me a card or given me their number, people committed to and passionate about helping kids. Suzette and Nicole were twin-sister pediatricians who studied the impact of trauma and mental health issues on at-risk children. I started the e-mail by expressing gratitude for their help with my life, for their commitment to others, and for their decision to look beyond paychecks and vacations in their life's work.

"We don't do anything that's easy," I concluded. "We do what's necessary."

What began as a kernel in my mind that day turned into PLOT, Preparing Leaders of Tomorrow, a nonprofit organization we founded dedicated to mentoring at-risk youth. PLOT provides a support system and college preparation to formerly incarcerated youth or those on the verge of falling into the system. Christine took on a lion's share of the administrative and legal paperwork. Everyone pitched in creating bylaws and setting up a board of directors and an advisory board, a mentor coordinator, all the scaffolding required to get it going.

An essential component is helping these kids get in touch with their feelings. "I have come to see that in teaching boys to deny their own pain," writes Geoffrey Canada, founder of the Harlem Children's Zone, "we inadvertently teach them to deny the pain of others." It's a huge gap and I try to approach kids emotionally, show them a man isn't about being macho. When I see them I hug them, talk to them softly, express what I'm feeling explicitly.

"Yo, Mr. Jim, you're soft," they'll say, not accustomed to my approach. Ten years ago I would've bristled at the label, but it rolls off me now.

I try to turn it into a teaching moment. That mentality—that enforced masculinity—kills as many people in our community as drugs and alcohol combined.

"What exactly is soft?" I'll ask, trying to get them to examine the perception. "Is it because I'm respectful? Is it because I'm speaking to you politely? Is it because I'm showing you love and respect? Why is that soft? Why do you think that?"

Of course, I know where it comes from. And it's hard to shake. Recently I was walking around my neighborhood with a girl and she held my hand. As she did I noticed some of my homeboys, people I grew up with, and this discomfort shot through me. What she felt was a beautiful moment, my body instinctively read as a threat. Things like holding a woman's hand shows weakness and weakness makes you stand out, putting a target on you in a million little ways. It's unhealthy and destructive, but it is part of the fabric of my community. I grew up in a household where my family didn't show love or affection, where we barely communicated. I wanted to accept her gesture, but that voice in my head wasn't silenced. It shows how pervasive it is: I'm trying to teach the next generation to shut that out, but am still hearing it myself.

21

Unfinished Products

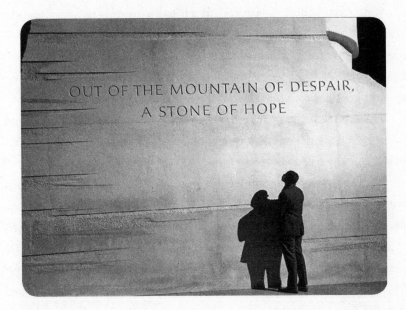

If you are silent about your pain, they'll kill you and say you enjoyed it.

—ZORA NEALE HURSTON

As I write this I'm in the process of obtaining my master's degree in public administration and embracing every opportunity to speak—to give voice to the voiceless; to meet with kids; to effect policy on local, state, or national levels. It's not a noble fight in my mind; it's a blatantly obvious one. There is something wrong if fighting for disenfranchised youth isn't a collective effort that emits from the very moral center of our country. This should be a given, especially in a country blessed with so much. I resist any attempts to treat me as a symbol, which strikes me as so far beside the point. Symbols are rarities, by definition, and I have no interest in being one. I'm working toward a world where my story is no longer a story.

With each milestone I force myself to tie things back to the individual or kind act that set it into motion. Sometimes it's immediate—like Christine forwarding me an e-mail—or distant, like the day Aunt Louloun shared her lone spoon of rice with me because she took on my hunger as her own.

There's the skinny white police officer from Long Island who brought me a Bible when I was young and asked me to pick a better path than the one I was on.

The time Dean Walton let me sleep on his couch even though it could've cost him his job because he simply could not allow the prospect of me being homeless.

All the people in the system who made it less of a machine, made sure I was treated as someone worthy of care—Christine and Marty; Ms. Lauren and Charles at Dean Street; Iza and Damon, who raised me like a son.

Prison is not a place someone goes to, a single point on the map. It's something much larger, akin to a force pushing and spreading through time and space. It strips away a person's life, humanity, and future, and radiates out into the lives of family, friends, and community. It impacts mothers and fathers, infects sons and daughters. It plagues blocks and neighborhoods and cities in a permanent way. Its power and weight and scope are undeniable.

One in nine black children in America has or has had a parent behind bars.[15] When you expand that out to brothers, uncles, and family friends, all the lives connected to that single statistic, it becomes startlingly clear that incarceration is swallowing these communities whole. The next generation grows up with it as a hard fact of their life and its poison seeps into every aspect of their being. It's an epidemic stripping away the humanity and futures of far too many young people whose poor choices don't make them criminals. They're growing up in something akin to combat and are just trying to survive.

Poverty is the underlying issue that feeds so many of these problems. According to the Pew Research Center, a staggering 38 percent of black children in America are living in poverty, which reads like nothing less than a pandemic.[16] A National Scientific Council on the Developing Child report says that the impacts of poverty "overcrowding, noise, substandard housing, separation from parent[s], exposure to violence, family turmoil, [and] economic hardship" can "last even after the child has been moved to a safe and loving home."[17] Studies have shown that these experiences create a buildup of cortisol—the stress hormone—that has disastrous effects on the health and mortality of this community.[18] Those of us who grew up in this world are not surprised at all by these findings. It's only apathy and willful ignorance that pretend they're not the beasts in the room. America, and by extension its justice system, continues to criminalize poverty.

The justice system—as it's practiced by lawmakers, prosecutors, and judges—needs to be reenvisioned and reconfigured. If we invest in our youth's future, I truly believe that there will be fewer violent crimes. In order to achieve this, we need to change not just policies, but hearts. Rehabilitation is the key to public safety. For far too long, justice has been practiced solely as punishment. I believe that such a narrow view is detrimental to the progress we need to make within the juvenile and criminal justice systems, as well as in society as a whole. Because of the adversarial nature of the legal system, advocates and prosecutors have been at odds. As such, the vital voice of prosecutors has been left out of this important conversation. I must admit that I too have failed to see that prosecutorial power can be a force for good instead of an engine for mass incarceration.

A few years ago, I was fortunate enough to work with both Adam Foss, a local prosecutor from Boston, and the late Brooklyn district attorney Kenneth Thompson. Both men became crucial voices for racial justice at a tense moment between law enforcement and minority communities. They used prosecutorial power to provide second chances in the form of programs and job training, worked to stop imprisonment for low-level drug offenses, helped gain amnesty for those with outstanding warrants, and developed internal units dedicated to reviewing wrongful convictions. As prosecutor Adam Foss has said: "Every day, thousands of times a day, prosecutors around the United States wield power so great that it can bring about catastrophe as quickly as it can bring about opportunity, intervention, support and, yes, even love."[19]

There also needs to be a concerted and systemic effort to separate violent crime from youthful or minor offenses. Lockup facilities and detention facilities—essentially junior prisons—just contribute to the hardening process. Juvenile justice facilities are exit ramps and they should function as such. Facilities can learn from, and should expand according to, the Boys Town model, which recognizes that it's not just a moral but a scientific issue: youth are apt to make poor decisions and have weak impulse control, but also are capable of great change because of their brains' plasticity. I benefited enormously from that safe environment, which focused on privileges and motivation, not punishment and intimidation. And I was saved by those people who recognized the possibility that, under the right circumstances, I could change. Hundreds of thousands of kids would benefit enormously from that same opportunity, and all of society would benefit.

I'm an advocate of keeping kids out of the system, but it was the people I encountered in the system who saved my life. Thus I'm an advocate for the *right* system, run by the right people. The best program in the world is a thin façade for care without the right people behind it. I remember once hearing a young woman talking to the federal Office of Juvenile Justice administrator Robert Listenbee, who has done so much for me and countless other young people. She emphasized that it's not enough to get people willing to work with kids—they have to like kids.

In addition, mentoring programs need to be expanded, incentivized, and funded so that at-risk youth can engage with role models in their community. Raise the Age asks for society to recognize the role of age and maturity in decision making, the undeniable biology at play. The Close to Home initiative looks to implement a circle of support and services around those who have already made poor decisions in an effort to help them make the correct ones. President Obama's task force asked police departments to respect the community around which they work, appreciate the humanity of the populations they are sworn to protect, and acknowledge the malicious impact of their own racial biases.

The United States of America accounts for 5 percent of the world's population but 25 percent of its prisoners. President Obama noted in a speech to the NAACP that our incarceration rate is four times higher than *China's*. In a global community where we think of ourselves as representing the pinnacle of justice and freedom, this is appalling. America too often uses prisons to solve problems they were not designed to solve. "When you're a hammer," the saying goes, "everything else just looks like a nail."

American society also spends far too much energy and focus on the effect instead of the cause. We don't offer legitimate education or job opportunities, and we don't offer a safe environment to all of our citizens. New York State spends approximately $260,000 a year to incarcerate a juvenile while spending less than $20,000 a year to educate one in its crumbling schools. Even if that education figure were doubled, and we spent $80,000 per year, per kid, we'd still save $180,000 per kid, all the while decreasing the chances that he or she would end up as an adult in the system. We're also improving the chance that they would become productive contributors to society—taxpayers, rather than tax burdens. And none of these numbers even factor in the immeasurable human cost. We comfortably spend billions of dollars incarcerating these teenagers, but refuse to invest in fixing their circumstances. By going after the symptoms instead of the root causes, we let the problems fester, grow, and multiply.

There is a reason to be optimistic with what the Obama administration put into place: Pell grants for prisoners, the Justice Department challenging states for incarcerating those who can't pay for their freedom, the president's aggressive clemency history (more than all of our presidents combined), severing the relationship with private prisons, and wide investigations into various police departments.

I'm fearful and despondent that President Trump and Attorney General Sessions appear committed to rolling back all of the progress made under President Obama. But I believe that policy makers and stakeholders will overcome their fears, get past the rhetoric, and make real efforts to uplift humanity—not through charity, but by offering genuine opportunities. We can't continue to victimize people for failing if we don't give them a chance to succeed.

The justice system is too often treated as an ugly corner of society that we ignore. But it feeds and affects so much of our day-to-day society. Marilyn J. Mosby, the Baltimore prosecutor at the center of the Freddie Gray murder, said, "I believe that we are the justice system. We, the members of the community, are the justice system because we are the victims of crimes. . . . We are the accused . . . We are the cops . . . We are the witnesses . . . We are the perpetrators . . . We are the judges. And as community members, we are the jury."

As painful as it is, I'm learning that social justice is a marathon, not a sprint. It's painful because lives are vanishing with each delay. Once I was just a vagabond kid looking for hustles. Now I'm doing it all over again, only the hustle is something so much bigger than me. My energy has been turned outward and downward—and I'm going to pull up whomever I can. "Any country, any society which does not care for its children," Nelson Mandela said, "is no nation at all."[20] Mandela implicitly understood that we are all tied to one another— inevitably and irrevocably—whether we want to accept it or not.

One day my son, Caleb, and I were hanging out with Marty and his wife, Amy. Marty casually said to my son that he's looking forward to visiting him one day in college. The comment was tossed off so naturally; by Marty's standards, attending college was as normal as the ability to speak. But it affected me in a way I couldn't even verbalize. Something that eluded me until my late teens was the expectation for my son at the tender age of three. I was reminded how enormous those small things are—that piece of exposure, those words of expectation—to a young mind.

As I finish writing this book, I've been reading David Brooks's *Road to Character*, in which he writes about a group of people who faced a "moral crisis," as he called it, and came out the other end. Brooks is a well-known conservative but that doesn't mean he doesn't extend great generosity of spirit to all those trying to make it.

> When they had quieted themselves, they had opened up space for grace to flood in. They found themselves helped by people they did not expect would help them. They found themselves understood and cared for by others in ways they did not imagine beforehand. . . .
>
> They find a vocation or calling. They commit themselves to some long obedience and dedicate themselves to some desperate lark that gives life purpose.

Recently, Mr. Walton called me up at work and told me one of his mentees, Luke, needed some help. Luke grew up in Bed Stuy as an A student who mostly stayed out of the trouble churning on his street. His mother had recently died and his stepfather kicked him out soon after his eighteenth birthday. After the passing of his sole nurturer he was left to face the cold world alone. The combination of rootlessness and homelessness led him to the street. He was lucky to find some mentors who talked him into entering Job Corps, a training and education program. He had landed a job interview the next day and needed clothes, but Mr. Walton was stuck at work.

I had never met Luke before, a shy and skinny kid who showed up at my office later that day—but that was only literally true. From my point of view not only had we met hundreds of times, we were the same person. In his eyes I saw the perseverance and beauty and struggle that I've seen in so many young faces.

At a clothing store in downtown Manhattan, I brought Luke to the same African gentleman who had sold my graduation suit a few years earlier. I convinced the salesman to take all the money I had for it, about seventy bucks, and told him he'd be helping out the next generation.

"Sure thing, man," he said. "No problem."

"Thank you, sir. We need more of you," I told him.

"Haha. You're kind. Just bring the next one to me too."

"Will do, will do. Let's just hope there's a lot more."

"You know it," he said. As I reached out my hand, he pulled me in for an easy hug. Luke stood at the door, ready to go, a shy smile across his face.

Afterward, I walk Luke to his train, tossing some possible interview questions he might have to field, assuring him nervousness is part of the deal, telling him stories about my first job experiences. As we're talking, he lets down his guard and his true self emerges, and I feel like I'm staring in a mirror. I think of my grandparents, who opened their doors to me; and Iza, who opened her heart to me. Of Damon, who treated me like a son. I think of Mr. Walton, who tried to be a bridge for me, whose heart I broke when he had to give up on me, whose presence again in my life seems a form of divine grace I can neither understand nor question.

We reach the subway station. Luke thanks me and heads down the stone steps, his new suit in a garment bag around his backpack. Then he turns around to wave. I see myself waving back.

Then he goes through the turnstile and mixes in with the busy New York crowd.

ACKNOWLEDGMENTS

I would like to express my sincerest gratitude to the many people who have helped with this book: My agent, Susan Golomb, for her faith in me; my editor, Jonathan Jao, for his guidance throughout this process; Sofia Groopman and all the people at Harper for their dedication; and my co-writer, Jon Sternfeld, for his patience, open-mindedness, willingness to educate me, and expertise. Thank you.

To those who have made me: Leonide Victorin, Molier Joseph, Aunt Michelle St. Germain, and Jacqueline Prince, thank you for sharing the little that you didn't have with me. There is no me without you. To Ms. Donna Oglio, you're tough for such a petite angel. Thanks for making me a better version of myself and helping me write down the first words for this book.

To Joanna Solfrian, you've been everything I can ask for as an advisor, counselor, mentor, and friend.

To Iza Cedeno and Damon Canada, you've been there at my lowest, angriest, and darkest moments, but you never wavered on your commitment to save me. It is rare to find people who will never give up on you. I love both of you for your selflessness.

To Christine Bella, there aren't enough words to describe my love for you. You have done more for me than I can ever repay you for. It brings me joy to know that I'm not special to you; this is what you do for every child you've come across. I'm blessed to know that you're stuck with me.

To my fada, Carlos Walton, words won't do me any justice here. I am me because of you. We've been through it all and, therefore, we'll continue to go through it all. Your love for us has put a lot of funeral homes out of business. You love those of us no one else bothered to love, which makes your love stronger than most. I love you more than I'm able to understand.

To Amy Cooney, this book doesn't exist without you. Thank you for loving me, Marty, and my son, CJ. I'm thankful to know that I'm part of the family.

To Marty Feinman, there isn't enough space here to express my gratitude and love for you. I know that I'm the most fortunate man living simply because I'm able to tell others that I'm guaranteed a space in that big heart of yours.

To Angelina Thompson, you're the greatest mother I know. I'm lucky to raise our greatest joy with you. Thank you.

To my mother, Miland Gelin, and father, Ricot St. Germain, thank you for giving me life. You've done your best, and I'm indebted to you both.

To my grandparents Marie Louisville and Luc St. Germain, I hope I'm making you proud in heaven.

To my brothers, Colin and Roothchild, and my sister, Geraldine St. Germain, thank you for carrying me through life. Love you all.

For all of the others who have played a role in my being, I couldn't mention you all, but you're no less significant to my journey.

To every young person I've encountered, to every child who has inherited a painful life or been born on the wrong side of privilege, I wrote this book for you. Although I don't speak for you, I hope you'll use what you can from it. Your struggle is no deficit; it is the fuel that will sustain you through this arduous journey known as life. Many are called, few are chosen. The more you fight, the more I will fight. I need you.

NOTES

1. Pope Francis. "Address of the Holy Father: Visit to Detainees at Curran-Fromhold Correctional Facility," Philadelphia, September 27, 2015, w2.vatican.va/content/francesco/en/speeches/2015/september/documents/papa-francesco_20150927_usa-detenuti.html.

2. Roy Baumeister and John Tierney. *Willpower: Rediscovering the Greatest Human Strength* (New York: Penguin Press, 2011), 174.

3. Desmond Tutu. "Why Desmond Tutu Thinks Bryan Stevenson Is 'Shaping the Moral Universe,'" *Vanity Fair,* May 2015, vanityfair.com/news/2015/04/bryan-stevenson-just-mercy-desmond-tutu.

4. Ta-Nehisi Coates. *The Beautiful Struggle* (New York: Spiegel & Grau, 2009), 20.

5. Bryan Stevenson. *Just Mercy: A Story of Justice and Redemption* (New York: Spiegel & Grau, 2015), 289.

6. Sampson Davis, George Jenkins, and Rameck Hunt, with Lisa Frazier Page. *The Pact: Three Young Men Make a Promise and Fulfill a Dream* (New York: Riverhead Books, 2003), 3.

7. Derived from a poem written by Dinos Christianopoulous.

8. Wes Moore. *The Other Wes Moore: One Name, Two Fates* (New York: Spiegel & Grau, 2011), 66.

9. Thomas Merton. *The Seven Storey Mountain* (New York: Mariner Books, 1999), Paperback edition, 92.

10. Jill Colvin. "Hundreds of Juvenile Offenders Being Relocated Closer to Home," *DNAinfo*, October 4, 2012, dnainfo.com/new-york/20121004/east-new-york/hundreds-of-juvenile-offenders-being-relocated-closer-home.

11. Ta-Nehisi Coates. *Between the World and Me* (New York: Spiegel & Grau, 2015), 82.

12. Commencement Speech, "Ready, Able and Willing," the Doe Fund, 2015.

13. NAACP. "Criminal Justice Fact Sheet," 2016, naacp.org/pages /criminal-justice-fact-sheet.

14. Coates, *The Beautiful Struggle,* 180.

15. Danielle Paquette. "One in Nine Black Children Has Had a Parent in Prison," *Washington Post,* October 27, 2015, washingtonpost .com/news/wonk/wp/2015/10/27/one-in-nine-black-children-have -had-a-parent-in-prison.

16. Eileen Patten, and Jens Manuel Krogstad. "Black Child Poverty Rate Holds Steady, Even as Other Groups See Declines," Pew Research Center, July 14, 2015, pewresearch.org/fact-tank/2015/07/14/black -child-poverty-rate-holds-steady-even-as-other-groups-see-declines.

17. Center on the Developing Child. "Excessive Stress Disrupts the Architecture of the Developing Brain," National Scientific Council on the Developing Child, Harvard University, January 2014, devel opingchild.harvard.edu/wp-content/uploads/2005/05/Stress_Dis rupts_Architecture_Developing_Brain-1.pdf.

18. "Trauma & Resilience," in *A Primer for Youth Defenders,* National Juvenile Defender Center, 2016 Annual Summit.

19. https://www.ted.com/talks/adam_foss_a_prosecutor_s_vision _for_a_better_justice_system/transcript?language=en.

20. Chris Niles. "Nelson Mandela: Any Society Which Does Not Care for its Children Is No Nation at All," UNICEF, July 17, 2013, unicef.org/infobycountry/southafrica_69771.html.

ABOUT THE AUTHORS

<u>Jim St. Germain</u> is the cofounder of Preparing Leaders of Tomorrow (PLOT), a nonprofit organization that provides mentoring to at-risk youth; and a board member with the National Juvenile Defender Center. He works as a residential care advocate for the City of New York, and was appointed by President Obama to the Coordinating Council on Juvenile Justice and Delinquency Prevention. Jim lives in Brooklyn, New York, with his son, Caleb.

<u>Jon Sternfeld</u> is a writer whose work includes *Crisis Point: Why We Must—and How We Can—Overcome Our Broken Politics in Washington and Across America* with Senators Trent Lott and Tom Daschle and *Strong in the Broken Places* with Quentin Vennie. He lives in New York.